MYTHS OF THE HINDUS & BUDDHISTS

MYTHS OF THE HINDUS & BUDDHISTS

BY

THE SISTER NIVEDITA

AND

ANANDA K. COOMARASWAMY

WITH THIRTY TWO ILLUSTRATIONS BY INDIAN ARTISTS UNDER THE SUPERVISION OF

ABANINDRO NATH TAGORE, C.I.E.

GYAN

Published by

Gyan Publishing House
5, Ansari Road
Daryaganj, New Delhi-110002
Phone: 011-47034999, 9811692060
E-mail: books@gyanbooks.com

Distribution Network
gyanbooks.com
India, USA, Canada, UK, Australia

ISBN: 978-81-212-6995-7 (PB)
First Published, 1913

2nd Impression 2024

Printed at: Gyan Press, Delhi.

MYTHS OF THE HINDUS & BUDDHISTS
Author: SISTER NIVEDITA AND ANANDA K. COOMARASWAMY

MYTHS OF THE HINDUS & BUDDHISTS

Créer un mythe, c'est-à-dire entrevoir derrière la réalité sensible une réalité supérieure, est le signe le plus manifeste de la grandeur de l'âme humaine et la preuve de sa faculté de croissance et de développement infinis.

A. SABATIER, 1879

I

THE VICTORY OF BUDDHA

ABANINDRO NĀTH TAGORE

Frontispiece

MYTHS OF THE HINDUS & BUDDHISTS

BY

THE SISTER NIVEDITA

(MARGARET E. NOBLE)

OF RĀMAKRISHNA-VIVEKĀNANDA

AND

ANANDA K. COOMARASWAMY

WITH THIRTY-TWO ILLUSTRATIONS BY INDIAN ARTISTS UNDER THE SUPERVISION OF

ABANINDRO NĀTH TAGORE C.I.E.

NEW YORK

HENRY HOLT & COMPANY

1914

PREFACE

SISTER NIVEDITA, to whom the present work was first entrusted, needs no introduction to Western or to Indian readers. A most sincere disciple of Swāmi Vivekānanda, who was himself a follower of the great Rāmakrishna, she brought to the study of Indian life and literature a sound knowledge of Western educational and social science, and an unsurpassed enthusiasm of devotion to the peoples and the ideals of her adopted country. Her chief works are *The Web of Indian Life*, almost the only fair account of Hindu society written in English, and *Kālī the Mother*, where also for the first time the profound tenderness and terror of the Indian Mother-cult are presented to Western readers in such a manner as to reveal its true religious and social significance. Through these books Nivedita became not merely an interpreter of India to Europe, but even more, the inspiration of a new race of Indian students, no longer anxious to be Anglicized, but convinced that all real progress, as distinct from mere political controversy, must be based on national ideals, upon intentions already clearly expressed in religion and art.

Sister Nivedita's untimely death in 1911 has made it necessary that the present work should be completed by another hand. The following parts of the text as here printed are due to Sister Nivedita: Mythology of the Indo-Aryan races (pp. 1–5); pp. 14–22 of the Introduction to the Rāmāyana; the whole of the Mahābhārata (*except* pp. 186–190); part of the section on Shiva (pp. 291–295); the comment on Kacha and Devayānī (pp. 339–342);

and the Story of Dhruva, Shani, Star-Pictures, etc. (pp. 378–388). The present writer is responsible for all else—rather more than two-thirds of the whole.

The illustrations are reproduced from water-colour drawings executed specially for this book by Indian artists under the supervision of Mr. Abanindro Nāth Tagore, C.I.E., Vice-Principal of the Calcutta School of Art, who has himself contributed some of the pictures.

The stories have thus the advantage, unique in the present series, of illustration by artists to whom they have been familiar from childhood, and who are thus well able to suggest their appropriate spiritual and material environment.

It may be well to explain briefly the principle on which these myths and legends have been selected and arranged. My aim has been to relate in a manner as close to the original as possible, but usually much condensed, such of the myths as are more or less familiar to every educated Indian, with whom I include all those illiterate but wise peasants and women whose knowledge of the *Purānas* has been gained by listening to recitations or reading, by visiting temples (where the stories are illustrated in sculpture), or from folk-songs or mystery-plays. The stories related here, moreover, include very much of which a knowledge is absolutely essential for every foreigner who proposes in any way to co-operate with the Indian people for the attainment of their desired ends—nowhere more clearly formulated than in mythology and art. Amongst these are, I hope, to be included not only such avowed lovers of Indian ideals as was Nivedita herself, but also civil servants and missionaries. The Indian myths here retold include almost all those which are commonly illustrated in Indian sculpture and painting. Finally, they include much that must very soon be recognized as belonging not only to India, but to the whole world; I feel that this is above all true of the Rāmāyana, which is surely the best tale of chivalry and truth and the love of creatures that ever was written.

ANANDA K. COOMARASWAMY

CONTENTS

ILLUSTRATIONS

Myths of the Hindus & Buddhists

CHAPTER I: MYTHOLOGY OF THE INDO-ARYAN RACES

The Study of Mythology

IN the early history of man Asia formed a vast breeding-ground of civilization of which countries like Egypt, Arabia, Greece, India, and China were the extremities. Egypt and Arabia were destined later, from their geographical positions, to be overrun and suffer destruction of their culture. Greece and pre-eminently India formed what may be called *culs-de-sac*. Here, as if up the long shores of some hidden creek, would be forced the tidal wave of one epoch after another, each leaving on the coast a tide-mark that perhaps none of its successors would be able entirely to cover. Hence, in India, we may hope to discover means of studying, as nowhere else in the world, the succession of epochs in culture.

Civilization develops by new conjunctions of tribes and races, each with its individual outlook, the result of that distinctive body of custom which has imposed itself upon them through the geographical conditions of whatever region formed their cradle-land and school. Western Asia is one of the central areas of the world. Here by the very necessities of the configuration the great highways from North to South and East to West meet, and mercantile cities—points of barter and exchange—will grow up at the crossways. Equally obvious is it that India and the remote parts of the Nile Valley will form seats of occupation and production. Here race upon race will settle and combine. Here agricultural nations will grow up. Here civilization will accumulate. And here we may look to see the gradual elaboration of schemes of thought which will not only bear their own history stamped upon them, but will in their turn become causes and sources of dynamic influence upon the world outside. It is not impossible to recover the story of the ideas which the Nile people have contributed to the world as we know it. But those people themselves, so we are informed, have irretrievably relaxed their hold upon their own past. Between them and it there is only broken continuity, a lapse of time that represents no process of cause and effect, but rather a perpetual interruption of such a series; for a single generation enamoured of foreign ways is almost enough in history to risk the whole continuity of civilization and learning. Ages of accumulation are entrusted to the frail bark of each passing epoch by the hand of the past, desiring to make over its treasures to the use of the future. It takes a certain stubbornness, a doggedness of loyalty, even a modicum of unreasonable conservatism maybe, to lose nothing in the long march of the ages; and, even when confronted with great empires, with a sudden extension of the idea of culture, or with the supreme temptation of a new religion, to hold fast what we have, adding to it only as much as we can healthfully and manfully carry.

The Genius of India

Yet this attitude is the criterion of a strong national genius, and in India, since the beginning of her history, it has been steadily maintained. Never averse to a new idea, no matter what its origin, India has never failed to put each on its trial. Avid of new thought, but jealously reluctant to accept new custom or to essay new expression, she has been slowly constructive, unfalteringly synthetic, from the earliest days to the present time.

The fault of Indian conservatism, indeed, has been its tendency to perpetuate differences without assimilation.

There has always been room for a stronger race, with its own equipment of custom and ideals, to settle down in the interstices of the Brāhmanical civilization, uninfluenced and uninfluencing. To this day Calcutta and Bombay have their various quarters—Chinese, Burmese, and what not—not one of which contributes to, or receives from, the civic life in the midst of which it is set. To this day the Baniyā of India is the Phœnix or Phœnician, perhaps of an older world. But this unmixingness has not been uniform. The personality of Buddha was the source of an impulse of religion to China and half a dozen minor nations. The Gupta empire represents an epoch in which foreign guests and foreign cultures were as highly welcomed and appreciated in India as to-day in Europe and America. And finally only the rise of Islām was effective in ending these long ages of intercourse which have left their traces in the faith and thought of the Indian people.

The Motives of Religion

Hinduism is, in fact, an immense synthesis, deriving its elements from a hundred different directions, and incorporating every conceivable motive of religion. The motives of religion are manifold. Earth-worship, sun-worship, nature-worship, sky-worship, honour paid to heroes and ancestors, mother-worship, father-worship, prayers for the dead, the mystic association of certain plants and animals: all these and more are included within Hinduism. And each marks some single age of the past, with its characteristic conjunction or invasion of races formerly alien to one another. They are all welded together now to form a great whole. But still by visits to outlying shrines, by the study of the literature of certain definite periods, and by careful following up of the special threads, it is possible to determine what were some of the influences that have entered into its making.

Now and again in history a great systematizing impulse has striven to cast all or part of recognized belief into the form of an organic whole. Such attempts have been made with more or less success in the compilation of books known as the *Purānas,* in the epic poem called the *Rāmāyana,* and most perfectly of all in the *Mahābhārata.* Each of these takes some ancient norm which has been perhaps for centuries transmitted by memory, and sets it down in writing, modifying it and adding to it in such ways as bring it, in the author's eyes, up to date.

The Mahābhārata

The Mahābhārata is the result of the greatest of the efforts thus made to conserve in a collected form all the ancient beliefs and traditions of the race. The name Mahābhārata itself shows that the movement which culminated in the compilation of this great work had behind it a vivid consciousness of the unity of the Bharata or Indian people. For this reason one finds in this work a great effort made to present a complete embodiment of the ideals to be found in the social organism, religion, ancient history, mythology, and ethics of the Indian people.

Hence if we want to follow Indian mythology from its dim beginnings to its perfect maturity through all its multiform intermediate phases we cannot have a better guide than the Mahābhārata. For in India mythology is not a mere subject of antiquarian research and disquisition; here it still permeates the whole life of the people as a controlling influence. And it is the living mythology which, passing through the stages of representation of successive cosmic process and assuming definite shape thereafter, has become a powerful factor in the everyday life of the people—it is this living mythology that has found place in the Mahābhārata.

It should be understood that it is the mythology which has left its clearest impress in the Mahābhārata that has attained a fully developed form, and exercised a potent influence on Indian society. Other myths have for a time appeared in a vague nebular form and then vanished like smoke, leaving little trace behind; they have not assumed any concrete forms in the memory of the race. Thus it is that we find a popular saying prevalent in Bengal that "Whatever is not in the Mahābhārata is not to be found in the land of Bharata [India]." In the Mahābhārata we find on the one hand the primal forms of mythology, and on the other its fully developed forms also. We find in this creation of the Indian mind a complete revelation of that mind.

In the infancy of the human mind men used to mix up their own fancies and feelings with the ways of bird and beast, the various phenomena of land and water, and the movements of sun and moon and stars and planets, and viewed the whole universe in this humanified form. In later times, when man had attained the greatest importance in the eyes of man, the glory of stellar worlds paled before human greatness.

In this book we have dealt with both these stages of mythology, the initial as well as the final. On the one hand, we have given some glimpses of the primal forms which mythology assumed after passing through the hazy indefiniteness of primitive ages. On the other, we have related more fully the stories of the age when mythology had reached its maturity.

CHAPTER II : THE RĀMĀYANA

Sources

VĀLMĪKI is a name almost as shadowy as Homer. He was, no doubt, a Brāhman by birth, and closely connected with the kings of Ayodhyā. He collected songs and legends of Rāma (afterwards called Rāma-Chandra, in distinction from Parashu-Rāma); and very probably some additions were made to his work at a later time, particularly the *Uttara Kanda.* He is said to have invented the *shloka* metre, and the language and style of Indian epic poetry owe their definite form to him. According to the Rāmāyana, he was a contemporary of Rāma, and sheltered Sītā during her years of lonely exile, and taught the Rāmāyana to her sons Kusa and Lava.

The material of the Rāmāyana, in its simplest form, the story of the recovery of a ravished bride, is not unlike that of another great epic, the *Iliad* of Homer. It is not likely, however, although the view has been suggested, that the *Iliad* derives from the Rāmāyana: it is more probable that both epics go back to common legendary sources older than 1000 years B.C.

The story of Rāma is told in one of the *Jātakas*, which may be regarded as a shorter version, one of many then current. Probably at some time during the last centuries preceding Christ the current versions of Rāma's saga were taken up by the Brāhman poet, and formed into one story with a clear and coherent plot; while its complete form, with the added *Uttara Kanda*, may be as late as A.D. 400. As a whole, the poem in its last redaction seems to belong essentially to the earlier phase of the Hindu renaissance, and it reflects a culture very similar to that which is visibly depicted in the Ajanta frescoes (first to seventh century A.D.); but of course the essential subject-matter is much more ancient. The version given in the present volume amounts to about one-twentieth of the whole Rāmāyana. It is a condensed translation, in which all the most essential matters are included; while no episode or figure of speech has been added for which the original does not afford authority.

Ethic of the Rāmāyana

Not the least significant feature of Vālmīki's epic lies in its remarkable presentation of two ideal societies: an ideal good and an ideal evil. He abstracts, as it were, from human life an almost pure morality and an almost pure immorality, tempered by only so much of the opposite virtue as the plot necessitates. He thus throws into the strongest relief the contrast of good and evil, as these values presented themselves to the shapers of Hindu society. For it should be understood that not merely the lawgivers, like Manu, but also the poets of ancient India, conceived of their own literary art, not as an end in itself, but entirely as a means to an end—and that end, the nearest possible realization of an ideal society. The poets were practical sociologists, using the great power of their art deliberately to mould the development of human institutions and to lay down ideals for all classes of men. The poet is, in fact, a philosopher, in the Nietzschean sense of one who stands behind and directs the evolution of a desired type. Results have proved the wisdom of the chosen means; for if Hindu society has ever as a whole approached the ideal or ideals which have been the guiding force in its development, it is through hero-worship. The *Vedas*, indeed, belonged essentially to the learned; but the epics have been translated into every vernacular by poets, such as Tulsi Dās and Kamban, ranking in power with Vālmīki himself. The material of the epics, moreover, as also of many of the *Purānas*, has been made familiar not only to the literate, but also to all the unlettered, not excepting women, by constant recitation, and also by means of the drama, in folk-song, and in painting. Until quite modern times no Hindu boy or girl grew up unfamiliar with the story of the Rāmāyana; and their highest aspiration was to be like Rāma or Sītā.

The Mythical Origin of Caste

It is in the *Rāmāyana*, and in the Laws of Manu (*c.* 500 B.C.) that we find the chief account of the ideal Hindu system of Colour (caste). The mythical origin of Colour, according to Manu, is as follows: Brāhmans are sprung from the mouth, Kshatriyas from the arm, Vaishyas from the thigh, and Shūdras from the foot of Brahmā. This myth is true in an allegorical sense; it is used more literally to give divine sanction to the whole system. But it must not be supposed that Manu or Vālmīki describes a state of society actually existing at any one time all over India. The history of Hindu society might much rather be written in terms of the degree of approach towards or divergence from the systems of the Utopists, Vālmīki and Manu. How powerful their influence still is, compared even with the force of custom, appears in the fact that it is at the present day the aim of many reformers by no means to abolish the caste system, but gradually to unite the sub-castes until none but the four main Colours remain as effective social divisions.

This development, combined with some provision for the transference from one caste to another of those who are able and willing to adopt the traditions and accept the discipline of a higher Colour, is what the present writer would also desire. Transference of caste, or the acquiring of Colour, is continually going on even now, by the absorption of aboriginal tribes into the Hindu system; but stories like those of Vishvāmitra illustrate the immense theoretical difficulty of such promotions. Against this extreme exclusiveness many protests have arisen in India, the most notable being that of Buddha, who, so far from accepting the divine right of a Brāhman by birth, taught that—

Not by birth does one become a Brāhman:
By his actions alone one becomes a Brāhman.

The strength of the hereditary principle has always prevailed against such reactions, and the most that reformers have actually accomplished is to create new caste groups.

Vālmīki's Ideal Society

Let us now examine very briefly the nature of Vālmīki's ideal society. From the first we are impressed with its complexity and with the high degree of differentiation of the interdependent parts of which it is constituted. It is founded on the conception of gradation of rank, but that rank is dependent, not upon wealth, but upon mental qualities only. The doctrine of reincarnation is taken for granted; and the conception of *karma* (that the fruit of actions bears inevitable fruit in another life) being combined with this, the theory logically followed that rank must be determined solely by heredity. He who deserved to be born as a Brāhman was born as a Brāhman, and he who deserved to be born as a Shūdra was born as a Shūdra. This is the theory which finds practical expression in the caste system, or, as it is known to Indians, the system of "Colour" (*varna*), in modern vernacular, "birth" (*jāti*). Fundamentally, there are four Colours: Brāhmans, the priests and philosophers; Kshatriyas, the ruling and knightly class; Vaishyas, traders and agriculturists; and Shūdras—servants of the other three, who alone are "twice-born," that is, receive priestly initiation in early manhood. Besides these, there are recognized a vast number of subdivisions of the four main classes, arising theoretically by intermarriage, and distinguishable in practice as occupation-castes.

For each Colour Hindu theory recognizes an appropriate duty and morality (*dharma*): to follow any but the "*own-dharma*" of a man's caste constituted a most disastrous sin, meriting condign punishment. In this conception of *own-dharma* there appears at once the profound distinction of Hindu from all absolutist moralities, such as the Mosaic or Buddhist. To take one concrete example, the Mosaic Decalogue lays down the commandment, "Thou shalt not kill," and this commandment is nominally binding equally upon the philosopher, the soldier, and the merchant—a somewhat illogical position. But Hinduism, permeated though it be by the doctrine of *ahimsa*, harmlessness, does not attempt to enforce it upon the Kshatriyas or Shūdras: it is the hermit and philosopher above all who must not kill or hurt any living thing, while the knight who shrank, in time of need, from slaying men or animals would not be praiseworthy as a humanitarian, but blameworthy as one who neglected to follow his own-morality. This very question is raised in the Rāmāyana, when Sītā suggests to Rāma that, as they are now dwelling in the forests, the resort of hermits, they should adopt the *yogī*-morality, and refrain from slaying, not merely beasts, but even the *rākshasas*;[1]

[1] *Rākshasas*, *daityas*, *yakshas*, and *asuras* are demons and devils constantly at war with men and gods.

but Rāma replies that he is bound both by knightly duty and by promise to protect the hermits, and that he must obey the ordinance of chivalry.

In its extreme form this doctrine of own-morality is represented as having been fully realized in practice only in the golden age, when none but Brāhmans practised asceticism, or attained to Perfect Enlightenment; in the second age the Brāhmans and Kshatriyas were equally powerful, and it is said that in this age Manu composed the *shāstras* (law-books) setting forth the duties of the four *varnas*; in the third age the Vaishyas also practised austerities; and in the fourth even the Shūdras engaged in austere penances. Thus the four ages represent a progressive deterioration from an ideal theocracy to a complete democracy. In the time of Rāma the beginning of the fourth age is already foreshadowed by the one Shūdra who became a *yogī*, and was slain by Rāma, not so much as a punishment as to avoid the consequential disturbance of society, already manifested in the untimely death of a Brāhman boy.

In an aristocratic society such as Vālmīki contemplates the severity of social discipline increases toward the summit: those who have the greatest power must practise the greatest self-restraint, partly because *noblesse oblige* partly because such austere discipline is the necessary condition without which power would rapidly melt away. It is needful to remember this essential character of a true aristocratic society, if we are to understand some of the most significant, and to the democrat and individualist the most incomprehensible and indefensible, episodes of the Rāmāyana. Upon the Kshatriya, and above all upon the king, devolves the duty of maintaining *dharma*; therefore he must not only protect men and gods against violence, as by slaying the rākshasas, but must himself for the sake of example conform to the rules of accepted morality, even when these rules have for him no personal significance whatever. It is thus that Rāma repudiates Sītā twice, though all the time perfectly satisfied in his own mind of her complete faithfulness. This repudiation of Sītā forms the most dramatic and remarkable feature of the whole story. Rāma and Sītā are brought together after a year's separation, and at the close of a long and arduous conflict: this moment, where modern sentiment would demand a "happy ending," is made the supreme test of character for both, and the final tragedy is only postponed by the appearance of the gods and justification of Sītā by ordeal. In these tragic episodes, forming the culminating moral crisis in the lives of both Rāma and Sītā, Vālmīki is completely and equally justified as a teacher and as an artist. Vālmīki's ideal society is almost free from sin, whereby he is the better enabled to exhibit the far-reaching effects of the ill-doing of single individuals and of only faults. Even Kaikeyī is not made ignoble: she is only very young and blind and wilful; but the whole tragedy of Rāma's life and the fulfilment of the purposes of the high gods follows on her wrongdoing.

Over against this human world of the silver age is drawn the sinful and inhuman world of the rākshasas, where greed and lust and violence and deceit replace generosity and self-restraint and gentleness and truth. But these evil passions are outwardly directed against men and gods and all those who are, for the rākshasas, aliens: amongst themselves there are filial affection and the uttermost of wifely devotion, there are indomitable courage and the truest loyalty. The city of the rākshasas is pre-eminently fair, built by Vishvakarman himself; they practise all the arts; they worship the gods, and by austerity and penance win great gifts of them: in a word, they flourish like the bay-tree, and if they are evil, at least they are not ignoble. Amongst them are found some, like Vibhishana, not evil at all. After all, then, these rākshasas are not inhuman at all, but their estate is an image of the *a-dharmic*, unrighteous, aspect of human society—an allegory which we should all understand were it presented to us to-day for the first time, like the Penguins of Anatole France.

The Story

The siege of Lankā is told in the original at great length and with grotesque humour. But its violence is redeemed by many incidents of chivalric tenderness and loyalty. Rāvana, once slain, is thought of by Rāma as a friend; Mandodarī grieves for him as Sītā herself might grieve for Rāma. The story is full of marvels, but the magic element has often a profound significance and is no merely fanciful embroidery. All the great powers possessed by the protagonists of one side or the other are represented as won by self-restraint and mental concentration, not as the fruit of any talisman fortuitously acquired. Thus the conflict becomes, in the last resort, essentially a conflict of character with character. Take again the case of the magic weapons, informed with the power of irresistible spells. Hanuman is struck down and paralysed with one of these, but no sooner are physical bonds added to the mental force than he is free. Here, surely, is clear evidence of an apprehension of the principle that to fortify with violence the power of wisdom is inevitably an unsuccessful policy.

In such ways the significance of Vālmīki's Rāmāyana becomes apparent to those who read or re-read it attentively, and its lasting influence on Indian life and character ideals becomes easily understandable. It is hardly possible to turn aside from this aspect of the myth of Rāma and Sītā without expressing profound regret that this great means of education should have been eliminated from modern educational systems in India—in the name of religious neutrality. For it would scarcely be going too far to say that no one unfamiliar with the story of Rāma and Sītā can be in any real sense a citizen of India, nor acquainted with morality as the greatest of Indian teachers conceived it. Perhaps one might go further and say that no one unfamiliar with the story of Rāma and Sītā can be a true citizen of the world.

The Rāmāyana as Animal Epos

Here and there throughout the world we come upon whispers and echoes of the great animal epos of primitive man. As a whole it no longer exists; it is no longer even recoverable. It can only be guessed at and inferred from a hint here, a fragment there. But nowhere in the modern world is the material for its restoration so abundant as in India. To this day in the Indian imagination there is a unique sympathy with animal expression. Man or boy, gentle and simple alike, telling some story of mouse or squirrel, will bring the tale to a climax with the very cries and movements of the creature he has watched. It is assumed instinctively that at least the fundamental feelings, if not the thoughts, of furred and feathered folk are even as our own. And it is here, surely, in this swift interpretation, in this deep intuition of kinship, that we find the real traces of the temper that went to the making long ago of Buddhism and Jainism, the gentle faiths.

The Rāmāyana as Animal Epos

The Indian people are human, and cruelty occurs amongst them occasionally. The fact that it is comparatively rare is proved by the familiarity and fearlessness of all the smaller birds and beasts. But in this unconscious attitude of the Indian imagination, in its mimicry and quick perception of the half fun, half pathos of the dumb creation, we have an actual inheritance from the childhood of the world, from that early playtime of man in which the four-footed things were his brethren and companions.

This whimsical spirit, this merry sense of kindred, speaks to us throughout the Buddhist Birth-Stories (*Jātakas*), as a similar feeling does in Æsop's Fables or in the tales of Uncle Remus. The *Jātakas*, it is true, deal with animal life as the vehicle of a high philosophy and a noble romance, instead of merely making it illustrate shrewd proverbs or point homely wit. The love of Buddha and Yashodarā formed the poetic legend of its age, and there was nothing incongruous to the mind of the period in making birds and beasts frequent actors in its drama. Swans are the preachers of gospels in the courts of kings. The herds of deer, like men, have amongst them chiefs and aristocrats, who will lay down their lives for those that follow them. Yet already, even here, we see the clear Aryan mind at work, reducing to order and distinctness the tangled threads of a far older body of thought. Out of that older substance are born the tendencies that will again and again come to the surface in the great theological systems of later times. Of it were shaped the heroes, such as Hanuman and Garuda, who step down into the more modern arena at every new formulation of the Hindu idea, like figures already familiar, to join in its action.

What we miss through all the poetry of this gradual Aryanizing is the element of awe—for this, though present, is perpetually growing less. The Aryan mind is essentially an organizing mind, always increasingly scientific, increasingly rational in its outlook upon things. The colour and caprice that make early mythologies so rich in stimulus for the imagination are almost always the contribution of older and more childlike races. To humanity, in its first morning-hours, there seemed to be in the animal something of the divine. Its inarticulateness, not then so far removed from man's own speech, constituted an oracle. Its hidden ways of life and sudden flashings forth upon the path were supernatural. The dim intelligence that looked out from between its eyes seemed like a large benevolence, not to be compassed or fathomed by mortal thought. And who could tell what was the store of wisdom garnered behind the little old face of the grey ape out of the forest, or hoarded by the coiled snake in her hole beside the tree?

The Attraction of the Animal

With all a child's power of wonder, the thought of man played about the elephant and the eagle, the monkey and the lion. Many tribes and races had each its own mystic animal, half worshipped as a god, half suspected of being an ancestor. With the rise of the great theological systems all this will be regimented and organized. From being gods themselves the mythical half-human creatures will descend, to become the vehicles and companions of gods. One of these will be mounted on the peacock, another on the swan. One will be carried by the bull, another by the goat. But in this very fact there will be an implicit declaration of the divine associations of the

II

GARUDA

NANDA LĀL BOSE

Page 16

subordinate. The emblem thus constituted will mark a compromise, a synthesis of two systems, two ideas—one relatively new, and one incomparably older and more primitive. For the same process that makes the Tenth Book of the *Rig-Veda* so markedly different from its predecessors, inasmuch as in it the religious consciousness of the Sanskrit-speaking people has begun to take note of the indigenous conceptions of the peoples of the soil, is characteristic of the advancing consciousness of Hinduism throughout the historic period. The Aryan brain, with its store of great nature-gods—gods of sky and sun and fire, of wind and waters and storm, gods who had so much in common with each other, throughout Aryan mythology, from the Hellespont to the Ganges—had gradually to recognize and include the older, vaguer, more dimly cosmic deities of various Asiatic populations. The process of this is perfectly clear and traceable historically. Only the rival elements themselves have to be assumed and enumerated. Of the growth of the mythology of Indra and Agni, of Vāyu and Varuna we can say very little. In all probability it was born outside India, and brought there, as to Greece, in a state of maturity. And similarly, we cannot trace the steps by which the Indian imagination came to conceive of the universe, or the god of the universe, as the Elephant-headed. Obviously, the idea was born in India itself, where the elephants ranged the forests and breasted the rivers. The appearance of the same worship in such countries as China and Japan is clearly a relic of some very ancient religious influence brought to bear upon them from the far south.

The Elephant-headed

What exactly is signified by this Ganesha, or Gaṇapati —Lord of the Multitudes, or was it primarily Lord of the Territory? What is the meaning of that white elephant-head borne on that red body? Vast and cosmic he certainly is. Is he at bottom the white cloud glistening in the evening against the crimson sun? In any case he stands to this day as the god of success and of worldly wisdom. His divine attribute is the simple one of fulfilling all desires. He is to be worshipped at the beginning of all worships, that they may be successful in their intention—a sure proof of long priority. In Japan it is said that he is known as the god of the villages, and that he has something a trifle rude in his worship. In itself this shows his great antiquity, though as lord of the villages in India he could not be so old as those of Southern India, which are always dedicated to the Earth-Mother, with an altar of rude stone.

How well we can enter into the tenderness and awe of the primitive Indian man for this his great god! The depths of the night would seem to be his vast form. All wisdom and all riches were in his gigantic keeping, He gave writing. He gave wealth. He was the starry universe itself. Success was his to bestow. All that was, was contained within him. How natural that he should be the Fulfiller of Desire! Ganesha is not the deity of a people who fear their god. He is gentle, calm, and friendly, a god who loves man and is loved by him. A genuine kindliness and a certain wise craft are written on his visage. But neither is he the god of any theological conception. He is obvious, simple, capable of a slight grossness, full of rude vigour and primal masculinity, destined from his birth to a marvellous future, both in faith and art, as the forefront of all undertakings that are to make for success. Less ancient than the primitive Mother of the Dekkan villages, he was nevertheless, it may be, the beginning of organized worship. He was already old when Buddhism was young. Above all, he is the god neither of priests nor of kings, neither of theocracies nor of nations, but in all probability of that old diffusive mercantile culture, the civilization of the Bharatas. To this day he is the god pre-eminently of merchants, and it is a curious fact that in the Indian city, when a merchant is made bankrupt, the event is notified to all comers by the office Ganeshas being turned upside down!

The Epic of Hinduism

First of the popular scriptures of Hinduism—written early in the Christian era, for the now consolidating nation—was the epic poem of Vālmīki known as the Rāmāyana. This is the world gospel of purity and sorrow, but also, no less notably, the fairy-tale of nature. Since the beginning of the reign of Ganesha the age of the making of Buddhism and the Jātaka had come and gone, and with the passing centuries the sway of the Aryan genius had been more and more clearly felt. As in every work of art we obtain a glimpse of the culture that precedes it, so in the Rāmāyana, while there is a great deal that is prophetic of developments to come, we also find ourselves transported into the child-world of an earlier age. Like all such worlds, it was one in which birds and beasts could talk and comport themselves as men. To the folk of that time, it is clear, the forest was a realm of mystery. It was inhabited by scholars and anchorites. It was full of beautiful flowers and fragrance; it was the haunt of sweet-singing birds; and it was cool and green. All holiness might be attained under its soothing influence. Any austerity might be practised in its ennobling solitudes. But it was also the home of deadly beasts of prey. And many of these were surrounded by an added and supernatural terror; for was it not known that the demon Mārīcha had the power to change his shape at will? Who, then, could tell whether even tiger or bear were what it seemed, or something more subtle and fearsome still? Amongst the evening shadows walked strange forms and malefic presences. Misshapen monsters and powerful fiends, owning allegiance to a terrible ten-headed kinsman in distant Lankā, ranged through its fastnesses. How often must the belated hunter have listened in horror to whispering sound from the darkness of trees and brushwood, feeling that he was acting as eavesdropper to the enemies of the soul!

But the gods were ever greater than the powers of evil. It was, after all, the twilight of divinity that hung so thick about the forest-sanctuary. Were there not there the *gandharvas* and *siddhas*—musical ministrants of the upper air? Were there not *apsarās*, the heavenly nymphs, for whose sake, at the moment of nightfall, we must not venture too near the edge of the forest pools, lest we catch them at their bathing and incur some doom? Were there not *kinnaras*, the human birds, holding instruments of music under their wings? Was it not known that amidst their silence slept Jatāyu, king for sixty thousand years of all the eagle-tribes, and that somewhere amongst them dwelt Sampati, his elder brother, unable to fly because his wings had been scorched off in the effort to cloak Jatāyu from sunstroke? And all about the greenwood came and went the monkey hosts, weird with a more than human wisdom, able at a word to make the leafy branches blossom into beauty, and yet unhappy strugglers with their own hot monkey-nature, ever imposing on them, like a spell, a strange unspeakable destiny of mischief and futility.

It is an organized society, this, that is predicated by the Indian imagination of the animal races. They have their families and genealogies, their sovereigns and political alliances, and their personal lot of tragedy or comedy. Throughout the dramatic phases of the Rāmāyana the counterplot is provided by the five great monkeys whom Sītā sees below her, seated on a hill-top, when she is being borne through the evening sky by Rāvana. Of these the chief is Sugriva, of the monster neck, who has lost wife and kingdom at the hands of his elder brother Bali, and waits to be avenged on him. Sugriva is thus a king in exile, surrounded by his counsellors and captains, in a sense the enchanted prince of fairy-tales. There are scholars who find in this tableau of the five chief monkeys on the mountain-top a fragment of some ancient cosmogony, already, it may be, a score of millenniums old.

Hanuman

But there moves through the Rāmāyana one being who, though also a monkey, is of a different order. In those parts of India where, as in the Himālayas or the interior of Mahārāshtra, the symbols of primitive Hinduism still abound, little chapels of Hanuman are as common as those of Ganesha, and the ape, like the elephant, has achieved a singular and obviously age-old conventionalism of form. He is always seen in profile, vigorously portrayed in low relief upon a slab. The image conveys the impression of a complex emblem rather than of plastic realism. But there is no question as to the energy and beauty of the qualities for which he stands. It may be questioned whether there is in the whole of literature another apotheosis of loyalty and self-surrender like that of Hanuman. He is the Hindu ideal of the perfect servant, the servant who finds full realization of manhood, of faithfulness, of his obedience; the subordinate whose glory is in his own inferiority.

Hanuman must have been already ancient when the Rāmāyana was first conceived. What may have been the first impulse that created him it is now useless to guess. But he is linked to a grander order than that of Sugriva and Bali, the princes whom he serves, inasmuch as he, like Jatāyu, is said to be the son of Vāyu, known in the Vedas as the god of the winds. In any case the depth and seriousness of the part assigned to him in the great poem assure him of unfading immortality. Whatever may have been his age or origin, Hanuman is captured and placed by the Rāmāyana amongst religious conceptions of the highest import. When he bows to touch the foot of Rāma, that Prince who is also a divine incarnation, we witness the meeting-point of early nature-worships with the great systems that are to sway the future of religion. But we must not forget that in this one figure those early systems have achieved the spiritual quality and made a lasting contribution to the idealism of man. In ages to come the religion of Vishnu, the Preserver, will never be able to dispense with that greatest of devotees, the monkey-god; and even in its later phases, when Garuda —the divine bird, who haunted the imagination of all early peoples—has taken his final place as the vehicle, or attendant, of Nārāyana, Hanuman is never really displaced. The wonderful creation of Vālmīki will retain to the end of time his domination over the hearts and consciences of men.

The Story of Rāma

The Story of Rāma as told by Vālmīki

One day the hermit Vālmīki inquired of the great *rishi*[1] Nārada whether he could tell of any man living perfect in goodliness, virtue, courage, and benevolence. Then Nārada related to him all the story that is now called the Rāmāyana, for such a man as Vālmīki desired to hear of was the great Rāma.

Vālmīki returned to his forest hut. As he passed through the woods he saw a bird-man and a bird-woman singing and dancing. But at that very moment a wicked hunter shot the bird-man with an arrow so that he died, and his mate bewailed him long and bitterly. Then the hermit was moved by pity and anger, and cursed the hunter and passed on. But as he walked on, his words recurred to him, and he found that they formed a couplet in a new metre: "Let this be called a *shloka*," he said.

Soon after he reached his hut there appeared to him the four-faced shining Brahmā, the Creator of the World. Him Vālmīki worshipped; but the unhappy bird-man and the new-made *shloka* filled his thoughts. Then Brahmā addressed him with a smile: "It was by my will that those words came from thy mouth; that metre shall be very famous hereafter. Do thou compose in it the whole history of Rāma; relate, O wise one, both all that is known and all that is as yet unknown to thee of Rāma and Lakshmana and Janaka's daughter, and all the tribe of rākshasas. What is unknown shall be revealed to thee, and the poem shall be true from the first word to the last. Moreover, this thy Rāmāyana shall spread abroad amongst

[1] A sage or priest of special authority, particularly one of the "seven rishis" who are priests of the gods and are identified with the stars of the Great Bear.

men so long as the mountains and the seas endure." So saying, Brahmā vanished.

Then Vālmīki, dwelling in the hermitage amongst his disciples, set himself to make the great Rāmāyan, that bestows on all who hear it righteousness and wealth and fulfilment of desire, as well as the severing of ties. He sought deeper insight into the story he had heard from Nārada, and thereto took his seat according to *yoga*[1] ritual, and addressed himself to ponder on that subject and no other. Then by his yoga-powers he beheld Rāma and Sītā, Lakshman, and Dasharatha with his wives in his kingdom, laughing and talking, bearing and forbearing, doing and undoing as in real life, as clearly as one might see a fruit held in the palm of the hand. He perceived not only what had been, but what was to come. Then only, after concentred meditation, when the whole story lay like a picture in his mind, he began to shape it into *shlokas*, of which, when it was finished, there were no less than twenty-four thousand. Then he reflected how it might be published abroad. For this he chose Kusi and Lava, the accomplished sons of Rāma and Sītā, who lived in the forest hermitage, and were learned in the Vedas, in music and recitation and every art, and very fair to see. To them Vālmīki taught the whole Rāmāyana till they could recite it perfectly from beginning to end, so that those who heard them seemed to see everything told of in the story passing before their eyes. Afterward the brothers went to Rāma's city of Ayodhyā, where Rāma found and entertained them, thinking them to be hermits; and there before the whole court the Rāmāyana was first recited in public.

1 *Yoga*, mental concentration; *lit.* union. *Yogī*, one who practises *yoga*, an ascetic or hermit.

Vishnu is born as Rāma & his Brothers

Dasharatha and the Horse Sacrifice

There was once a great and beautiful city called Ayodhyā—that is, "Unconquerable"—in the country of Koshala. There all men were righteous and happy, well read and contented, truthful, well provided with goods, self-restrained and charitable and full of faith. Its king was Dasharatha, a veritable Manu amongst men, a moon amongst the stars. He had many wise counsellors, amongst whom were Kashyapa and Mārkandeya, and he had also two saintly priests attached to his family, namely, Vāshishtha and Vāmadeva. To another great sage, Rishyasringa, he gave his daughter Santā. His ministers were such men as could keep their counsel and judge of things finely; they were well versed in the arts of policy and ever fair-spoken. Only one desire of Dasharatha's was unsatisfied: he had no son to carry on his line. Because of this, after many vain austerities, he determined at last on the greatest of all offerings—a horse sacrifice; and calling the family priests and other Brāhmans, he gave all necessary orders for this undertaking. Then, returning to the inner rooms of the palace, he told his three wives what had been set afoot, whereat their faces shone with joy, like lotus-flowers in early spring.

When a year had passed the horse that had been set free returned, and Rishyasringa and Vāshishtha performed the ceremony, and there was great festivity and gladness. Then Rishyasringa told the king that four sons would be born to him, perpetuators of his race; at which sweet words the king rejoiced exceedingly.

Vishnu is born as Rāma and his Brothers

Now at this time all the deities were there assembled to receive their share of the offerings made, and being assembled together they approached Brahmā with a petition. "A certain wicked rākshasa named Rāvana greatly oppresses us," they said, "whom we suffer patiently because thou hast granted him a boon—not to be slain by gandharvas, or yakshas, or rākshasas, or gods. But now his tyranny becometh past endurance, and, O Lord, thou shouldst devise some method to destroy him." To them Brahmā replied: "That evil rākshasa disdained to ask from me immunity from the attack of men: by man only he may and shall be slain." Thereat the deities rejoiced. At that moment there arrived the great God Vishnu, clad in yellow robes, bearing mace and discus and conch, and riding upon Garuda. Him the deities reverenced, and prayed him to take birth as the four sons of Dasharatha for the destruction of the wily and irrepressible Rāvana. Then that one of lotus-eyes, making of himself four beings, chose Dasharatha for his father and disappeared. In a strange form, like a flaming tiger, he reappeared in Dasharatha's sacrificial fire and, greeting him, named himself as the messenger of God. "Do thou, O tiger amongst men," said he, "accept this divine rice and milk, and share it amongst thy wives." Then Dasharatha, overjoyed, carried the divine food and gave a portion of it to Kaushalyā, and another portion to Sumitrā, and another to Kaikeyī, and then the fourth portion to Sumitrā again. In due time four sons were born of them, sharing the self of Vishnu—from Kaushalyā, Rāma; from Kaikeyī, Bharata; and from Sumitrā, Lakshmana and Satrughna; and these names were given them by Vāshishtha.

Meanwhile the gods created mighty monkey-hosts, brave and wise and swift, shape-shifters, hardly to be slain, to be the helpers of the heroic Vishnu in the battle with the rākshasas.

Vishnu is born as Rāma & his Brothers

The four sons of Dasharatha grew up to early manhood, excelling all in bravery and virtue. Rāma especially became the idol of the people and the favourite of his father. Learned in the Vedas, he was no less expert in the science of elephants and horses and in riding cars, and a very mirror of courtesy. Lakshmana devoted himself to Rāma's service, so that the two were always together. Like a faithful shadow Lakshman followed Rāma, sharing with him everything that was his own, and guarding him when he went abroad to exercise or hunt. In the same way Satrughna attached himself to Bharata. So it was till Rāma reached the age of sixteen.

Now there was a certain great rishi named Vishvāmitra, originally a Kshatriya, who by the practice of unheard-of austerities had won from the gods the status of *brahmā-rishi.* He dwelt in the Shaiva hermitage called Siddhāshrāma, and came thence to ask a boon from Dasharatha. Two rākshasas, Mārīcha and Suvāhu, supported by the wicked Rāvana, continually disturbed his sacrifices and polluted his sacred fire; none but Rāma could overcome these devils. Dasharatha welcomed Vishvāmitra gladly, and promised him any gift that he desired; but when he learnt that his dear son Rāma was required for so terrible and dangerous a service, he was cast down, and it seemed as though the light of his life went out. Yet he could not break his word, and it came to pass that Rāma and Lakshman went away with Vishvāmitra for the ten days of his sacrificial rites. But though it was for so short a time, this was the beginning of their manhood and of love and strife.

Vāshishtha cheered Dasharatha's heart, assuring him of certain victory for Rāma. So, with his father's blessing, Rāma set out with Vishvāmitra and his brother Lakshman.

A cool breeze, delighted at the sight of Rāma, fanned their faces, and flowers rained down upon them from the sky. Vishvāmitra led the way; the two brothers, carrying their bows and swords, wearing splendid jewels and gloves of lizard-skin upon their fingers, followed Vishvāmitra like glorious flames, making him bright with the reflection of their own radiance.

Arrived at the hermitage, Vishvāmitra and the other priests began their sacrifice; and when the rākshasas, like rain-clouds obscuring the sky, rushed forward in horrid shapes, Rāma wounded and put to flight Mārīcha and Suvāhu, and slew the others of those evil night-rangers. After the days of sacrifice and ritual at Siddhāshrāma were over, Rāma asked Vishvāmitra what other work he required of him.

Rāma weds the Daughter of Janaka

Vishvāmitra replied that Janaka, Rāja of Mithila, was about to celebrate a great sacrifice. "Thither," he said, "we shall repair. And thou, O tiger among men, shalt go with us, and there behold a wonderful and marvellous bow. This great bow the gods gave long ago to Rāja Devarata; and neither gods nor gandharvas nor asuras nor rākshasas nor men have might to string it, though many kings and princes have essayed it. That bow is worshipped as a deity. The bow and Janaka's great sacrifice shalt thou behold."

Thus all the Brāhmans of that hermitage, with Vishvāmitra at their head, and accompanied by Rāma and Lakshman, set out for Mithila; and the birds and beasts dwelling in Siddhāshrāma followed after Vishvāmitra, whose wealth was his asceticism. As they went along the forest paths Vishvāmitra related ancient stories to the two brothers, and especially the story of the birth of Gangā, the great river Ganges.

Janaka welcomed the ascetics with much honour, and appointing them to seats according to their rank, he asked who those brothers might be that walked amongst men like lions or elephants, godlike and goodly to be seen. Vishvāmitra told King Janaka all the history of Dasharatha's sons, their journey to Siddhāshrāma and fight with the rākshasas, and how Rāma had now come to Mithila to see the famous bow.

Next day Janaka summoned the brothers to see the bow. First he told them how that bow had been given by Shiva to the gods, and by the gods to his own ancestor, Devarata. And he added : " I have a daughter, Sītā, not born of men, but sprung from the furrow as I ploughed the field and hallowed it. On him who bends the bow I will bestow my daughter. Many kings and princes have tried and failed to bend it. Now I shall show the bow to you, and if Rāma succeed in bending it I shall give him my daughter Sītā."

Then the great bow was brought forth upon an eight-wheeled cart drawn by five thousand tall men. Rāma drew the bow from its case and strove to bend it ; it yielded easily, and he strung and drew it till at last it snapped in two with the sound of an earthquake or a thunder-clap. The thousands of spectators were amazed and terrified, and all but Vishvāmitra, Janaka, Rāma, and Lakshman fell to the ground. Then Janaka praised Rāma and gave orders for the marriage to be prepared, and sent messengers to Ayodhyā to invite Rāja Dasharatha to his son's wedding, to give his blessing and consent.

Thereafter the two kings met and Janaka bestowed Sītā upon Rāma, and his second daughter Urmilā on Lakshman.

To Bharata and Satrughna Janaka gave Mandavyā and Srutakirtī, daughters of Kushadhwaja. Then those four princes, holding each his bride's hand, circumambulated the sacrificial fire, the marriage dais, the king, and all the hermits thrice, while flowers rained down from heaven and celestial music sounded. Then Dasharatha and his sons and their four brides returned home, taking with them many presents, and were welcomed by Kaushalyā and Sumitrā and the slender-waisted Kaikeyī. Having thus won honour, wealth, and noble brides, those four best of men dwelt at Ayodhyā, serving their father.

Now, of those four sons, Rāma was dearest to his father and to all men of Ayodhyā. In every virtue he excelled; for he was of serene temper under all circumstances of fortune or misfortune, never vainly angered; he remembered even a single kindness, but forgot a hundred injuries; he was learned in the Vedas and in all arts and sciences of peace and war, such as hospitality, and policy, and logic, and poetry, and training horses and elephants, and archery; he honoured those of ripe age; he regarded not his own advantage; he despised none, but was solicitous for the welfare of every one; ministering to his father and his mothers, and devoted to his brothers, especially to Lakshman. But Bharata and Satrughna stayed with their uncle Ashwapati in another city.

Rāma to be installed as Heir-Apparent

Now Dasharatha reflected that he had ruled for many, many years, and was weary, and he thought no joy could be greater than if he should see Rāma established on the throne. He summoned a council of his vassals and counsellors and neighbouring kings and princes who were accustomed to reside in Ayodhyā, and in solemn words,

III

RĀMA'S MARRIAGE

K. Venkatappa

Page 30

like the thunder of drums, addressed this parliament of men:

"Ye well know that for many long years I have governed this realm, being as a father to those that dwell therein. Thinking not to gain my own happiness, I have spent my days in ruling according unto *dharma*.[1] Now I wish for rest, and would install my eldest son Rāma as heir-apparent and entrust the government to him. But herein, my lords, I seek for your approval; for the thought of the dispassionate is other than the thought of the inflamed, and truth arises from the conflict of various views." The princes rejoiced at the king's words, as peacocks dance at the sight of heavy rain-clouds. There arose the hum of many voices, as for a time the Brāhmans and army-leaders, citizens and countrymen considered together. Then they answered:

"O aged king, assuredly we wish to see Prince Rāma installed as heir-apparent, riding the elephant of state, seated beneath the umbrella of dominion."

Again the king inquired of them for greater certainty: "Why would ye have Rāma to your ruler?" and they replied:

"By reason of his many virtues, for indeed he towers among men as Sakra amongst the gods. In forgiveness he is like the Earth, in debate like Brihaspati. He speaks the truth, and is a mighty bowman. He is ever busied with the welfare of the people, and not given to detraction where he finds one blemish amongst many virtues. He is skilled in music and his eyes are fair to look upon. Neither his pleasure nor his anger is in vain; he is easily approached, and self-controlled, and goes not forth to war or the protection of a city or a province

[1] *Dharma*, righteousness, the established code of ethics.

without victorious return. He is beloved of all. Indeed, the Earth desires him for her Lord."

Then the king summoned Vāshishtha, Vāmadeva, and other of the Brāhmans, and charged them to make ready for Rāma's installation. Orders were given for the purveyance of gold and silver and gems and ritual vessels, grains and honey and clarified butter, cloth as yet unworn, weapons, cars, elephants, a bull with gilded horns, a tiger-skin, a sceptre and umbrella, and heaped-up rice and curds and milk for the feeding of hundreds and thousands. Flags were hoisted, the roads were watered, garlands hung on every door; knights were notified to be present in their mail, and dancers and singers to hold themselves in readiness. Then Dasharatha sent for Rāma, that long-armed hero, like the moon in beauty, and gladdening the eyes of all men. Rāma passed through the assembly, like a moon in the clear starry autumn sky, and bending low worshipped his father's feet. Dasharatha lifted him and set him on a seat prepared for him, golden and begemmed, where he seemed like an image or reflection of his father on the throne. Then the aged king spoke to Rāma of what had been decided, and announced that he should be installed as heir-apparent. And he added wise counsel in these words:

"Though thou art virtuous by nature, I would advise thee out of love and for thy good: Practise yet greater gentleness and restraint of sense; avoid all lust and anger; maintain thy arsenal and treasury; personally and by means of others make thyself well acquainted with the affairs of state; administer justice freely to all, that the people may rejoice. Gird thee, my son, and undertake thy task."

Then friends of Kaushalyā, Rāma's mother, told her all that had been done, and received gold and kine and gems in reward for their good tidings, and all men with delighted minds repaired to their homes and worshipped the gods.

Then again the king sent for Rāma and held converse with him. "My son," he said, "I shall install thee to-morrow as heir-apparent; for I am old and have dreamt ill dreams, and the astrologers inform me that my life-star is threatened by the planets Sun and Mars and Rāhu. Therefore do thou, with Sītā, from the time of sunset, observe a fast, well guarded by thy friends. I would have thee soon installed, for the hearts even of the virtuous change by the influence of natural attachments, and none knoweth what may come to pass." Then Rāma left his father and sought his mother in the inner rooms. He found her in the temple, clad in silk, worshipping the gods and praying for his welfare. There, too, were Lakshman and Sītā. Rāma reverenced his mother, and asked her to prepare whatever should be necessary for the night of fasting, for himself and Sītā. Turning then to Lakshman, "Do thou rule the Earth with me," he said, "for this is thy good fortune not less than mine. My life and kingdom I desire only because of thee." Then Rāma went with Sītā to his own quarters, and thither Vāshishtha also went to bless the fast.

All that night the streets and highways of Ayodhyā were crowded with eager men; the tumult and the hum of voices sounded like the ocean's roar when the moon is full. The streets were cleaned and washed, and hung with garlands and strings of flags and banners; lighted lamps were set on branching cressets. The name of Rāma was on every man's lips, and all were expectant of the morrow, while Rāma kept the fast within.

The Scheming of Kaikeyī

All this time Bharata's mother, Kaikeyī, had not heard a word of Rāja Dasharatha's intention. Kaikeyī was young and passionate and very beautiful; by nature she was generous, but not so kind or wise that she might not be swayed by the crooked promptings of her own desires or another's instigation. She had a faithful old humpbacked nurse of an evil disposition; Mantharā was her name. Now Mantharā, hearing the rejoicings and learning that Rāma was to be installed as heir-apparent, hurried to inform her mistress of this misfortune to Bharata, as Rāma's honour seemed to her narrow view. "O senseless one," she said, "why art thou idle and content when such misfortune is thine?" Kaikeyī asked her what evil had befallen. Mantharā answered with words of anger: "O my lady, a terrible destruction awaits thy bliss, so that I am sunk in fear immeasurable and afflicted with heaviness and grief; burning like a fire, I have sought thee hurriedly. Thou art verily a Queen of Earth; but though thy Lord speaks blandly, he is crafty and crooked-hearted within, and wills thee harm. It is Kaushalyā's welfare that he seeks, not thine, whatever sweet words he may have for thee. Bharata is sent away, and Rāma is to be set upon the throne! Indeed, my girl, thou hast nursed for thy husband a poisonous snake! Now quickly act, and find a way to save thyself and Bharata and me." But Mantharā's words made Kaikeyī glad: she rejoiced that Rāma should be heir, and giving a jewel to the humpbacked maid, she said: "What boon can I give thee for this news? I am glad indeed to hear this tale. Rāma and Bharata are very dear to me, and I find no difference between them. It is well that Rāma should be set upon the throne. Have thanks for thy good news."

Then the humpbacked servant was the more angry, and cast away the jewel. "Indeed," she said, "thou art mad to rejoice at thy calamity. What woman of good sense is gladdened by deadly news of a co-wife's son's preferment? Thou shalt be as it were Kaushalyā's slave, and Bharata but Rāma's servant."

But still Kaikeyī was not moved to envy. "Why grieve at Rāma's fortune?" she said. "He is well fitted to be king; and if the kingdom be his, it will be also Bharata's, for Rāma ever regards his brothers as himself." Then Mantharā, sighing very bitterly, answered Kaikeyī: "Little dost thou understand, thinking that to be good which is thy evil fortune. Thou wouldst grant me a reward because of the preferment of thy co-wife! Know surely that Rāma, when he is well established, will banish Bharata to a distant land or to another world. Bharata is his natural enemy, for what other rival has he, since Lakshmana desires only Rāma's weal, and Satrughna is attached to Bharata? Thou shouldst save Bharata from Rāma, who shall overcome him as a lion an elephant: thy co-wife, Rāma's mother, too, will seek to revenge on thee that slight thou didst once put on her. Sorry will be thy lot when Rāma rules the earth. Thou shouldst, while there is time, plan to set thy son upon the throne and banish Rāma."

Thus Kaikeyī's pride and jealousy were roused, and she grew red with anger and breathed deep and hard, and answered Mantharā:

"This very day Rāma must be banished and Bharata installed as heir. Hast thou any plan to accomplish this my will?"

Then Mantharā reminded her of an ancient pledge: how long ago in a great battle with the rākshasas Dasharatha had been wounded and almost slain; how Kaikeyī had found him unconscious on the field of battle, and borne him to a place of safety and there healed him; how Dasharatha had granted her two boons, and she reserved those boons to ask them from him when and as she would. "Now," said Mantharā, "ask thy husband for these boons: to establish Bharata as heir upon the throne, and banish Rāma to the forests for fourteen years. During those years Bharata shall be so well established and make himself so dear to the people that he need not fear Rāma. Therefore do thou enter the Anger-chamber,[1] casting off thy jewels, and, putting on a soiled garment, vouchsafe no word or look to Dasharatha. Thou art his dearest wife, to whom he can refuse nothing, nor can he endure to see thee grieved. He will offer thee gold and jewels, but do thou refuse every offer but the banishment of Rāma and the establishment of Bharata."

Thus was Kaikeyī led to choose that as good which was in truth most evil; stirred up by the humpbacked servant's words, the fair Kaikeyī started up like a mare devoted to her foal and rushed along an evil path. She thanked and praised the humpbacked Mantharā, and promised her many rich rewards when Bharata should be set upon the throne. Then she tore off her jewels and beautiful garments, and flung herself down upon the floor of the Anger-chamber; she clasped her breasts and cried: "Know that either Rāma shall be banished and my son installed, or I shall die: if Rāma goes not to the forest, I will not desire bed or garland, sandal-paste or ointment, meat or drink, or life itself." So, like a starry sky hidden

[1] A room set apart for an offended queen.

by heavy clouds, that royal lady sulked and gloomed; like a bird-woman struck down by poisoned shafts, in her distress like a serpent's daughter in her wrath.

Then, while it was still long before the dawn, Dasharatha bethought him to inform Kaikeyī of the coming ceremony. Not finding her in her painted bower nor in his own rooms, he learnt that she had gone to the Anger-chamber. There he followed, and beheld his youngest wife lying upon the ground like an uprooted vine or an ensnared doe. Then that hero, like a forest elephant, tenderly touched the lotus-eyed queen and asked what ailed her. "If thou art sick there are physicians; or if thou wouldst have any who deserve a punishment rewarded, or those who should be rewarded punished, name thy wish: I can deny thee nothing. Thou knowest that I can refuse no request of thine; ask then for whatsoever thou desirest and be comforted."

Thus consoled, she answered: "None has injured me; but I have a desire which, if thou wilt grant, I will tell thee of." Then Dasharatha swore by Rāma himself that he would accomplish whatever she desired.

Then Kaikeyī revealed her dreadful wish, calling the Heaven and Earth and Day and Night and household gods and every living thing to witness that he had promised to fulfil her will. She reminded him of that old war with the asuras when she had saved his life and he had granted her two boons. Thus the king was snared by Kaikeyī, like a deer entering a trap. "Now those boons," she said, "which thou art pledged to grant me here and now, are these: let Rāma, clad in deer-skin, lead a hermit's life in Dandaka forest for fourteen years, and Bharata be established as heir-apparent. Do thou now prove thy royal word, according to thy race and character and birth. Truth, so the hermits tell us, is of supreme benefit to men when they reach the next world."

Dasharatha's Dilemma

Then Dasharatha was overwhelmed with grief and swooned away, and, coming to himself again, he prayed Kaikeyī to waive her right. For long he pleaded with her, weeping heavy tears and thinking all an evil dream; but Kaikeyī only answered with exhortations to keep his sworn word, reminding him of many ancient exemplars of truth, such as Saivya, who gave his own flesh to the hawk that pursued the dove he had protected, or Alarka, that gave his eyes to a Brāhman. "If thou dost not fulfil what has been promised, thou art for ever disgraced, and here and now shall I take my own life," she said. Then Dasharatha, urged by Kaikeyī like a goaded horse, cried out: "I am bound fast by the bond of truth: this is the root of all my seeming madness. My only wish is to behold Rāma."

Now dawn had come, and Vāshishtha sent Rāma's charioteer to tell the king that all was ready for the ceremony. Hardly able to say anything for grief, the king sent that charioteer to fetch Rāma to his side. So, leaving Sītā with happy words, Rāma drove through the gay streets to his father's palace; those who had not the fortune to see Rāma, or to be seen by him, despised themselves, and were despised by all.

Rāma greeted the king and Kaikeyī dutifully, but Dasharatha, altogether broken down and crushed to earth, could only murmur faintly, "Rāma, Rāma." Grieved at heart, Rāma wondered if he had done anything amiss, or if any misfortune had befallen his father. "O mother," he said to Kaikeyī, "what sorrow has overtaken my father's heart?" Then she answered shamelessly: "O Rāma, nothing ails thy father, but somewhat he has to tell thee, and since thou art his dearest son, he cannot frame the speech that injures thee. Yet thou shouldst perform what he has promised me. Long ago the Lord of the Earth promised me two boons: now in vain he would set up a dyke, after the water has all passed away—for thou knowest that truth is the root of all religion. If thou wilt accomplish whatever good or evil he ordains, I shall tell thee all." Rāma answered: "Dear lady, do not speak such words to me; for if he order, I can jump into the fire or drink strong poison. Know that I shall carry out his wish: Rāma's promise never fails." Then Kaikeyī told him the story of the boons, and she said: "These are the boons I have been promised: that thou shouldst dwell as a hermit in Dandaka forest for fourteen years, with dress of bark and matted hair, and that Bharata should be installed as heir-apparent on the throne to-day. Thy father is too much grieved to even glance at thee; but do thou save his honour by redeeming those great pledges he has given."

Rāma was not grieved or angered by these cruel words, but answered quietly: "Be it as thou sayest. I am only sorry for my father's grief. Let messengers be sent at once for Bharata, while I, not questioning his wish, go to the forest. Even though he has not himself commanded me, thy order is sufficient. Allow me now to see my mother and to comfort Sītā, and do thou serve and tend both Bharata and our father, for this is right." Then Rāma, followed by Lakshman hot with anger, but himself unmoved, sought his mother, and found her making offerings to Vishnu and other deities. Gladly she greeted him, and he reverently her. Then he told her all that had befallen: how Bharata should be appointed heir, and himself should live for fourteen years an exile in the forest. Like a great *sāl* tree felled by the woodman's axe, she sank to the ground and wept inconsolably. "O my son," she said, "hadst thou not been born, I should have grieved only because I had no son; but now a greater sorrow is mine. I am the eldest of the queens, and have ever endured many things from the younger wives. Now I shall be as one of Kaikeyī's maidservants, or even less. She is ever of sour mood to me; how may I now, neglected by my husband, meet her eyes? Twenty-seven years of thy life have I expected an end of grief, and now I know not why death delays to carry me away. All the almsgiving and austerity have been in vain. Yet, O my darling, I shall follow thee even to the forest, as a cow follows after her young one; for I cannot bear the days till thy return, nor dwell amongst the co-wives. Do thou take me with thee, like a wild hind." But Lakshman urged his brother to resist, with angry and impatient words, vowing to fight for Rāma and blaming Dasharatha bitterly. Kaushalyā then joined her prayer to Lakshman's, and would seek death if Rāma left her. But Rāma, unmoved by lust of Empire, answered Lakshman that Kaikeyī had been but an instrument in the hands of Destiny; that others of his line had fulfilled hard tasks commanded by their fathers; that he would follow the same path, for one obeying a father could not suffer degradation. "And, O gentle brother," he said, "I am determined to obey my father's order." To Kaushalyā he answered: "The king has been ensnared by Kaikeyī, but if thou dost leave him when I am gone he will surely die. Therefore do thou remain and serve him, according to thy duty. And do thou pass the time in honouring the gods and Brāhmans." Then Kaushalyā was calmed and blessed her son, commending him to the gods and rishis and holysteads and trees and mountains and deer of the forest and all creatures of the sky to guard him. Then with sacred fire and Brāhman ritual she blessed his going and walked sunwise thrice about him, and he went to Sītā.

Sītā, who knew nothing of what had befallen, rose and greeted him with trembling limbs, for he could no longer hide his grief. Then Rāma told her all that had been done, and he said: "Now Bharata is king thou shouldst not praise me, even amongst thy friends; so mayst thou dwell in peace as one favourable to their party. Do thou thus dwell here in peace; rise betimes, worship the gods, bow to the feet of my father Dasharatha, and honour my mother Kaushalyā, and after her my other mothers with equal love and affection. Look on Bharata and Satrughna as thy sons or brothers, for they are dearer to me than life. Thus live thou here, while I go forth into the forest."

Sītā will follow Rāma into Exile

Then Sītā answered: "I can only mock at such unmeet words, not fitting to be heard, much less to be spoken by a great prince such as thou. For, O my lord, a father, mother, son, brother, or daughter-in-law indeed abide by the result of their own actions; but a wife, O best of men, shares in her husband's fate. Therefore I have been ordered, no less than thou, to exile in the forest. If thou goest there I shall go before thee, treading upon thorns and prickly grass. I shall be as happy there as in my father's house, thinking only of thy service. I shall not cause thee trouble, but will live on roots and fruits. I will precede thee walking and follow thee in eating. And there will be pools, with wild geese and other fowl and bright with full-blown lotus-flowers, where we may bathe. There shall I be happy with thee, even for a hundred or a thousand years!"

But Rāma strove to dissuade her by recounting a tale of hardships and dangers endured by forest-dwellers, as of fierce and wild animals, poisonous serpents, a bed of leaves, scanty food, arduous ritual, hunger, thirst, and fear. But Sītā, with tears in her eyes, answered patiently: "These evils seem to me like so many blessings if thou art with me, nor will I live forsaken. Moreover, it was prophesied by Brāhmans of my father's house that I should dwell in a forest, and a yogini came to my mother when I was a girl and told the same tale. Know that I am wholly bound to thee, as was Sāvitrī to Satyāvan; thy company is heaven to me and thy absence hell. Following thee, I shall be blameless, for a husband is as God to a wife. Do thou take me to share equally thy joy and sorrow, else will I drink poison, or burn in fire, or drown in water!" So she prayed, while the big tears trickled down her face like drops of water from the petals of a lotus.

Then Rāma granted her desire: "O fair one, since thou fearest not the forest thou shalt follow me and share my righteousness. Do thou bestow thy wealth on Brāhmans and make haste to be ready for the journey." Then Sītā's heart was gladdened, and she bestowed her wealth on Brāhmans and fed the poor and made all ready for the way.

Lakshman also Follows

Now Lakshman, too, with tears in his eyes, held Rāma's feet and spoke to him: "If thou wilt go thus to the forest full of elephants and deer, I shall also follow, and together we shall dwell where the songs of birds and the humming of bees delight the ear. I shall go before thee on the way, finding the path, carrying bows and hoe and basket; daily

I shall fetch the roots and fruits thou needest, and thou shalt sport with Sītā on the hill-sides, while I do every work for thee." Nor could Rāma by any argument dissuade him. "Take leave, then, of all thy relatives," said Rāma, "and bring away from my guru's[1] house the two suits of mail and burnished weapons given to me as bridal gifts by Janaka. Distribute my wealth amongst the Brāhmans." Then Rāma, Sītā, and Lakshman went to farewell their father and the mothers of Rāma. Then a noble Brāhman named Sumantra, seeing Dasharatha broken by grief, and moved to pity at the going forth of Rāma, prayed Kaikeyī to relent, clasping his hands and using smooth but cutting speech; but that noble lady's heart was hardened, and she might not in any wise be moved. But when Dasharatha wished to send Ayodhyā's wealth and men with Rāma to the forest she paled and choked with anger, for she required that Rāma should go destitute and that the wealth should belong to Bharata. But Rāma said: "What have I to do with a following in the forest? What avails it to keep back the trappings of a goodly elephant when the elephant itself is renounced? Let them bring me dresses of bark, a hoe and basket." Then Kaikeyī brought a dress of bark, one each for Rāma and Lakshman and Sītā. But Sītā, clad in robes of silk, seeing the robe of a nun, trembled like a doe before the snare and wept. Then would they persuade Rāma to leave Sītā to dwell at home, abiding his return; and Vāshishtha rebuked Kaikeyī. "This was not in the bond," said he, "that Sītā should go forth to the forest. Rather let her sit in Rāma's seat; for of all those that wed, the wife is a second self. Let Sītā rule the earth in Rāma's stead, being Rāma's self, for be sure that Bharata

[1] *Guru*, a teacher, especially in matters of religion and philosophy, here also of martial exercises.

will refuse to take the throne that should be Rāma's. Behold, Kaikeyī, there is not a person in the world who is not a friend to Rāma: even to-day thou mayst see the beasts and birds and serpents follow him, and the trees incline their heads toward him. Therefore let Sītā be well adorned and have with her cars and goods and servants when she follows Rāma."

Then Dasharatha gave her robes and jewels, and laying aside the dress of bark, Sītā shone resplendent, while the people muttered against Kaikeyī, and Sumantra yoked the horses to Rāma's car. Rāma's mother bade farewell to Sītā, counselling her in the duties of women, to regard her lord as God, though exiled and deprived of wealth; to whom Sītā answered: "The moon may sooner lose its brightness than I depart from this. The lute without strings is silent, the car lacking wheels is motionless, so a woman parted from her lord can know no happiness. How should I disregard my lord, who have been taught the greater and the lesser duties by those above me?"

Then Rāma, taking leave of Dasharatha and of his mothers, said with praying hands: "If I have ever spoken discourteously, by lack of thought, or inadvertently done any wrong, do ye pardon it. I salute all ye, my father and mothers, and depart." Then Sītā, Rāma, and Lakshman walked sunwise thrice about the king and turned away.

Then Rāma and Lakshman, and Sītā third, ascended the flaming car of gold, taking their weapons and coats of mail, the hoe and basket, and Sītā's goods bestowed by Dasharatha; and Sumantra urged on the goodly horses, swift as the very wind. Men and beasts within the city were stricken dumb with grief, and, bereft of wit, rushed headlong after Rāma, like thirsty travellers seeing water;

even Rāma's mother ran behind the car. Then Rāma said to the charioteer, "Go thou swiftly," for, like a goaded elephant, he might not bear to look behind. Soon Rāma was far away, beyond the sight of men gazing at the car's track. Then Dasharatha turned to Kaikeyī and cursed her with divorce from bed and home, and seeing the city with empty streets and closed stalls, "Take me speedily to Rāma's mother, Kaushalyā's chamber; only there may I find any rest."

Rāma and Sītā and Lakshman go into Exile

Driving fast for two days, Rāma reached the boundary of Koshala, and, turning back toward Ayodhyā, bade farewell to land and people. "O best of cities," said he, "I say it to thee and to the deities that guard and dwell with thee: returning from my forest home, my debt paid off, thee and my father and my mother I will see again." Then they left Koshala, rich in wealth and kine and Brāhmans, and passed through other smiling lands until they reached the blessed Gangā, crystal clear, resorted to by every creature, haunted by gods and angels, sinless and sin-destroying. There Guha, king of Nishādha, greeted them and fed their horses and kept guard over them all night, and when the dark cuckoo's note and the peacock's cry were heard at dawn he sent for a splendid ferry-boat. Then Rāma asked for starch-paste, and he and Lakshman dressed their hair in matted locks, after the fashion of hermits dwelling in the forest. Rāma said farewell to Guha, and Sumantra the charioteer he bade go back to Ayodhyā, though he prayed to follow farther. Then as they crossed, Sītā prayed to Gangā for safe return after fourteen years, vowing to worship that River-Queen with many offerings.

That night they dwelt by a great tree on the farther bank and ate boar's flesh slain by Rāma and Lakshman;

and those two brothers vowed to protect Sītā and each other, whether in solitude or amongst men. Lakshman should walk in front, then Sītā, and Rāma last. They talked also of Ayodhyā, and Rāma, fearing Kaikeyī's evil heart, would have Lakshman return to care for Kaushalyā; and he railed against Kaikeyī and somewhat blamed his father, swayed by a woman's will. But Lakshman comforted his brother so that he wept no more. "Thou shouldst not grieve," he said, "grieving Sītā and me; and, O Rāma, I can no more live without thee than a fish taken out of water—without thee I do not wish to see my father, nor Satrughna, nor Sumitrā, nor Heaven itself." Then Rāma was comforted, and slept with Sītā under the banyan-tree, while Lakshman watched.

Next day they reached the holy place where Gangā joins with Jamna at Prayāg; there they came to the hermitage of Bharadwaja, guided by the wreathing smoke of his sacrificial fire, and they were welcome guests. Bharadwaja counselled them to seek the mountain of Chitrakuta, ten leagues from Prayāg. "There is a fit abode for thee," he said, "graced with many trees, resounding with the cries of peacocks, and haunted by great elephants. There are herds of elephants and deer. Thou shalt range the woods with Sītā, and shalt delight in rivers, meadows, caves, and springs, in the cries of cuckoos and the belling of the deer, and in pleasant fruits and roots." Then he taught them how to come there, crossing the Jamna and passing the great banyan-tree Shyāmā, the Dusky, and thence by a fair sandy road through the Jamna forests.

So Rāma and Sītā and Lakshman took leave of Bharadwaja and crossed the Jamna by a raft, and came to Shyāmā. Immediately on arrival there, Sītā prayed to Jamna, vowing many offerings of kine and wine for Rāma's safe return. To Shyāmā Sītā also prayed, saluting him with folded hands: "O great tree, I bow to thee. May my lord's vow be all fulfilled, and we again behold Kaushalyā and Sumitrā." Then as they went along the forest path, Sītā, seeing trees and flowers unknown, asked Rāma many questions, as of their names and virtues; and Lakshman brought her flowers and fruits to pleasure her; and the rippling streams, and the cries of cranes and peacocks, and the sight of elephants and monkeys delighted her.

On the second day they reached the Chitrakuta mountain, where was the hermitage of Vālmīki. Greeted by that rishi, Rāma told him all that had befallen. Then Lakshman fetched divers sorts of wood, and those brothers built a goodly house with doors and thatched with leaves. Then Lakshman slew a deer and cooked it, and Rāma made ritual offerings to the divinities of that very place, and after communion with the deities he entered the well-wrought thatched house with Sītā and Lakshman, and they rejoiced with happy hearts and cast off grieving for Ayodhyā.

Dashâratha's Grief and Death

Meanwhile Ayodhyā was a place of grief and mourning, without comfort for king or people. On the fifth day of Rāma's exile, just when Kaushalyā for a moment yielded to her sorrow and reproached her lord, there came into Dasharatha's mind a recollection of a sin committed in a past life by means of an arrow-finding-its-mark-by-sound —which sin now bore the fruit of exile and death. Remembering this sin, he told Kaushalyā the same night how it had been committed :

"I was then so skilled a bowman as to earn the name of

one who, aiming by sound alone, can hit the mark. Thou, O lady, wert then unwedded, and I was a youthful prince. It was when rain first fell after the days of burning heat; frogs and peacocks were rejoicing, trees were shaken by the wind and rain, the hills were hidden by the heavy showers. On such a pleasant day I went forth to hunt by the river Sarayu, and there I heard a sound like the filling of a water-jar or the roaring of an elephant. Then I shot an arrow in the direction of the sound, for it was dark, so that nothing could be seen. Then I heard moans and cries, and I found a hermit by the bank, pierced by my shaft; he told me of his estate and bade me seek his aged parents in the hermitage near by, and therewith died, and I lamented him. Then I sought his father and his mother, who were anxious in mind because of his delay, and confessed to them my deed; and the rishi, who by his curse might have burned me to a cinder, spared my life because I freely told him all that had befallen. But when the funeral pyre was ready, and those aged ones, called by a vision of their son, burned their bodies with his upon the pyre, they twain cursed me with a lesser curse, that in the end I should meet my death by grieving for a son.

"Thou knowest, gentle lady, that the fruit of good or evil actions is reaped by the doer thereof. Childish is anyone who does any action not considering consequences! He that fells a mango grove and waters other trees may hope for fruit when he beholds the flower; but when the season for fruit cometh he will grieve! So is it now with me: I die of grief for Rāma's exile. I scarcely see thee, my senses are no longer keen; I am like a smoking lamp that burns low when there is but little oil remaining. O Rāma, O Kaushalyā, O unhappy Sumitrā, O cruel Kaikeyī!" Thus lamenting, Rāja Dasharatha died.

When news of this spread abroad next day Ayodhyā was plunged in deeper grief, for in a kingless country all goes amiss, rain does not fall, there are no rejoicings, nor prosperity, nor safety; a kingdom without a king is like a river without water, a wood without grass, a herd of kine without a keeper; a king is father and mother, and compasseth the welfare of all men and creatures. Considering thus, the palace officers and family priests took counsel, headed by Vāshishtha, to send envoys to Bharata, with a message that he should come at once for a matter that might not be delayed; but these envoys should not tell him anything of Rāma's exile or the king's death. Riding in well-horsed cars, those envoys, going very swiftly, reached on an evening the wealthy city of Girivraja, in Kekaya, where Bharata was lodged with his maternal uncle.

That same night Bharata dreamt many evil dreams and might not be comforted. "Either I or Rāma or Lakshman or the king is about to die," he said. Then the envoys entered and were well received. Bharata inquired if all was well with his father and mothers and brothers, and was assured that it was even so. Then the ambassadors delivered their message, and Bharata told his uncle and his grandfather, and took leave to go to Ayodhyā. They conferred on him many gifts, as woollen cloths and deer-skins and elephants and dogs and swift horses; but he, filled with anxiety because of the dreams and the very hasty journey of the envoys, had little pleasure in the gifts, and taking with him Satrughna, he departed quickly to Ayodhyā.

Kaikeyī's son beheld that best of cities at sunrise on the seventh day. Seeing that all was dark and silent in that place of sadness, and beholding many inauspicious sights foreboding ill, Bharata entered the royal palace with a heavy heart. Not seeing his father in his quarters, he sought his mother Kaikeyī and touched her feet. She rose from her golden seat delighted, and asked him of his welfare and his journey. This he told her, and himself asked for the king. "Where is that lord of men," he said, "for I would fain touch his feet? He is most often here with thee, but thy room and couch are empty. Is he, then, with Kaushalyā?" Then Kaikeyī, blinded by lust of glory and deeming that desirable for Bharata which he indeed considered evil, answered him: "Thy father has gone the way of everything that lives." Then long and sadly he bewailed, and said at last: "Happy for Rāma and those who were present when my sire yet lived, and might perform his death-bed rites. Now, where is Rāma, who is my father, brother, and friend? I am his servant; I take refuge at his feet. Do thou inform him that I am here. And do thou tell me how my father died and what were his last words." Then Kaikeyī told him how his father died, and these were his last words, she said: "Blessed are they that shall see Rāma and the strong-armed Lakshman returning here with Sītā." Then Bharata apprehended fresh misfortune, and asked his mother whither Kaushalyā's son and Sītā and Lakshman had gone. "Rāma has gone with Sītā and Lakshman, wearing hermits' robes, to Dandaka forest," she answered, and told him the whole story of the boons, expecting that he would be pleased. But he was bitterly angered, and reproached Kaikeyī as Dasharatha's murderer: "Like a burning coal, born for the destruction of our race art thou, whom my father unwittingly embraced. Thou didst little know my love of Rāma! Only for his sake it is, who calls thee mother, that I renounce thee not. Know that this kingdom is too great a burden for me, and even were it not I would not receive it. Now I shall bring back Rāma from the forest and will serve him. But thou shalt suffer misery in this world and the next; all that befits thee is to die by fire, or exile, or with a cord about thy neck!"

Then came Kaushalyā and Vāshishtha and greeted Bharata; and, guided by that skilful sage, Bharata performed all his father's funeral rites, and with his mothers walked sunwise around the burning pyre, and after ten days' mourning gathered up the ashes. Then, as he still grieved out of all measure, Vāshishtha counselled him, discoursing of the birth and death of beings and the pairs[1] that appertain to every creature. Thus comforted, those chiefs of men held up their heads again, like Indra's shining banner stained by sun and rain.

The Regency of Bharata

On the fourteenth day the ministers requested Bharata to take his seat upon the throne; but he refused, and gave orders to prepare an expedition to go in search of Rāma. When all was ready he mounted a car and set out on the way; with him went six thousand other cars, and a thousand elephants, and a hundred thousand cavalry, and men of rank, and citizens, as merchants and traders, potters and weavers and armourers, goldsmiths and washermen and actors, and beside these many learned men and well-respected Brāhmans.

Passing through Guha's realm, the host was entertained by him, and again by Bharadwaja at Prayāg. One word Bharadwaja spoke to Bharata. "Thou shouldst not blame Kaikeyī," he said. "This exile of the king is for the good of men and gods and asuras and hermits."

[1] "The pairs," *i.e.* the pairs of opposites, pleasure, pain, &c., inseparable from life.

From Prayāg the mighty host marched on to Chitrakuta, and came to Rāma's hermitage. Then Bharata advanced alone, and fell at his brother's feet. This was the fashion of Rāma: he sat in the leaf-thatched house, crowned with matted locks and clad in a black deer's skin; like a flame he was and lion-shouldered, mighty-armed and lotus-eyed; lord of this sea-girt world he seemed, like to the ever-living Brahmā; and by his side were Lakshmana and Sītā. Then Bharata wept to see his brother thus, who was used to royal state. But Rāma raised him from the ground and kissed his head and asked him of Dasharatha and his own well-being. Then Bharata related all that had come to pass, and prayed Rāma to return to Ayodhyā and rule; but Rāma would not. "How can I, commanded by my father and mother to dwell in the forest, do any otherwise? Thou shouldst rule, in accordance with his will; thou shouldst not blame Kaikeyī, for obedience is the duty alike of sons and wives and disciples, nor is a mother's wish less binding than a father's." Then Bharata answered: "If the kingdom is mine, I have the right to bestow it upon thee; do thou accept it." But Rāma would not consent to this, nor be moved by any argument, whether of Bharata, or of his mother, or of Vāshishtha, or of any of that host. Then Bharata prayed Rāma for his golden sandals, and, bowing down to them, vowed thus: "For these fourteen years I shall dwell as a hermit without the walls of Ayodhyā, making over to thy sandals the task of government. If then thou comest not, I shall die by fire." To this plan Rāma agreed, and, embracing Bharata and Satrughna, said, "So be it." One thing he added: "Do thou not cherish resentment against Kaikeyī, but be kindly toward her; this both myself and Sītā pray thee." Then Bharata walked sunwise about Rāma, and, placing the sandals on an elephant, took them back to Ayodhyā, followed by all that host of men. There he installed the sandals on the throne, and, living in retirement, carried on the government as their minister.

Now, for two reasons, Rāma would no longer dwell at Chitrakuta: first, inasmuch as hosts of rākshasas, out of hatred of him, annoyed the hermits of that place; and, secondly, because the host of men from Ayodhyā had trampled and defiled the place; and, moreover, it reminded him too sharply of his brother's grief and the citizens' and queen-mother's. He went, therefore, with Sītā and Lakshman toward Dandaka, and entered that deep forest like the sun that is hidden by a mass of clouds.

The Forest Life

Rāma and Sītā and Lakshman wandered through the forest, welcome guests at every hermitage. The great sages dwelling in the hermitages also complained against those devilish rangers of the night, and besought Rāma's protection against them, which he freely promised; and when the gentle Sītā one day suggested that they should lay down their arms, abandoning the rule of knights for that of saints, and ceasing from hostility even against the rākshasas—" The very bearing of weapons changeth the mind of those that carry them," she said—Rāma answered that it might not be, for he was pledged by knightly duty and personal promise.

So Rāma dwelt in the forest for ten years, staying a month, a season, or a year at one or another hermitage. Once a fierce rākshasa named Virādha seized Sītā and would have carried her off, but Rāma and Lakshman with huge labour slew him. Another time they met a mighty vulture; but he was a friend, and announced himself as Jatāyu and a friend of Rāma's father. Jatāyu promised Rāma his help, and to guard Sītā when Rāma and Lakshman went abroad together.

Last of all, Rāma and Sītā and Lakshman came to Panchāvati, where stretched a fair lawn beside the river Godāverī, whose banks were overhung by flowery trees. The waters swarmed with fowl, throngs of deer dwelt in the woods, the cries of peacocks resounded, the hills were covered with good trees and flowers and herbs. There Lakshman built a spacious bamboo house, well thatched with leaves and with a well-smoothed floor. Thither Jatāyu also came; and Rāma, Sītā, and Lakshman were contented, like the gods in Heaven.

Now Rāma was seated with Sītā, talking to Lakshman, when there came to Panchāvati a fearful and hideous rākshasī, sister of Rāvana; and when she saw Rāma, immediately she desired him. Her name was Surpanakhā. Refused by Rāma, she sought to become Lakshman's wife, and, repulsed by him, she returned to Rāma and would have slain Sītā. Then Lakshman seized his sword and cut off her nose and ears, and she fled away bleeding, till she met her brother Khara, younger brother of Rāvana. His anger at her misfortune knew no bounds, and he sent fourteen rākshasas to slay those brothers and Sītā and bring their blood for Surpanakhā to drink. But Rāma slew all those evil creatures with his arrows.

Then Khara was indeed filled with furious anger, and set out himself with fourteen thousand rākshasas, every one shape-shifters, horrible, proud as lions, big of mouth, courageous, delighting in cruelty. As this host drove on many evil omens befell; but Khara was fey and not to be turned aside from what he deemed a small matter—to slay three human beings.

Rāma, perceiving the oncoming host, sent Lakshman with Sītā to a secret cave, and cast on his mail, for he would fight alone; and all the gods and spirits of the air and creatures of heaven came to behold the battle. The rākshasas came on like a sea, or heavy clouds, and showered their weapons upon Rāma, so that the wood-gods were afraid and fled away. But Rāma was not afraid, and troubled the rākshasas with his marrow-piercing shafts, so that they fled to Khara for protection. He rallied them, and they came on again, discharging volleys of uprooted trees and boulders. It was in vain; for Rāma, alone and fighting on foot, slew all the fourteen thousand terrible rākshasas and stood face to face with Khara himself. A dreadful battle was theirs, as if between a lion and an elephant; the air was dark with flying shafts. At last a fiery arrow discharged by Rāma consumed the demon. Then the gods, well pleased, showered blossoms upon Rāma, and departed whence they came. And Sītā and Lakshman came forth from the cave.

Rāvana's Wrath

But news of the destruction of the rākshasas was brought to Rāvana, and he who brought the news advised Rāvana to vanquish Rāma by carrying Sītā away. Rāvana approved this plan, and sought out the crafty Mārīcha to further his ends. But Mārīcha advised Rāvana to stay his hand from attempting the impossible, and Rāvana, being persuaded for that time, went home to Lankā.

Twenty arms and ten heads had Rāvana: he sat on his golden throne like a flaming fire fed with sacrificial offerings. He was scarred with the marks of many wounds received in battle with the gods; of royal mien and gorgeously apparelled was that puissant and cruel rākshasa.

His wont was to destroy the sacrifices of Brāhmans and to possess the wives of others—not to be slain by gods or ghosts or birds or serpents. Now Surpanakhā came to her brother and showed her wounds, and told him of Rāma and Sītā, and taunted him for unkingly ways in that he took no revenge for the slaughter of his subjects and his brother; then she urged him to bring away Sītā and make her his wife. So he took his chariot and fared along by the sea to a great forest to consult again with Mārīcha, who dwelt there in a hermitage practising self-restraint.

Mārīcha counselled Rāvana not to meddle with Rāma. "Thou wouldst get off easily," he said, "if Rāma, once angered, left a single rākshasa alive, or held his hand from destroying thy city of Lankā." But Rāvana was fey, and boasted that Rāma would be an easy prey. He blamed Mārīcha for ill-will toward himself, and threatened him with death. Then Mārīcha out of fear consented, though he looked for no less than death from Rāma when they should meet again. Then Rāvana was pleased, and, taking Mārīcha in his car, set out for Rāma's hermitage, explaining how Sītā should be taken by a ruse.

The Golden Deer

Mārīcha, obedient to Rāvana, assumed the form of a golden deer and ranged about the wood near Rāma's hut: its horns were like twin jewels, its face was piebald, its ears like two blue lotus-flowers, its sleek sides soft as the petals of a flower, its hoofs as black as jet, its haunches slender, its lifted tail of every colour of the rainbow—a deer-form such as this he took! His back was starred with gold and silver, and he ranged about the forest lawns seeking to be seen by Sītā. And when she saw him she was astonished and delighted, and called to Rāma and Laksh-

IV

THE DEATH OF MĀRĪCHA

K. VENKATAPPA

Page 56

man, and begged Rāma to catch or kill the deer for her, and she urged him to the chase. Rāma, too, was fascinated by the splendid deer. He would not heed Lakshman's warning that it must be a rākshasa disguised. "All the more, then, must I slay it," said Rāma, "but do thou watch over Sītā, staying here with the good Jatāyu. I shall be back again in a very little while, bringing the deer-skin with me."

Now vanishing, now coming near, the magic deer led Rāma far away, until he was wearied out and sank upon the ground under a shady tree; then it appeared again, surrounded by other deer, and bounded away. But Rāma drew his bow and loosed an arrow that pierced its breast, so that it sprang high into the air and fell moaning on the earth. Then Mārīcha, at the point of death, assumed his own shape, and remembering Rāvana's command, he bethought him how to draw Lakshman also away from Sītā, and he called aloud with Rāma's voice, "Ah, Sītā! Ah, Lakshman." At the sound of that awful cry Rāma was struck with nameless fear, and hurried back to Panchāvati, leaving Mārīcha dead.

Now Sītā heard that cry, and urged Lakshman to go to Rāma's help, upbraiding him with bitter words; for he knew Rāma to be unconquerable, and himself was pledged to guard Sītā from all danger. But she called him a monster of wickedness, and said that he cared nothing for Rāma, but desired herself; and he might not endure those words, and though many an ill omen warned him, she forced him thus to go in search of Rāma. So he bowed to her and went away, but often turning back to glance at Sītā, fearing for her safety.

Sītā Stolen

Now Rāvana assumed the shape of a wandering yogī; carrying a staff and a beggar's bowl, he came towards Sītā waiting all alone for Rāma to come back. The forest knew him: the very trees stayed still, the wind dropped, the Godāverī flowed more slowly for fear. But he came close to Sītā, and gazed upon her, and was filled with evil longings; and he addressed her, praising her beauty, and asked her to leave that dangerous forest and go with him to dwell in palaces and gardens. But she, thinking him a Brāhman and her guest, gave him food and water, and answered that she was Rāma's wife, and told the story of their life; and she asked his name and kin. Then he named himself Rāvana and besought her to be his wife, and offered her palaces and servants and gardens. But she grew angry beyond all measure at that, and answered: "I am the servant of Rāma, lion amongst men, immovable as any mountain, vast as the mighty ocean, radiant as Indra. Wouldst thou draw the teeth from a lion's mouth, or swim the sea with a heavy stone about thy neck? As well mightst thou seek the Sun or Moon as me! Little like is Rāma unto thee, but different as is a lion from a jackal, an elephant from a cat, the ocean from a tiny stream, or gold from iron. Indra's wife thou mightst carry off, and live; but if thou takest me, the wife of Rāma, thy death is certain, and I, too, shall surely die." And she shook with fear, as a plantain-tree is shaken by the wind.

But Rāvana's yellow eyes grew red with anger and the peaceful face changed, and he took his own horrid shape, ten-faced and twenty-armed; he seized that gentle thing by the hair and limbs, and sprang into his golden ass-drawn car, and rose up into the sky. But she cried aloud to Lakshman and to Rāma. "And O thou forest and flowery trees," she cried, "and thou Godāverī, and woodland deities, and deer, and birds, I conjure you to tell my lord that Rāvana has stolen me away."

Then she saw the great vulture Jatāyu on a tree, and prayed him for help; he woke from sleep and, seeing Rāvana and Sītā, spoke soft words to the rākshasa, advising him to leave his evil course. Jatāyu warned him that Rāma would surely avenge the wrong with death, "and while I live thou shalt not take away the virtuous Sītā, but I will fight with thee and fling thee from thy car." Then Rāvan, with angry eyes, sprang upon Jatāyu, and there was a deadly battle in the sky; many weapons he showered on Jatāyu, while the king of birds wounded Rāvana with beak and talons. So many arrows pierced Jatāyu that he seemed like a bird half hidden in a nest; but he broke with his feet two bows of Rāvana's, and destroyed the sky-faring car, so that Rāvana fell down on to the earth, with Sītā on his lap. But Jatāyu by then was weary, and Rāvana sprang up again and fell upon him, and with a dagger cut away his wings, so that he fell down at the point of death. Sītā sprang to her friend and clasped him with her arms, but he lay motionless and silent like an extinguished forest fire. Then Rāvana seized her again and went his way across the sky. Against the body of the rākshasa she shone like golden lightning amidst heavy clouds, or a cloth of gold upon a sable elephant. All nature grieved for her: the lotus-flowers faded, the sun grew dark, the mountains wept in waterfalls and lifted up their summits like arms, the woodland deities were terrified, the young deer shed tears, and every creature lamented. But Brahmā, seeing Sītā carried away, rejoiced, and said, "Our work is accomplished now," foreseeing Rāvana's death. The hermits were glad and sorry at once: sorry for Sītā, and glad that Rāvana must die.

Now, as they drove through the sky in such a fashion Sītā saw five great monkeys on a mountain-top, and to them she cast down her jewels and her golden veil, unobserved of Rāvana, as a token for Rāma. But Rāvana left behind the woods and mountains, and crossed the sea, and came to his great city of Lankā[1]—and set her down in an inner room, all alone and served and guarded well. Spies were sent to keep a watch on Rāma. Then Rāvana returned and showed to Sītā all his palace and treasure and gardens, and prayed her to be his wife, and wooed her in every way; but she hid her face and sobbed with wordless tears. And when he urged her again she took a blade of grass and laid it between Rāvana and herself, and prophesied his death at Rāma's hands and the ruin of all rākshasas, and utterly rejected him. Then he turned from prayer to threats, and, calling horrid rākshasas, gave her to their charge, and commanded them to break her spirit, whether by violence or by temptation. There was the gentle Sītā, like a sinking ship, or a doe amongst a pack of dogs.

Rāma's Wrath

Now Rāma, returning from the chase of Mārīcha, was heavy-hearted; meeting Lakshman, he blamed him much for leaving Sītā. The jackals howled and birds cried as they hurried back. As they came near to the hermitage the feet of Rāma failed him, and a trembling shook his frame; for Sītā was not there. They ranged the groves of flowering trees, and the river banks where lotus-flowers were open, and sought the mountain caves, and asked the

[1] Lankā, according to the usual view, Ceylon.

V

RĀVANA FIGHTING WITH JATAYU

K. VENKATAPPA

Page 60

river and the trees and all the animals where Sītā was. Then Rāma deemed that rākshasas had eaten her, taking revenge for Khara. But next they came to where Jatāyu had fought with Rāvana, and saw the broken weapons and the car and the trampled ground; and Rāma raged against all beings, and would destroy the very heavens and earth, unless the gods gave back his Sītā. Then they perceived the dying Jatāyu, and deeming him to be a rākshasa that had eaten Sītā, Rāma was about to slay him. But Jatāyu spoke feebly, and related to Rāma all that had befallen, so that Rāma, throwing down his bow, embraced the friendly bird and lamented for his death; and Jatāyu told of Rāvana and comforted Rāma with assurances of victory and recovery of Sītā. But therewith his spirit fled away, and his head and body sank down upon the ground; and Rāma mourned over his friend:

"Ah, Lakshmana," he said, "this kingly bird dwelt here contented many years, and now is dead because of me: he has given up his life in seeking to rescue Sītā. Behold, amongst the animals of every rank there are heroes, even amongst birds. I am more sorry for this vulture who has died for me than even because of Sītā's loss."

Then Lakshman brought wood and fire, and they burned Jatāyu there with every right and offering due to twice-born men, and spoke the *mantras* for his speedy coming to the abodes of the shining gods; and that king of vultures, slain in battle for a good cause, and blest by Rāma, attained a glorious state.

Then Rāma and Lakshman set out to search for Sītā far and wide; it was but a little time before they met a horrid rākshasa, and it was no light matter for them to come to their above in battle with him. But he, wounded to death, rejoiced, for he had been cursed with that form by a hermit until Rāma should slay and set him free. Rāma and Lakshman burnt him on a mighty pyre, and he rose from it and, mounting upon a heavenly car, he spoke to Rāma, counselling him to seek the help of the great monkey Sugriva and the four other monkeys that dwelt on the mountain Rishyamūkha. "Do not thou despise that royal monkey," he said, "for he is puissant, humble, brave, expert, and graceful, good at shifting shapes, and well acquainted with the haunts of every rākshasa. Do thou make alliance with him, taking a vow of friendship before a fire as witness, and with his help thou shalt surely win back Sītā." Then he departed, bidding them farewell and pointing out the way to Rishyamūkha; and they, passing by Matanga's hermitage, came to that wooded mountain, haunt of many birds, beside the Pampa lake.

Rāma's Alliance with Sugriva

It was not long before Rāma and Lakshman reached the Rishyamūkha mountain, where Sugriva dwelt. Now this Sugriva lived in exile, driven from home and robbed of his wife by his cruel brother Vāli; and when he saw the two great-eyed heroes bearing arms, he deemed them to have been sent by Vāli for his destruction. So he fled away, and he sent Hanuman disguised as a hermit to speak with the knights and learn their purpose. Then Lakshman told him all that had befallen, and that Rāma now sought Sugriva's aid. So Hanuman, considering that Sugriva also needed a champion for the recovery of his wife and kingdom, led the knights to Sugriva, and there Rāma and the monkey-chief held converse. Hanuman made fire with two pieces of wood, and passing sunwise about it, Rāma and Sugriva were made sworn friends, and each bound himself to aid the other. They gazed at each other intently, and neither had his fill of seeing the other. Then Sugriva told his story and prayed Rāma for his aid, and he engaged himself to overcome the monkey-chief's brother, and in return Sugriva undertook to recover Sītā. He told Rāma how he had seen her carried away by Rāvana, and how she had dropped her veil and jewels, and he showed these tokens to Rāma and Lakshman. Rāma knew them, but Lakshman said: "I do not recognize the bracelets or the ear-rings, but I know the anklets well, for I was not used to lift my eyes above her feet."

Now, says the story, Rāma fared with Sugriva to Vāli's city, and overcame Vāli, and established Sugriva on the throne. Then four months of the rainy season passed away, and when the skies grew clear and the floods diminished, Sugriva sent out his marshals to summon the monkey host. They came from Himālaya and Vindhyā and Kailās, from the east and from the west, from far and near, from caves and forests, in hundreds and thousands and millions, and each host was captained by a veteran leader. All the monkeys in the world assembled there, and stood before Sugriva with joined hands. Then Sugriva gave them to Rāma for his service, and would place them under his command. But Rāma thought it best that Sugriva should issue all commands, since he best understood the ordering of such a host, and was well acquainted with the matter to be accomplished.

The Search for Sītā

As yet neither Rāma nor Lakshman nor Sugriva knew more of Rāvana than his name; none could tell where he dwelt or where he kept Sītā hidden. Sugriva therefore dispatched all that host under leaders to search the four quarters for a month, as far as the uttermost bound of any land where men or demons dwelt, or sun shone. But he trusted as much in Hanuman as in all that host together; for that son of the wind-god had his father's energy and swiftness and vehemence and power of access to every place in earth or sky, and he was brave and politic and keen of wit and well aware of conduct befitting the time and place. And much as Sugriva relied on Hanuman, Hanuman was even more confident of his own power. Rāma also put his trust in Hanuman, and gave him his signet-ring to show for a sign to Sītā when he should discover her.

Then Hanuman bowed to Rāma's feet, and departed with the host appointed to search the southern quarter, while Rāma remained a month with Sugriva expecting his return. And after a month the hosts came back from searching the north and west and east, sorry and dejected that they had not found Sītā. But the southern host searched all the woods and caves and hidden places, till at last they came to the mighty ocean, the home of Varuna, boundless, resounding, covered with dreadful waves. A month had passed and Sītā was not found; therefore the monkeys sat dejected, gazing over the sea and waiting for their end, for they dared not return to Sugriva.

But there dwelt a mighty and very aged vulture named Sampati in a neighbouring cave, and he, hearing the monkeys talking of his brother Jatāyu, came forth and asked for news of him. Then the monkeys related to him the whole affair, and Sampati answered that he had seen Sītā carried away by Rāvana and that Rāvana dwelt in Lankā, a hundred leagues across the sea. "Do ye repair thither," he said, "and avenge the rape of Sītā and the murder of my brother. For I have the gift of foresight,

VI

RĀMA SENDING HIS SIGNET-RING TO SĪTĀ

K. VENKATAPPA

Page 64

and even now I perceive that Rāvan and Sītā are there in Lankā."

Sītā found in Lankā

Then the monkeys grew more hopeful, but when they marched down to the shore and sat beside the heaving sea they were again downcast, and took counsel together sadly enough. Now one monkey said he could bound over twenty leagues, and another fifty, and one eighty, and one ninety; and Angada, son of Vāli, could cross over a hundred, but his power would not avail for the return. Then Jambavan, a noble monkey, addressed Hanuman, and recalled his birth and origin, how the wind-god had begotten him and his mother Anjana had borne him in the mountains, and when he was still a child he had thought the sun to be a fruit growing in the sky, and sprang easily three thousand leagues toward it; how Indra had cast a bolt at him, breaking his jaw; how the wind-god in anger began to destroy the heavens and earth, till Brahmā pacified him and granted him the boon that his son should be invulnerable, and Indra gave him the boon of choosing his own death. "And do thou, heroic monkey, prove thy prowess now and bound across the ocean," he said, "for we look on thee as our champion, and thou dost surpass all things in movement and in vehemence."

Then Hanuman roused himself, and the monkey host rejoiced. Swelling with pride and might, he boasted of the deed he would accomplish. Then he rushed up the mountain Mahendra, shaking it in his wrath and frightening every beast that lived in its woods and caves. Intent upon achieving a hard task, where no friend could help and no foe hindered, Hanuman stood with head uplifted like a bull, and praying to the sun, to the mountain wind, to the Self-create and to all beings, he set his heart in the work to be accomplished. He grew great, and stood, like a fire, with bristling hair, and roared like thunder, brandishing his tail; so he gathered energy of mind and body. "I will discover Sītā or bring Rāvana away in chains," he thought, and therewith sprang up so that the very trees were dragged upward by his impetus and fell back again behind him. He hurtled through the air like a mountain, his flashing eyes like forest fires, his lifted tail like Sakra's banner. So Hanuman held his way across the ocean. Nor, when the friendly ocean lifted up Mount Mainaka, well wooded and full of fruits and roots, would Hanuman stay to rest, but, rising up, coursed through the air like Garuda himself. Then a grim rākshasī named Sinhikha rose from the sea and caught him by the shadow, and would devour him; but he dashed into her mouth and, growing exceeding great, burst away again, leaving her dead and broken. Then he perceived the farther shore, and thinking his huge form ill-fitted for a secret mission, he resumed his natural size and shape, and so alighted on the shore of Lankā, nor was he ever so little wearied or fatigued.

On the mountain summit Hanuman beheld the city of Lankā, girt with a golden wall, and filled with buildings huge as cloudy mountains, the handiwork of Vishvakarman. Impatiently he waited for the setting of the sun; then, shrinking to the size of a cat, he entered the city at night, unseen by the guards. Now Lankā seemed to him like a woman, having for robe the sea, for jewels cow-pens and stables, her breasts the towers upon her walls; and behold, as he entered in, she met him in a terrible shape and barred his way. Then Hanuman struck her down, though gently, considering her a woman, and she yielded to him, and bade him accomplish his affair. Hanuman made his way to the palace of Rāvana, towering on the mountain-top, girt with a wall and moat. By now the moon was full and high, sailing like a swan across the skyey sea, and Hanuman beheld the dwellers in the palace, some drinking, some engaged in amorous dalliance, some sorry and some glad, some drinking, some eating, some making music, and some sleeping. Many a fair bride lay there in her husband's arms, but Sītā of peerless virtue he could not find; wherefore that eloquent monkey was cast down and disappointed. Then he sprang from court to court, visiting the quarters of all the foremost rākshasas, till at last he came to Rāvana's own apartments, a very mine of gold and jewels, ablaze with silver light. Everywhere he sought for Sītā, and left no corner unexplored; golden stairs and painted cars and crystal windows and secret chambers set with gems, all these he beheld, but never Sītā. The odour of meat and drink he sniffed, and to his nostrils there came also the all-pervading Air, and it said to him, "Come hither, where Rāvana lies." Following the Air, he came to Rāvana's sleeping-place. There lay the lord of the rākshasas upon a glorious bed, asleep and breathing heavily; huge was his frame, decked with splendid jewels, like a crimson sunset cloud pierced by flashes of lightning; his big hands lay on the white cloth like terrible five-hooded serpents; four golden lamps on pillars lit his bed. Around him lay his wives, fair as the moon, decked in glorious gems and garlands that never faded. Some, wearied with pleasure, slept where they sat; one clasped her lute like an amorous girl embracing her lover; another fair one, skilled in the dance, made graceful gestures even in her sleep; others embraced each other. There, too, was Mandodarī, Rāvana's queen, exceeding all others in her splendour and loveliness; and Hanuman guessed she must be Sītā, and the thought enlivened him, so that he waved his arms and frisked his tail and sang and danced and climbed the golden pillars and sprang down again, as his monkey-nature moved him.

But reflection showed his error, for he said: "Without Rāma, Sītā would not eat or drink or sleep or decorate her person, nor would she company with any other than he; this is some other one." So Hanuman ranged farther through the palace, searching many a bower in vain. Many fair ones he beheld, but never Sītā, and he deemed she must be slain or eaten by the rākshasas. So he left the palace and sat awhile in deep dejection on the city wall. "If I return without discovering Sītā," he reflected, "my labour will have been in vain. And what will Sugriva say, and the sons of Dasharatha, and the monkey host? Surely Rāma and Lakshman will die of grief, and after them Bharata, and then Satrughna, and then the queen-mothers, and seeing that, Sugriva, Rāma's friend, will die too, and the monkey-queens, and Angada, and all the monkey race! No more shall the noble monkeys assemble amongst the woods and mountains or in secret places and indulge in games; but a loud wailing will arise when I return, and they will swallow poison, or hang themselves, or jump down from lofty mountains. Therefore I must not return unsuccessful; better that I should starve and die. It is not right that all those noble monkeys should perish on my account. I shall remain here and search Lankā again and again; even this Asoka wood beyond the walls shall be examined."

Then Hanuman bowed to Rāma and Sītā, to Shiva, to Indra and to Death, to the Wind, the Moon and Fire, and to Sugriva, and praying to these with thought intent, he ranged the Asoka wood with his imagination and met with Sītā. Then he sprang from the wall like an arrow from a bow, and entered the wood in bodily shape. The wood was a place of pleasure and delight, full of flowering trees and happy animals; but Hanuman ravaged it and broke the trees. One beautiful Asoka tree stood alone, amongst pavilions and gardens, built round with golden pavements and silver walls. Hanuman sprang up this tree and kept watch all about, thinking that Sītā, if she were in the forest, would come to that lovely place. He saw a marble palace, with stairs of coral and floors of shining gold, and there lay one imprisoned, weak and thin as if with fasting, sighing for heavy grief, clad in soiled robes, and guarded by horrid rākshasīs, like a deer among the dogs or a shining flame obscured by smoke.

Then Hanuman considered that this must be Sītā, for she was fair and spotless, like a moon overcast by clouds, and she wore such jewels as Rāma had described to him. Hanuman shed tears of joy and thought of Rāma and Lakshman. But now, while he yet sat hidden on the tree, Rāvana had waked, and that lordly rākshasa came with a great train of women to the Asoka wood. They followed their heroic husband like lightnings following a cloud, and Hanuman heard the sound of their tinkling anklets as they passed across the golden pavements.

Hanuman speaks with Sītā

Rāvan came toward Sītā, and when she saw him she trembled like a plantain-tree shaken by the wind, and hid her face and sobbed. Then he wooed her in every way, tempting her with wealth and power and comfort; but she refused him utterly, and foretold his death at

Rāma's hands. But Rāvana waxed wood-wrath, and gave a two-month term, after which, if she yielded not, she should be tortured and slain; and leaving her to the horrid rākshasī guards with orders to break her will, Rāvana returned with his wives to his apartment. Then Sītā, shrinking from the horrible she-demons, threatening her with death and torture, and reviling Rāma, crept to the foot of the Asoka tree where Hanuman was hidden.

Hanuman reflected that there was need for him to speak with Sītā; but he feared to frighten her, or to attract the notice of the guard and bring destruction on himself, for, though he had might to slay the rākshasa host, he could not, if wearied out, return across the ocean. So he sat hidden in the branches of the tree and recited Rāma's virtues and deeds, speaking in gentle tones, till Sītā heard him. She caught her breath with fear and looked up into the tree, and saw the monkey; eloquent was he and humble, and his eyes glowed like golden fire. Then he came down out of the tree, ruddy-faced and humbly attired, and with joined palms spoke to Sītā. Then she told him that she was Sītā and asked for news of Rāma, and Hanuman told her all that had befallen and spoke of Rāma and Lakshman, so that she was wellnigh as glad as if she had seen Rāma himself. But Hanuman came a little nearer, and Sītā was much afraid, thinking him to be Rāvana in disguise. He had much ado to persuade her that he was Rāma's friend; but at last, when she beheld the signet-ring, it seemed to her as if she were already saved, and she was glad and sorry at once—glad to know that Rāma was alive and well, and sorry for his grief.

Then Hanuman suggested that he should carry Sītā on his back across the sea to Rāma. She praised his strength, but would not go with him, because she thought she might fall from his back into the sea, especially if the rākshasas followed them, and because she would not willingly touch any person but Rāma, and because she desired that the glory of her rescue and the destruction of the rākshasas should be Rāma's. "But do thou speedily bring Rāma hither," she prayed. Then Hanuman praised her wisdom and modesty, and asked for a token for Rāma; and she told him of an adventure with a crow, known only to herself and Rāma, that had befallen long ago at Chitrakuta, and she gave him a jewel from her hair, and sent a message to Rāma and Lakshman, praying them to rescue her. Hanuman took the gem and, bowing to Sītā, made ready to depart. Then Sītā gave him another message for Rāma, by which he might know surely that Hanuman had found her. "Tell him, 'One day my brow-spot was wiped away, and thou didst paint another with red earth —thou shouldst remember this. And, O Rāma, do thou come soon; for ten months have passed already since I saw thee, and I may not endure more than another month'; and good fortune go with thee, heroic monkey," she said.

Hanuman burns Lankā

But Hanuman was not satisfied with finding Sītā; he dashed about the Asoka grove and broke the trees and spoiled the pavilions, like the Wind himself. The rākshasīs sent messages to Rāvana for help, and he, hearing that a mighty monkey was destroying his servants, sent the powerful Jambumāli, bow in hand, to slay Hanuman forthwith; and, indeed, he wounded him with a sharp arrow as he sat upon a temple roof, but Hanuman hurled a bolt at him and crushed him utterly. Then a host of heroic rākshasas, led by Prince Aksha, proceeded against

Hanuman and met their death; next Indrajit was sent against him, and an awful battle was joined, whereat the very gods were amazed. He sent a million shafts against the monkey, but he, ranging the sky, escaped them all; then Indrajit paused, and with concentrated mind pondered over the true character of Hanuman, and with spiritual insight perceived that he was not to be slain by weapons. Therefore he devised a way to bind him, and he loosed a Brahmā shaft at him. Therewith Hanuman was bound, and knew the bond unbreakable, and he fell to earth; but he reflected that it would be well for him to converse with Rāvana, and therefore he struggled not, but let the rākshasas bear him off. But they, seeing him still, bound him yet closer, pitifully moaning the while, with cords and bark. But that binding was the means of his release, for the binding power of a Brahmā weapon is broken at once if another bond is added to it. But the wily monkey gave no sign that the bonds were loosed; and the fierce rākshasas, crying to each other, "Who is he? what does he want?" and "Kill him! burn him! eat him!" dragged him before Rāvana.

Questioned by Rāvana's minister, Hanuman answered that he was indeed a monkey, come to Lankā as Rāma's envoy to accomplish his commands and to behold Rāvana; and he told the story of Rāma up till then, and gave Rāvaṇa sound advice, to save his life by surrendering Sītā. Rāvana was furious and would have Hanuman slain; but the counsellors reminded him that the punishment of death could not justly be inflicted upon one who named himself an envoy. Then Rāvana cast about for a fitting penalty, and bethought him to set Hanuman's tail afire. Then the rākshasas bound the monkey's tail with cotton soaked in oil and set it all ablaze. But the heroic monkey cherished

VII

BURNING OF LANKĀ

K. VENKATAPPA

Page 72

a secret plan; he suffered the rākshasas to lead him about Lankā that he might the better learn its ways and strength. Then word was taken to Sītā that that monkey with whom she had conversed was led about the streets of Lankā and proclaimed a spy, and that his tail was burning. Thereat she grieved, and praying to the Fire, she said: "As I have been faithful to my lord, do thou be cool to Hanuman." The Fire flamed up in answer to her prayer, and at that very moment Hanuman's sire blew cool between the flame and Hanuman.

Perceiving that the fire still burnt, but that his tail was icy-cold, Hanuman thought that it was for Rāma's sake and Sītā's and his sire's that the heat was chilled; and he snapped his bonds and sprang into the sky, huge as a mountain, and rushed to and fro in Lankā, burning the palaces and all their treasures. And when he had burnt half Lankā to the ground and slaughtered many a rākshasa, Hanuman quenched his tail in the sea.

Hanuman returns to Rāma

Then all at once he repented of his rash deed, for he thought that Sītā must have died in the fire. "It is a small matter to have burnt Lankā," he reflected, "but if Sītā has lost her life I have failed altogether in my work, and will rather die than return in vain to Rāma." But again he thought: "It may be that that fair one has been saved by her own virtue; the fire that scorched me not has surely never hurt that noble lady." Therewith he hastened back to the Asoka tree and found her seated there, and he greeted her, and she him, and once more they spoke of Rāma, and Hanuman foretold that he would speedily rescue Sītā and slay the rākshasas. Then Hanuman sprang up like a winged mountain and fared across the sea, now clearly seen, now hidden by the clouds, till he came to Mahendra, flourishing his tail and roaring like the wind in a mighty cavern. And all the monkey host rejoiced exceedingly to see and hear him, knowing that he must have found Sītā; they danced, and ran from peak to peak, and waved the branches of trees and their clean white cloths, and brought fruits and roots for Hanuman to eat. Then Hanuman reported all that he had done to Angada and Jambavān, while the monkey host sat round about the three there on Mahendra's summit.

When all had been told, Angada turned to the monkey host and said: "O noble monkeys, our work is done, and the time has come for us to return to Sugriva without delay"; and they answered him: "Let us go." Then Angada leapt up into the air, followed by all the monkeys, darkening the sky as if with clouds and roaring like the wind; and coming speedily to Sugriva, Angada spoke first to the heavy-hearted Rāma, and gave him tidings of Sītā and praised the work of Hanuman. Then Rāma talked with Hanuman, and asked him many a question as to the welfare of the slender-waisted Sītā; and Hanuman told him all, and gave her message regarding the matter of the crow and of the painted brow-spot, and showed to Rāma the jewel from Sītā's hair entrusted to him as a token. Rāma wept at the sight of that goodly gem: it was grief to him to behold it and not Sītā herself; but he rejoiced to know that Sītā lived and that Hanuman had found her.

Then Rāma praised Hanuman as the best of servants, who had done more even than was required of him; for a servant, merely good, does what is commanded and no more, and a bad servant is one who does not even that which his master orders. "Hanuman," he said, "has done his work and more, and sorry am I that I cannot do him any service in return. But affection tells of all," and therewith Rāma embraced the self-controlled and great-hearted Hanuman like a brother.

Next, Sugriva spoke and issued orders for a march of all the host toward the far south to lay a siege to Lankā, while Hanuman reported to Rāma all that he had learnt of the strength and fortifications of the city, saying: "Do thou regard the city as already taken, for I alone have laid it waste, and it will be an easy matter for such a host as this to utterly destroy it."

Now the monkey army went on its way, led by Sugriva and Rāma, and the monkeys skipped for joy and bounded gleefully and sported one with another. With them went many friendly bears, ruled by Jambavān, guarding the rear. Passing over many mountains and delightful forests, the army came at length to Mahendra, and beheld the sea before them; thence they marched to the very shore, beside the wave-washed rocks, and made their camp. They covered all the shore, like a second sea beside the tossing waves. Then Rāma summoned a council to devise a means for crossing over the ocean, and a guard was set, and orders issued that none should wander, for he feared the magic of the rākshasas.

Vibhishana deserts the Rākshasas

Meanwhile Rāvana in Lankā called another council, for "Victory follows from taking counsel," as the sages say. "Ye know how the monkey Hanuman harried Lankā, and now Rāma has reached the ocean shore with a host of bears and monkeys, and he will dry the sea or bridge it and besiege us here. Do ye consider the means of protection for the city and the army"—thus spake Rāvana to his counsellors. And his generals advised him to entrust the battle to his son, Prince Indrajit, while others, as Prahasta, Nikumbha, and Vajrahanu, boasted that they alone would swallow up the monkey army. But Vibhishana, younger brother of Rāvana, advised another course. "Force," said he, "is only to be resorted to when other means have failed, viz. conciliation, gifts, and sowing dissension. Moreover, force avails only against such as are weak or are displeasing to the gods. What but death can result from a conflict with Rāma, self-controlled and vigilant and strong with the might of all the gods? Who ever thought that Hanuman should have done so much? and from this thou shouldst be warned and yield up Sītā to her lord, to save thyself and us." And playing a perilous part, he followed his brother to his own chamber and saluted him, and spake yet further for his welfare. "From the day that Sītā came," he said, "the omens have been evil: fire is ever obscured by smoke, serpents are found in kitchens, the milk of kine runs dry, wild beasts howl around the palace. Do thou restore Sītā, lest we all suffer for thy sin." But Rāvana dismissed his brother angrily, and boasted that he would hold Sītā as his own, even if all the gods should war against him.

Now the reason why Rāvana had never up till now used force to Sītā was this, that Brahmā, one time when Rāvana had ill-used a celestial dame, laid upon him a curse that if ever again he did the like against his victim's will his head should break in a hundred pieces. And by now Rāvana was thin and passion-worn and weary, like a horse spent with a long journey, and he desired to compass Rāma's death and make Sītā his own. Therefore he took counsel again with his generals for war, but again Vibhishana opposed him, till Rāvana cursed him angrily as cowardly and treasonable. Then Vibhishana deemed the time had come when he could suffer no more of such insults, and rising into the air with his four personal followers, he said to Rāvana that he had spoken for his welfare, "but the fey refuse advice, as a man on the brink of death refuses medicine." So saying he passed through the sky across the sea and came to the monkey host, and announced himself as come to make alliance with Rāma. Most of the monkey leaders were for slaying him, for they put little faith in a rākshasa, even if he were not a disguised spy; but Rāma spoke him fair, and engaged, in return for his assistance in the war, to set him on the throne of Lankā when Rāvana should have been slain.

"*Adam's Bridge*"

Then Hanuman and Sugriva and Rāma took counsel with Vibhishana how to cross the ocean, and he deemed that Rāma should seek the aid and the friendship of Ocean for the building of a bridge. This was agreed upon, and Rāma, spreading a couch of sacrificial grass, lay down upon it, facing the east, with praying hands toward the sea, resolving, "Either the ocean shall yield or I will die." Thus Rāma lay three days, silent, concentred, following the rule, intent upon the ocean; but Ocean answered not. Then Rāma was angered, and rose and took his bow, and would dry up the sea and lay Varuna's home bare; and he loosed dreadful shafts at him that flamed and pierced the waters, awakening mighty storms, distressing the *nāgas* and the *makaras* of the sea, so that the god-hermits haunting the sky cried out "Alas!" and "Enough!" But Ocean did not show himself, and Rāma, threatening him, set to his bow a Brahmā arrow blest with a Brahmā charm, and drew. Then heaven and earth were darkened and the mountains trembled, lightnings flashed, and every creature was afraid, and the mighty deep was wrought with violent movement. Then Ocean himself rose from mid-sea like the sun from Meru. Jewelled and wreathed was he and decked with many gems, and followed by noble rivers, such as Gangā, Sindhu, and others. He came to Rāma with joined palms and spoke him fair:

"O Rāma," said he, "thou knowest that every element has its own inherent qualities. Mine is this, to be fathomless and hard to cross. Neither for love nor fear can I stay the waters from their endless movement. But thou shalt pass over me by means of a bridge, and I will suffer it and hold it firm." Then Rāma was appeased, but the Brahmā arrow waited to find its mark and might not be restrained. Rāma inquired from Ocean: "Where shall I let it strike?" and Ocean answered: "There is a part of my domain toward the north haunted by evil wights; there let it fall." Then Rāma let fly the flaming shaft, and the water of the sea toward the north was dried and burnt, and where the sea had been became a desert. But Rāma blessed the desert and made it fruitful.

Then Ocean said to Rāma: "O kind one, there is a monkey here named Nala, and he is Vishvakarmā's son and has his sire's skill. Full of energy is he, and he shall build the bridge across me, and I shall bear it up." Then Ocean sank again beneath the waters. But Nala said to Rāma: "Ocean has spoken truth: only because thou didst not ask me I hid my power till now."

Now all the monkeys, following Nala's orders, gathered trees and rocks and brought them from the forests to the shore, and set them in the sea. Some carried timber, some used the measuring-rods, some bore stones; huge was the tumult and noise of crags and rocks thrown into

VIII

BUILDING OF RĀMA'S BRIDGE

K. VENKATAPPA

Page 78

the sea. The first day fourteen leagues were made, and on the fifth day the bridge was finished, broad and elegant and firm—like a line of parting of the hair on Ocean's head. Then the monkey host passed over, Rāma and Lakshman riding upon Sugriva and Angada. Some monkeys went along the causeway, others plunged into the sea, and others coursed through the air, and the noise of them drowned the sound of the ocean waves.

Lankā Besieged

Dreadful were the omens of war that showed themselves: the earth shook, the clouds rained blood, a fiery circle fell from the sun. But the monkeys roared defiance at the rākshasas, whose destruction was thus foretold. Then Rāma, beholding Lankā towering up to pierce the heavens, built by Vishvakarma, wrought, as it were, of mind rather than matter, hanging in the sky like a bank of snow-white clouds, was downcast at the thought of Sītā prisoned there; but he arrayed the host of bears and monkeys and laid siege to Lankā.

Meanwhile Rāvana's spies, sent in monkey shape to gather news, brought tidings thereof to Lankā, and, advising him of Rāma's resistless power, counselled that Sītā should be surrendered; but Rāvana was enraged, and drove the spies away disgraced, and sent others in their place, but ever with the same result. No help was there, then, but to give battle or yield up Rāma's bride; but Rāvana took counsel first to betray Sītā to his will. He told her that the monkey host had been dispersed and Rāma slain, and a rākshasī came in, bringing the semblance of Rāma's head and bow, and Sītā knew them, and was grieving out of all measure, and crying aloud with many lamentations, and she prayed Rāvana to slay her by Rāma's head that she might follow him. But therewith came in a messenger from the rākshasa general calling Rāvana to the battle, and he turned to the field of war; and when he left, the head and bow immediately vanished, and Sītā knew them to have been but counterfeits and vain illusions.

Rāma Wounded

Now Vibhishana's four rākshasa followers had spied on Lankā, and knew the disposition of Rāvana's forces; and Rāma laid siege to the four gates of Lankā accordingly, establishing the monkey Nilā at the eastern gate, guarded by the rākshasa general Prahasta; Angada at the western gate, guarded by Mahāparshwa; Hanuman at the southern gate, guarded by Prince Indrajit; and himself attacked the north gate, guarded by Rāvana. Then Rāma sent Angada as an envoy to Rāvana, challenging him to the fight; but Rāvana, forgetting the respect due to an envoy, would have slain him; and Angada sprang away and broke the palace roof, and returned to Rāma. Then the monkeys advanced in order and swarmed about the walls, flooding the moat and striking terror into the hearts of the rākshasas; scaling parties climbed the walls and battered down the gates with trees and stones, shouting "Victory for Rāma and for Sugriva!" The rākshasas sallied forth in turn with horrid trumpetings and joined in battle with the monkeys, and all the air was filled with the noise of fighting, and terrible confusion arose of friend and foe and man and beast, and the earth was strewn with flesh and wet with gore. Thus an equal battle raged till evening; but the rākshasas waited for the night, and eagerly desired the setting of the sun, for night is the rākshasas' time of strongest might. So night fell, and the demons ranged, devouring monkeys by thousands.

Then those of Rāma's party rallied and for a time prevailed, and Indrajit was beaten back. But he, resorting to his magic, became invisible, and showered deadly wounding arrows upon Rāma and Lakshman; fighting in crooked ways, he bound them fast so that they fell helpless to the ground, covered with a thousand wounds.

Sugriva, Hanuman, Vibhishana, and all the leaders of the monkeys stood round about those wounded heroes with tear-filled eyes; but Indrajit, unseen of any save his uncle Vibhishana, rejoiced, and let fly many a shaft that wounded Hanuman and Nilā and Jambavān. Then Indrajit returned to Lankā as a victor, and his father welcomed him; and for a while the fighting ceased.

Now Vibhishana rallied the frightened monkeys, and comforted Sugriva, saying: "This is no time for giving way to grief. Rāma is not dying. Do thou gather the forces and inspire them with fresh hope." But the monkeys were panic-stricken, and if even a straw moved they deemed it to be a rākshasa. And Rāvana meanwhile, taking Sītā on his car, showed to her Rāma and Lakshman lying on the field, senseless and pierced with many arrows, wounded and lying in the dust; and she deemed them to be dead, and wailed—but Rāvana brought her back to Lankā.

Meanwhile Rāma came to himself, and seeing Lakshman seeming to be dead, he made great lamentation, and praising what the monkeys had done, though unsuccessful, he gave them leave to go whither they would across the bridge and seek their homes. And Vibhishana, too, had no more taste for battle or desire for the throne of Lankā. But Sugriva comforted them and gave them fresh courage, and the monkey-chief Sushena told of a magic herb that grows by the Milky Ocean, and can restore the dead to life, "and let the Wind-god's son go thither for it," he said.

The Coming of Garuda

But as he spoke a stormy wind arose, lashing the sea and shaking the very mountains, and suddenly the monkeys beheld Garuda sailing through the air like a flaming fire. As Garuda came nigh, the arrows fell from the wounded heroes like frightened serpents darting away; and when he bent in salutation and touched their faces with his hands, the sons of Dasharatha were healed, and they came to their former strength and radiance, and more. Then Rāma questioned Garuda who he was, and he answered: "I am thy friend, thy life free-ranging external to thyself, Garuda, and I have come to aid thee, hearing that thou wert bound by the magic shafts of Indrajit. Now thou shouldst take warning how the rākshasas fight with cunning and magic, and thou shouldst never trust them in the field. I take my way: thou needst not wonder how friendship came to be between us; thou shalt know all after the battle is achieved. Surely thou shalt slay Rāvana and win back Sītā." With this Garuda, embracing Rāma and Lakshman, embracing, too, the monkey-chiefs, rose into the sky and sailed away upon the wind.
Then the monkey-chiefs, seeing Rāma and Lakshman restored to life and power, began to roar and frisked their tails; drums and kettledrums were struck, and seizing trees, hundreds and thousands of monkeys advanced again upon the gates of Lankā. The rangers of the night issued forth under Dhumrāksha ("Grey-eye"), and there was a deadly onset. The monkeys bit and tore and fought with trees and stones, and the rākshasas killed and wounded them with arrows and cleft them with their axes and crushed

them with their maces. Then seeing the monkeys hard beset, Hanuman, seizing a heavy rock, advanced on Dhumrāksha, and, casting it down upon his car, crushed it to dust; then Hanuman laid about him lustily, and armed with a mountain-top he rushed on Dhumrāksha again. But the rākshasa brought down his mace on Hanuman's head and wounded him sore; then Hanuman, heedless of the wound, let fly the mountain-top at Dhumrāksha, and crushed him to the ground like a falling hill. Seeing their leader slain, the rākshasas retired.

Heavy Fighting

Short was the peace ere Rāvana sent out another leader of the rākshasas, the deadly Thunder-tooth ; him Angada met as he drove the monkey host before him, piercing five and nine with every shaft, and engaged in deadly duel, till at last he severed the demon's neck and laid him low. Then Rāvana sent out Akampana (" Unconquerable "), and he was slain by Hanuman, with all his host. Then Rāvana was somewhat shaken and foreboded ill, but he sent for Prahasta ("Long-hand"), his foremost general; and he gathered another host, and sallied forth upon a splendid car by the eastern gate, accompanied by his counsellors, Man-slayer and Noisy-throat and Tall. That encounter was the death of many hundred rākshasas and monkeys, and the occasion of many a deed of heroism. Prahasta from his shining car sped thousands of monkey-slaying shafts, and a very river of blood flowed between the opposing hosts. Then Nilā, Agni's son, brandishing an uptorn tree, rushed on Prahasta ; but he wounded the monkey with showers of arrows. At last his bow was shattered in the conflict, and the twain fought hand to hand, with tooth and nail. Then Prahasta struck Nilā a deadly blow with his mace, and Nilā flung a tall tree at Prahasta's breast; but he lightly avoided that and rushed on Nilā. Then Nilā flung a mighty crag at the rākshasa, shattering his head, so that he fell slain. The rākshasa host drew back; like water rushing through a broken dyke, they melted away and entered Lankā, stricken with grief and fear.

Rāvana was inflamed with wrath to learn of Prahasta's death, and his heart sank, but he boasted that he would himself destroy Rāma and Lakshman with a thousand shafts, and mounted his own shining car and led a rākshasa host against the monkeys; he seemed like the Destroyer himself, accompanied by ghosts and flesh-devouring monsters with burning eyes. Big-belly and Goblin and Man-destroyer and Three-heads, fighters with mountain-peaks and flaming maces, came with Rāvana. But he, when they were face to face with the besiegers, dismissed the host to take their ease, and himself advanced to fight alone. Then first Sugriva hurled a mountain-top at him, but Rāvana severed it with his golden shafts, so that it fell vainly to the earth, and he sped a deadly flaming shaft at the monkey-king that bore him to the ground groaning with pain. Then other monkey-chiefs together rushed at Rāvana, but these in like fashion he destroyed, so that they cried to Rāma for help. Lakshman prayed for that battle, and Rāma granted him, and he took the field; but already Hanuman was pressing Rāvana hard, so that he cried: "Well done, monkey; thou art a foe in whom I may rejoice." Therewith he struck the Wind-god's son a heavy blow so that he shuddered and fell back, and Rāvana turned to fight with Nilā. But the Fire-god's son, flaming with anger, sprang on to Rāvana's car and darted like fire from point to point; and Rāvana's heart sank, but he took a deadly shaft and aimed at Nilā, and laid him low, at the very point of death. But then Lakshman took up the battle, and showers of arrows were loosed by either hero, so that both were sorely wounded; and a flaming dart struck Rāma's brother down. Then Rāvana seized him; but he that could raise Himālaya could not lift Lakshman from the ground, for he remembered that he was a very part of Vishnu himself, and he stayed immovable. Then Hanuman returned and struck the rākshasa king a staggering blow so that he fell back, senseless and bleeding, on the platform of his car; and Hanuman lifted Lakshman easily and bore him away to Rāma. Nor was it long before both Rāvana and Lakshman came to their senses; and Rāma, mounted upon Hanuman's back, engaged in a dreadful battle with the king of Lankā. Rāma destroyed his car, and wounded Rāvana with bolts, and cut his crown atwain with a fiery disc, and struck him with an arrow, so that he grew weak and faint; then, sparing his life, he sent him back to Lankā, saying: "Thou hast accomplished deeds of heroism, and I see thee faint; do thou retire to Lankā now, for thou shalt feel my power in another battle." So the generous Rāma spared his foe, and all the gods and quarters and the seas and creatures of earth rejoiced to see the rākshasa king cast down.

Pot-ear Awakened

Now Rāvana bethought him of his brother Kumbhakarna ("Pot-ear"). He would ever sleep, now six, now eight, now ten months at a time, and would wake only to gorge, and then sleep again. But he was the hardest fighter and the very best of the rākshasas in battle; and now he had already slept nine months, when Rāvana sent a host to waken him. They found him sleeping in his cave; he lay like a mountain, drunk with sleep, and vast as Hell, his rank breath sweeping all before him, smelling of blood and fat. The rākshasas made ready for him heaps of deer and buffaloes, steaming rice and jars of blood, mountains of food piled up as high as Meru; then set about to wake him. They winded conchs and shouted and beat on drums, so that the very birds in the sky fell dead of fear; but Pot-ear slept the harder, and the rākshasas could hardly stand against the tornado of his breath. Then they girded their cloths the tighter, and ten thousand of them yelled together, and struck heavy blows at him with logs of wood, and beat a thousand kettledrums at once. Then they waxed angrier, and set themselves to work in earnest; some bit his ears, some poured a thousand pots of water in them, some wounded him with spears and maces, and some drove a thousand elephants against him. Therewith at last he woke, and yawned, and yawned again, so that a very storm was raging; and the pangs of hunger assailed him, and he looked about for food. Then he beheld the feast, and fell to heartily, and ate and drank; and when the rākshasas thought him filled, they stood around him and bowed, and informed him of all that had befallen, and prayed his help. Then he, already half asleep again, roused himself, and boasted that he would regale the rākshasas with an abundant feast of monkey flesh and blood; "and myself shall swill the blood of Rāma and Lakshman," said he.

So Pot-ear bathed, and, going to his brother, bade him take heart. He drank two thousand flasks of wine, and marched out like a moving mountain, clad in golden mail, to attack the monkeys. The monkeys fled in terror, but Pot-ear caught them and rushed about devouring them by handfuls, so that the blood and fat dripped from his mouth. Then Rāma, with Hanuman and Angada and other brave monkeys, fell on him with trees and mountain-tops, swarming round him like clouds about a mountain; and Pot-ear, half asleep as yet, began to rouse himself and fight in earnest. Hanuman, from the sky, cast down the mountain-peaks on him; but he swallowed twenty and thirty monkeys at a mouthful, and slew them by hundreds at every stroke, and wounded Hanuman, and raged from side to side.

Pot-ear Slain

Then Pot-ear sped a second deadly shaft at Hanuman; but he caught it and broke it with his hands, and all the monkeys shouted, so that the rākshasa was daunted and turned away. But therewith Pot-ear flung a mountain-top and struck Sugriva down, and he lifted him and carried him away. The monkeys were scattered and their king a prisoner. But Sugriva roused himself and turned on Pot-ear and wounded him and got away; and the battle was joined again, and Lakshman fought against the rākshasa. Then Rāma took up the battle, and wounded his foe with many shafts, and shot away an arm, destroying a hundred monkeys in its fall. Then with a second shaft he cut away the other arm, and with two keen-edged discs he cut away the demon's legs, and with a shaft of Indra he struck away his head; and he fell like a great hill and crashed down into the sea, and the gods and heroes rejoiced.

Rākshasa Successes

Then Rāvana grew ever more heavy of heart; but Prince Indrajit came to his father and vowed to slay Rāma and

Lakshman that day, and he sallied forth. But first he offered libations unto Fire, and sacrificed a goat; and the bright, smokeless Fire-god, with his flickering tongue, rose up to take the offering, and he bestowed a Brahmā weapon on Indrajit, and blessed his bow and car with charms. Armed with that weapon, Indrajit slew countless hosts of monkeys, and laid low Sugriva and Angada and Jambavān and Nilā and other chiefs, but himself remained invisible. Then Rāma, seeing him thus weaponed and unassailable, counselled a semblance of defeat. And Indrajit returned victorious to Lankā.

Hanuman fetches Healing Herbs

Then Vibhishana and Hanuman ranged the field, beholding thousands of slain and wounded, a horrid sight and grim; and they came nigh to the king of bears, Jambavān, and asked if he yet lived. He answered faintly, recognizing Vibhishana's voice, and asked if Hanuman was alive; then Hanuman bowed to Jambavān and held his feet. Jambavān rejoiced, and despite his wounds he spoke to the Wind-god's son:

"Do thou labour for this host of bears and monkeys, for only thou canst save them. Thou shalt bound over the sea, and reach Himālaya, king of mountains, and bring thence the four life-giving herbs that grow on him, and return forthwith with healing for the monkey host."

Then Hanuman roared and sprang; and he passed across the sea and over hills and woods and rivers and cities till he came to Himālaya and beheld its hermitages. He ranged the mountain, but the herbs were hidden from him; and angered and impatient, Hanuman rooted up the whole mountain and sprang with it into the air and returned to Lankā, welcomed by all the host. And the slain and wounded monkeys rose up whole, as if from restful sleep, healed by the savour of the four medicinal herbs. But all the slain rākshasas had been cast into the sea. Then Hanuman took the mountain-peak again to Himālaya and returned to Lankā.

Now Sugriva, perceiving that few rākshasas lived to guard the city, stormed the gates, and a host of monkeys bearing flaming brands entered and burnt and ravaged her. The second night had now come on, and the burning city glowed in the darkness, like a mountain blazing with forest fires. But Rāvana sent out a host against the monkeys time and again. First Kumbha and Nikumbha led the rākshasas, and were slain in deadly battle; then Mahārāksha, son of Khara, in turn was slain, and Indrajit went out again. He fought invisible as ever, and sorely wounded Rāma and Lakshman. Then Indrajit retired, and came forth again, riding on a car with an illusory magic figure of Sītā; and he rode up and down the field, holding her by the hair and striking her, and he cut her down in the sight of all the monkey host. Hanuman, believing in the false show, stayed the battle and brought the news to Rāma; and Rāma fell down, like a tree cut off at the root. But while they grieved, Indrajit went to the altar at Nikhumbila to make sacrifices to the god of Fire.

Rāvana's Son is Killed

Meanwhile Vibhishana came to Rāma and found him overwhelmed with grief, and Lakshman told him that Sītā had been slain by Indrajit. But Vibhishana guessed this to have been a vain show, less possible than for the ocean to be dried up. "It is a device," he said, "to delay the monkey army till Indrajit shall have completed a sacrifice to Fire and have won as a boon to be invincible in battle. Therefore grieve not, but hasten to prevent his offerings, lest the very gods be in danger if he complete them." Then Rāma rose, and with Lakshman and Vibhishana pursued the son of Rāvana; and they overtook him ere he reached Nikhumbila, mounted on a fiery car. Then befell the worst and fiercest of conflicts that had yet been: Lakshman bore the brunt of that battle, and it is said that the ancestors and gods, the birds and snakes, protected Lakshman from the deadly shafts. And this was at last the manner of Indrajit's death: Lakshman took an Indra shaft, and making an act of truth, he prayed its indwelling deity: "If Rāma be righteous and truthful, the first of all men in heroism, then slay this son of Rāvana"; and drawing the straight-speeding arrow to his ear, he loosed it, and it severed the rākshasa's neck, that head and trunk fell to the ground, and all the rākshasas, seeing their leader slain, cast down their arms and fled. And all the monkeys rejoiced, for no rākshasa hero remained alive save Rāvana himself. Then Rāma welcomed the wounded Lakshman with great affection, and ordered Sushena to administer medicines to him and to the wounded monkeys; and the monkey-chief applied a potent drug to Lakshman's nose, and, smelling it, the outward-going of his life was stayed, and he was healed.

Bitterly Rāvana grieved for his son. "The triple worlds, and this earth with all its forests, seem to me vacant," he cried, "since thou, my hero, hast gone to the abode of Yama, who shouldst have performed my funeral rites, not I thine"; and he burned with rage and sorrow. Then he determined to slay Sītā in revenge, but his good counsellor Supārshwa held him back, saying: "Thou mayst not slay a woman; but when Rāma is slain thou shalt possess her."

All Lankā was resounding with the lamentations of the rākshasīs for the rākshasas slain in battle, and Rāvana sat in fury, devising means to conquer Rāma: he gnashed his teeth and bit his lips and laughed, and went with Big-belly and Squint-eye and Great-flank to the field of battle, followed by the last of the demon army, and boasting: "I shall make an end of Rāma and Lakshman to-day."

Rāvana's Fury

Nor could the monkeys stand before him, but were destroyed like flies in fire; but Sugriva engaged in single fight with Squint-eye and made an end of him; and therewith both armies joined again, and there was deadly slaughter on either hand, and either army shrank like a pond in summer. Next Big-belly was slain by Sugriva, and Angada was the death of Great-flank, so that the monkeys roared with triumph. But now Rāvana came on, bearing a Brahmā weapon, and scattering the monkeys right and left.

He stayed not ere he came to the sons of Dasharatha: he took his way where Rāma stood aside, with great eyes like the petals of a lotus, long of arm, unconquerable, holding a bow so huge it seemed to be painted on the sky. Rāma set arrows to the bow and drew the string, so that a thousand rākshasas died of terror when they heard it twang; and there began a deadly battle between the heroes. Those arrows pierced the king of Lankā like five-hooded serpents, and fell hissing to the ground; but Rāvana lifted up a dreadful asura weapon, and let fly at Rāma a shower of arrows having lion- and tiger-faces, and some with gaping mouths like wolves. Rāma answered these with shafts faced like the sun and stars, like meteors or lightning flashes, destroying the shafts of Rāvana. Then Rāvana fought with other celestial weapons, and he lifted a Rudra shaft, irresistible and flaming, hung with eight noisy bells, and hurled it at Vibhishana; but Lakshman came before it, saving Vibhishana from death. Rāma, seeing that weapon falling upon Lakshman, prayed it: "Peace be to Lakshman! Be thou frustrated, and let thy energy depart"; but the blazing dart struck Lakshman's breast and laid him low, nor could any monkey draw the shaft out of him. Rāma stooped and drew it forth and broke it in twain, and then, albeit grieved out of measure for Lakshman and angered by his grief, Rāma called to Hanuman and Sugriva, saying: "Now is the time appointed come at last. To-day I shall accomplish a deed of which all men and gods and every world shall tell as long as the earth supports a living creature. To-day my sorrow shall have an end, and all that for which I have laboured shall come to pass."

Then Rāma set his mind upon the battle, but Hanuman went again to Himālaya and brought the mount of healing herbs for Lakshman, and Sushena took the life-giving plant and made Lakshman to smell its savour, so that he rose up whole and well; and Lakshman embraced his brother, and urged him to achieve his promise that very day. Sakra sent down from Heaven his car and his charioteer, named Mātalī, to aid the son of Dasharatha in his fight, and Rāma went about and greeted it, and, mounting upon it, seemed to light the whole world with his splendour. But Rāvana loosed at him a rākshasa weapon, and its golden shafts, with fiery faces vomiting flames, poured over Rāma from every side and changed to venomous serpents. But Rāma took a Garuda weapon and loosed a flight of golden arrows, changing at will to birds, and devouring all the serpent arrows of the rākshasa.

Then the presiding deities of all the weapons came to stand by Rāma, and what with this auspicious omen and other happy signs, Rāma began to harass Rāvana sorely, and wounded him, so that his charioteer, beholding him as if at the point of death, turned away from the field of battle. Then the revered Agastya, come thither with the gods to witness the defeat of Rāvana, drew near to Rāma and taught him: "Rāma, Rāma, great-armed hero, my child, hearken to the eternal secret, the Heart of the Sun, whereby thou mayst overcome every foe. Do thou worship Sun, lord of the world, in whom dwells the spirit of all the gods. Hail! Hail! O thousand-rayed, hail to Āditya! Thou wakener of the lotus! Thou source of life and death, destroyer of all darkness, light of the soul, who wakest when all sleep, and dwellest in every heart! Thou art the gods and every sacrifice and the fruits thereof. Do thou worship with this hymn the lord of the universe, and thou shalt conquer Rāvana to-day."

Rāvana Slain

Then Rāma hymned the Sun, and purified himself with water-sippings, and was glad; and he turned to deal with Rāvana, for the rākshasa had come to himself again and was eager for the battle. Each like a flaming lion fought the other; head after head of the Ten-necked One did Rāma cut away with his deadly arrows, but new heads ever rose in place of those cut off, and Rāvana's death seemed nowise nearer than before—the arrows that had slain Mārīcha and Khara and Vāli could not take the king of Lankā's life away. Then Rāma took up the Brahmā weapon given to him by Agastya: the Wind lay in its wings, the Sun and Fire in its head, in its mass the weight of Meru and Mandara. Blessing that shaft with

Vedic *mantras*, Rāma set it on his bow and loosed it, and it sped to its appointed place and cleft the breast of Rāvana, and, bathed in blood, returned and entered Rāma's quiver humbly.

Thus was the lord of the rākshasas slain, and the gods rained flowers on Rāma's car and chanted hymns of praise, for their desired end was now accomplished—that end for which alone Vishnu had taken human form. The heavens were at peace, the air grew clear and bright, and the sun shone cloudless on the field of battle.

Rāvana Mourned

But Vibhishana lamented for his brother sadly, and Rāma comforted him, saying: "A hero slain in battle should not be mourned. Success in battle is not for ever: why shouldst thou grieve that one who put to flight Indra himself should fall at last? Do thou rather perform his funeral rites. Take comfort, too, at this: with death our enmity is ended, and Rāvana is as dear to me as thee."

Then there issued out of Lankā a host of weeping rākshasīs, seeking their lord and wailing bitterly; and Mandodarī made this lament:

"O thou great-armed, younger brother of Vaisrāvana, who could stand before thee? Gods and rishis thou hast daunted; not to be borne is it that a man, fighting on foot, hath slain thee now! But thy death has come to pass because of Sītā, and I am a widow. Thou didst not heed my words, nor didst thou think how many fairer damsels thou hadst than her. Alas! how fair thou wert and how kind thy smile: now thou art bathed in blood and pierced with shafts! Thou wert wont to sleep on a couch of gold; but now thou liest in the dust. Why dost thou fare away and leave me alone? Why dost thou not welcome me?" But the other wives of Rāvana consoled her and lifted her up, saying: "Life is uncertain for all, and all things change." Meanwhile Vibhishana made ready the funeral pyre, and Rāvana was taken to the burning-ground and burnt with every rite and honour due to heroes. Rāvana's wives returned to Lankā, and the gods departed to their own place. Then Lakshman, taking water brought from the ocean by Sugriva in a golden jar, anointed Vibhishana as lord of the city of Lankā and king of the rākshasas, and thereat the monkeys and rākshasas both rejoiced.

Sītā brought to Rāma

But now Rāma called Hanuman to him, and sent him to search for Sītā and inform her of all that had befallen; and he found her still by the Asoka tree, guarded by rākshasīs. Hanuman stood before her humbly and told his tale, and she gave him the message: "I desire to behold my lord." Then the radiant monkey came to Rāma and gave him Sītā's message. Rāma wept thereat and was plunged in thought, and with a heavy sigh he said to Vibhishana: "Do thou bring Sītā hither quickly, bathed and fitly adorned with sandal-paste and jewels." He repaired to her and gave her Rāma's command; she would have gone to him unbathed. "But thou shouldst do according to thy lord's word," he said. "So be it," she replied, and when she had made her ready, worthy bearers brought her on a palanquin to Rāma. Rāma, beholding her who had long been the prisoner of Rāvana, and overcome with sorrow, was stricken at once with fury, joy, and grief. "O lord of rākshasas, O gentle king," said he to Vibhishana, "do thou bring Sītā near to me." Then Vibhishana drove away the crowd of monkeys, bears, and rākshasas, and the attendants with canes and drums roughly hustled the assembled host. But Rāma bade them desist, and ordered that Sītā should leave her palanquin and come to him on foot, saying to Vibhishana: "Thou shouldst rather comfort than harass these our own folk. No sin is there when women are seen abroad in time of war or danger, at an own-choice,[1] or at marriage. Sītā is in danger now, and there can be no wrong in seeing her, the more so as I am here to guard her." Vibhishana, cast down at that rebuke, brought Sītā humbly up to Rāma; and she stood shamefast, hiding as it were her true self in her outward shape, beholding Rāma's face with wonder, joy, and love. At the sight of him her sorrow vanished, and she shone radiant like the moon.

But Rāma, seeing her stand humbly near him, could no more hold back his speech, and cried: "O gentle one, I have subdued thy foe and wiped away the stain upon my honour. The work of Hanuman, in crossing the deep and harrying Lankā; of Sugriva, with his army and his counsel; and of Vibhishana, hath borne its fruit, and I have fulfilled my promise, by my own might accomplishing the duty of a man." Then Sītā looked on Rāma sadly, like a deer, with tear-filled eyes; and Rāma, seeing her so near, but bethinking him of honour in the sight of men, was torn in twain. "I have wiped away the insult to our family and to myself," said he, "but thou art stained by dwelling with another than myself. What man of high degree receives back a wife who hath lived long in another's house? Rāvan has held thee on his lap and gazed on thee with lustful eyes. I have avenged his evil deed, but I am unattached to thee. O gentle one, I am forced by a sense of honour to renounce thee, for how should Rāvana have overlooked thee, so fair and dainty as thou art, when he

[1] *Swayamvara*, choice of a husband from assembled suitors: see the story of Nala and Damayantī, page 356.

had thee at his will? Do thou choose what home thou wilt, whether with Lakshman, or Bharata, or Sugriva, or with Vibhishana."

Then Sītā, hearing that cruel speech of Rāma, little like his wonted words, trembled like a swaying vine, and wept with heavy tears, and she was ashamed before that great assembly. But she wiped the tears from her face, and answered him: "Ah, why dost thou speak thus roughly and unkindly? Seeing the ways of other women, thou wilt trust in none! But, O thou long-armed hero, I am my own sufficient witness to my purity. It was not with my consent that another touched my person. My body was not in my power; but my heart, that lies under my own sway, is set on thee alone. O thou my lord and source of honour, our affection increased by living continually together for a long time; and now, if thou dost not know my faithfulness, I am undone for ever. O king, why didst thou not renounce me when Hanuman came? Then would I have given up my life, and thou needst not have undertaken all thy labour, nor laid a burden on thy friends. Thou art angered; like a common man thou seest naught in me but womanhood. I am called the daughter of Janaka, but, in sooth, I was born of Earth; thou knowest not my true self."

Then Sītā turned to Lakshman, and said with faltering speech: "O son of Sumitra, build me a funeral pyre; therein is my only refuge. Branded with an undeserved stigma, I will not live." Lakshman, wrought with grief and anger, turned to Rāma, and in obedience to his gesture he prepared the funeral pyre.

Sītā's Ordeal

Then Sītā, circumambulating Rāma, standing with downcast eyes, approached the fire; with folded hands she stood and prayed: "Inasmuch as my heart has never turned from Rāma, do thou, O Fire, all men's witness, guard me; since Rāma casts me away as stained, who in sooth am stainless, do thou be my refuge." Then Sītā went about the pyre and entered the burning flames, so that all, both young and old, assembled there were overcome with grief, and the noise of uttermost wailing and lamentation arose on every hand.

Rāma stayed immovable and rapt; but the gods came down to Lankā in their shining cars and, folding their hands, prayed Rāma to relent. "Thou that dost protect the worlds, why dost thou renounce the daughter of Janaka, leaving her to choose the death by fire? How can it be thou knowest not what thyself art? Thou wast in the beginning, and shalt be at the end: thou art first of all the gods, thyself the grandsire and creator. Why dost thou treat Sītā after the fashion of a mere man?" said they. To whom Rāma replied: "I know myself only as a man, Rāma, the son of Dasharatha; now let the grandsire tell me who I am and whence I came."

Then Brahmā answered: "Hearken, thou whose virtue lies in truth! O Lord, thou art Nārāyana, bearing disc and mace; thou art the one-tusked boar; thou goest beyond the past, the present, and the future; thine is the bow of Time; thou art creation and destruction; thou art the slayer of all enemies, thou the forgiveness and control of passions; thou art the refuge of all gods and hermits; thou art manifest in every creature, in cows and Brāhmans, in every quarter, in sky and river and mountain-peak; a thousand limbs, a thousand eyes, a thousand heads are thine; thy heart am I, thy tongue Sarasvatī; the closing of thy eye is night, its opening day: Sītā is Lakshmi and thou Vishnu and Krishna. And, O Rāma, now Rāvana is slain, do thou ascend to Heaven, thy work accomplished. Naught shall they lack whose hearts are set on thee, nor fail who chant thy lay."

Then Fire, hearing those happy words, rose up with Sītā on his lap, radiant as the morning sun, with golden jewels and black curling hair, and he gave her back to Rāma, saying: "O Rāma, here is thy Sītā, whom no stain has touched. Not in word or thought or look has Sītā turned aside from thee. Albeit tempted every way, she did not think of Rāvana even in her inmost heart. As she is spotless, do thou take her back." Rāma, staying silent for a while, with shining eyes pondered the speech of Agni; then he answered: "Because this fair one dwelt long time in Rāvana's house, she needed vindication before the assembled folk. Had I taken her unproved, the people would complain that Rāma, son of King Dasharatha, was moved by desire, and set at naught social law. I know well that Sītā's heart is set on me alone, and that her own virtue was her sufficient refuge from the assaults of Rāvana; she is mine as the sun's rays are the sun's. I can no more renounce her, but rather it behoves me to obey your happy words." Thus the glorious son of Dasharatha regained his bride, and his heart was glad.

Visions of the Gods

But now Shiva took up the word, and revealed to Rāma his father Dasharatha stationed on a shining car amongst the gods, and Rāma and Lakshman bowed to him; and he, beholding his dearest son, took Rāma on his lap, and spake: "Even in heaven amongst the gods I am not happy, lacking thee. I call to mind even now Kaikeyī's word, and thou hast redeemed my pledge and freed me from every debt. Now I have heard that thou art the primal

male incarnate for the compassing of Rāvana's death. Kaushalyā shall be glad to see thee return victorious. Blessed are those that shall behold thee installed as Lord of Ayodhyā! Thy term of exile is ended. Do thou rule with thy brothers now in Ayodhyā and have long life!"
Then Rāma prayed his father: "Do thou now forgive Kaikeyī, and take back thy dreadful curse wherewith thou didst renounce her and her son." Then Dasharatha said: "So be it"; and to Lakshman: "May good befall thee, thou truth and honour, and thou shalt attain a lofty place in heaven. Do thou attend on Rāma, whom all the gods adore with folded hands." And to Sītā he said: "Thou shouldst not feel resentment forasmuch as Rāma renounced thee; for thy welfare it was done. Now hast thou attained a glory hard to be won by women! Thou knowest well the duty of a wife. It needs not for me to tell thee that thy husband is thy very god," Then Dasharatha in his car returned to Indra's heaven.
Next Indra, standing before Rāma, with folded hands addressed him, saying: "O Rāma, first of men, it may not be for naught that we are come to thee. Do thou pray for such a boon as thou desirest." Then Rāma spoke, delighted: "O Lord of Heaven and foremost of the eloquent, do thou grant me this, that all the monkeys slain in battle return to life and see again their wives and children. Do thou restore those bears and monkeys that fought for me and laboured hard and recked nothing of death. And let there be flowers and fruits and roots for them, and rivers of clear water, even out of season, wherever they may go." And Indra granted that great boon, so that a host of monkeys rose up, asking like wakened sleepers: "What has happened?" Then the gods, once more addressing Rāma, said: "Do thou return to Ayodhyā, sending the

monkeys on their way. Comfort Sītā, seek out thy brother Bharata, and, being installed as king, do thou bestow good fortune on every citizen." Therewith the gods departed, and the happy army made their camp.

Rāma's Return

When morning dawned, Rāma, taking the car Pushpaka, given to him by Vibhishana, stood ready to depart. Self-moving was that car, and it was very fairly painted and large; two stories it had, and windows and flags and banners and many chambers, and it gave forth a melodious sound as it coursed along the airy way. Then said Vibhishana: "What more may I do?" and Rāma answered: "Do thou content these bears and monkeys who have accomplished my affair with divers jewels and wealth; then shall they fare to their homes. And do thou rule as one who is righteous, self-controlled, compassionate, a just collector of revenues, that all may be attached to thee." Then Vibhishana bestowed wealth on all the host, and Rāma was taking leave of all the bears and monkeys and of Vibhishana; but they cried out: "We wish to go with thee to Ayodhyā." Then Rāma invited them gladly, and Sugriva and Vibhishana and all the host mounted the mighty car; and the car rose up into the sky, drawn by golden geese, and sailed on its airy way, while the monkeys, bears, and rākshasas took their ease.

But when they passed by the city of Kishkindhā, Sugriva's capital, Sītā prayed Rāma to take with him to Ayodhyā Tārā, the wife of Sugriva, and the wives of other monkey-chiefs; and he stayed the car while Sugriva brought Tārā and the wives of other monkeys. And they mounted and set forth towards Ayodhyā. They passed across Chitrakuta and Jamna and the Ganges where it divides in three, and at last beheld Ayodhyā, and bowed to her; and all the bears and monkeys and Vibhishana rose up in delight to see her, shining fair as Amarāvatī, the capital of Indra.

It was the fifth day after the last of fourteen years of exile when Rāma greeted the hermit Bharadwāja, and from him learnt that Bharata awaited his return, leading a hermit's life and honouring the sandals. And Bharadwāja gave him a boon, that the trees along the road to Ayodhyā should bear flowers and fruit as he went, even though out of season. And so it was that for three leagues, from Bharadwāja's hermitage to Ayodhyā's gate, the trees bore flowers and fruits, and the monkeys thought themselves in heaven. But Hanuman was sent in advance to bring back tidings from Ayodhyā and Bharata, and speedily he went, in human form. He came to Bharata in his hermitage garbed as a yogī, thin and worn, but radiant as a mighty sage, and ruling the earth as viceroy of the sandals. Then Hanuman related to him all that had befallen Rāma since the brothers parted in Chitrakuta, and Bharata's heart was filled with gladness, and he gave orders to prepare the city and to worship all the gods with music and flowers, and that all the people should come forth to welcome Rāma. The roads were watered and the flags hoisted, and the city was filled with the sound of cavalry and cars and elephants. Then Rāma came, and Bharata worshipped him and bathed his feet and humbly greeted him; but Rāma lifted him up and took him in his arms. Then Bharata bowed to Sītā, and welcomed Lakshman, and embraced the monkey-chiefs, naming Sugriva "our fifth brother"; and he praised Vibhishana.

Then Rāma came to his mother and humbly touched her feet, and he made salutation to the priests. Next Bharata brought the sandals and laid them at Rāma's

IX

THE RETURN OF RĀMA

K. Venkatappa

Page 102

feet, and with folded hands he said: "All this, thy kingdom, that thou didst entrust to me, I now return: behold, thy wealth of treasure, palace, and army is tenfold multiplied." Then placing his brother on his lap, Rāma fared on to Bharata's hermitage, and there descending, Rāma spake to the good car: "Do thou return to Vaishrāvan—I grant thee leave." For that self-coursing car had been taken by Rāvana from his elder brother; but now at Rāma's word it returned to the God of Wealth.

Rāma installed with Sītā

Then Bharata restored the kingdom to his brother, saying: "Let the world behold thee to-day installed, like the radiant midday sun. None but thou can bear the heavy burden of an empire such as ours. Do thou no more dwell in lonely places, but sleep and rise to the sound of music and the tinkle of women's anklets. Do thou rule the people as long as the sun endures and as far as earth extends." And Rāma said: "So be it."

Then skilful barbers came, and Rāma and Lakshman bathed and were shorn of their matted locks and dressed in shining robes; and Dasharatha's queens attended Sītā and decked her in splendid jewels, while Kaushalyā decked the monkeys' wives, and the priests gave orders for the coronation. Then Rāma mounted a car driven by Bharata, and Satrughna held the umbrella, and Lakshman waved a chowry and Vibhishana another. Sugriva rode on an elephant, and the other monkeys followed riding on elephants to the number of nine thousand, and with music and the noise of conchs the lord of men entered his own city. Four golden jars were given to Hanuman and Jambavān and Vegadarshi and Rishabha to fetch pure water from the four oceans, and they rose into the sky and brought the holy water from the utmost bounds of ocean, north and south and east and west. Then Vāshishtha, setting Rāma and Sītā upon their golden throne, sprinkled that first of men and consecrated him as king of Ayodhyā. Thereat the gods rejoiced, and the gandharvas sang and the apsaras danced; the earth was filled with crops, the trees bore fruit and flowers, and all men were glad and merry. And Rāma conferred upon the Brāhmans gifts of gold and ornaments, and cows and horses; to Angada he gave a golden jewelled chain such as are worn by the gods, and to Sītā a necklace of matchless pearls and other ornaments and splendid robes. But she, holding the pearls in her hand, glanced at her lord, and from him to Hanuman, remembering his goodly service; and Rāma, reading her wish, granted her leave, and she gave the necklace to Hanuman. And the Wind-god's son, exemplar of energy, renown, capacity, humility, and courage, wearing that garland, shone like a mountain illumined by the moon and fleecy clouds. And to every other hero Rāma gave due gifts of jewels and wealth.

Then Sugriva and Hanuman and Jambavān, with all the host, returned to their own homes, and Vibhishana repaired to Lankā; but Rāma governed Ayodhyā, and in his time men lived for a thousand years, and due rains fell, and the winds were ever favourable, and there was no distress from sickness or from wild beasts or from invasion, but all men were glad and merry.

Rāma Reigns

Then, while Rāma sat on the throne, all the great hermits came to visit him who had regained his kingdom. They came from east and west and north and south, led by Agastya, and Rāma worshipped them and appointed for them splendid seats of sacrificial grass and gold-embroidered deer-skin. Then the sages praised Rāma's fortune, especially inasmuch as he had slain Rāvana's son, mightier than Rāvana himself, and had delivered men and gods from fear. Then Rāma questioned the sages about the former history of Rāvana and Rāvana's son, and they related to him at length the story of the rākshasas' origin—how they had come to Lankā; how Rāvana, Kumbhakarna, and Vibhishana had won each a boon from the grandsire; what evil deeds had been done by Rāvana; and how the gods had appointed Vishnu to take human form to achieve his death. Likewise they told of the origin and deeds of the monkeys Vāli and Sugriva and Hanuman. "And, O Rāma!" they said, "in the golden age the demon sought to fight with thee; for those whom the gods destroy go to the heaven of the gods till they are born again on earth; those whom Vishnu slays go to Vishnu's heaven, so that his very wrath is a blessing. And it was for this that Rāvana stole Sītā away and thou didst assume a human form for his destruction, O great one, know that thou art Nārāyana: do thou recollect thyself. Thou art the eternal Vishnu, and Sītā is Lakshmī."

Rāma himself and all the assembled folk—Rāma's brothers, the monkey-chiefs, the rākshasas under Vibhishana, the vassal kings, and the Brāhmans, Kshatriyas, Vaishyas, and Shudras of Ayodhyā—marvelled at the words of the great sages; and Agastya took leave of Rāma and departed, and night fell.

Hanuman Rewarded

The monkeys dwelt at Ayodhyā more than a month, feasting on honey and well-cooked meats and fruits and roots, though it seemed to them but a moment, because of their devotion toward Rāma. Then the time came for them to go to their own city, and Rāma embraced them all with affection and gave them goodly gifts. But Hanuman bowed and begged this boon, that he might ever be devoted to Rāma alone, and that he might live on earth so long as the story of Rāma's deeds was told of amongst men; and Rāma granted it, and took from his own neck a jewelled chain and put it upon Hanuman. One by one the monkeys came and touched the feet of Rāma, and then went their way; but they wept for sorrow of leaving him.

Sītā's Second Trial

Then Rāma governed Ayodhyā for ten thousand years; and at length it came to pass that Sītā had conceived. Then Rāma asked her if she had any longing, and she replied that she desired to visit the hermitages of the sages by the Ganges; and Rāma said: "So be it"; and the visit was fixed for the morrow.

The same night it happened that Rāma was engaged in converse with his counsellors and friends, and he asked them: "What do the citizens and countrymen say of Sītā and my brothers and Kaikeyī?" And one replied that they spoke often of Rāma's great conquest of Rāvana. But Rāma pressed for more definite reports, and a counsellor replied: "The people do indeed speak of thy great deeds and thy alliance with the bears and monkeys and rākshasas; but they murmur inasmuch as thou hast taken Sītā back, albeit she was touched by Rāvana and dwelt long time in his city of Lankā. For all that, they say, thou dost still acknowledge her. 'Now we, too, will pass over the misdoings of our wives, for subjects always follow the customs of their king.' Such, O king, is the talk."

Then Rāma's heart sank, and he sent away the counsellors and sent for his brothers, and they came and stood by him with folded hands and touched his feet. But they saw that he was heavy-hearted and that his eyes were full of tears, and waited anxiously for him to speak. Then Rāma told them what he had learnt. "I am crushed by these slanders," he said, "for I am of an illustrious family, and Sītā is no less nobly born. And Sītā, to prove her innocence, submitted to ordeal by fire before you all, and Fire and Wind and all the gods declared her stainless. Even now my heart knows her to be blameless. But the censure of the folk has pierced me: ill is ill-fame for such as I, and preferable were death than this disgrace. Do thou, therefore, Lakshman, make no question, but take Sītā with thee to-morrow to Vālmīki's hermitage beside the Ganges, as if fulfilling the desire she spoke of even now; and by my life and arms, do ye not seek to move me from this, lest I deem you to be my foes." And Rāma's eyes were full of tears, and he went to his own apartment sighing like a wounded elephant.

The next morning Lakshman brought a goodly car and came to Sītā, saying: "Rāma hath commanded me to take thee to the hermitages by the Ganges in accordance with thy wish." Then Sītā, taking costly gifts with her, mounted the car most eagerly. On the second day they came to the Ganges bank, whose water takes away all sin; but Lakshman stood and wept aloud. Then Sītā asked him why he wept. "For," she said, "it is but two days since thou didst see Rāma: he is dearer to me than life, but I am not so sad as thou. Do thou take me across the river to visit the hermits there and present my gifts, and then shall we return; and, indeed, I am eager to see my lord again, whose eyes are like the petals of the lotus, the lion-breast, the first of men." So Lakshman sent for boatmen, and they went across. When they were come to the other side, Lakshman stood by Sītā with folded hands and prayed her to forgive him and not deem him at fault, saying: "This is a matter too sore for words, so I but tell thee openly that Rāma now renounces thee, inasmuch as the citizens have spoken against thee; he has commanded me to leave thee here, as if in satisfaction of thy own desire. But do not grieve, for well I know that thou art guiltless, and thou mayst dwell with Vālmīki, our father's friend. Do thou remember Rāma always and serve the gods, so mayst thou be blest!" Then Sītā fell down fainting; but she came to herself and complained bitterly: "Alas! I must have greatly sinned in a past life to be thus divided from my lord, though blameless. O Lakshman, formerly it was no hardship for me to live in the forest, for I was able to be Rāma's servant. But how can I live there all alone now, and what reply can I make to those who ask what sin I have committed to be banished thus? I would fain be drowned in these waters, but I may not bring about the destruction of my lord's race. Do thou as Rāma has ordered, but take this message from me to him: 'Thou knowest, O Rāma, that I am unstained and devoted utterly to thee. I understand that it is for the avoiding of ill-fame that thou dost renounce me, and it is my duty to serve thee even in this. A husband is a woman's god, her friend and *guru*. I do not grieve for what befalls me, but because the people have spoken ill of me.' Do thou go and tell these things to Rāma." Then Lakshman crossed the river again and came to Ayodhyā; but Sītā went to and fro without any refuge and began to cry aloud. Then Vālmīki's sons found her there, and Vālmīki came to the river-side and comforted her, and brought her to the hermitage and gave her to the hermits' wives to cherish with affection.

Lakshman found his brother sunk in grief and with his eyes filled with tears, and he was sorry, and touched his feet and stood with folded hands, and said: "O sire, I have done all that thou didst command, and have left that peerless lady at Vālmīki's hermitage. Thou shouldst not grieve therefor; for such is the work of time, whereat the wise grieve not. Where there is growth there is decay; where there is prosperity there is also ruin; where there is birth there must be also death. Therefore, attachment to wife, or sons, or friends, or wealth is wrong, for separation is certain. Nor shouldst thou give way to grief before the folk, lest they blame thee again."

Then Rāma was comforted, and praised the words and love of Lakshman; and he sent for the priests and counsellors who waited, and occupied himself again with the affairs of state. But none had come that day for any affair, for in Rāma's time there was no disease or poverty, and none sought redress. But as Lakshman went away he saw a dog, that waited by the gate and barked, and he asked it what was its affair. Then the dog replied: "I wish to tell it to Rāma himself, who is the refuge of all creatures, and proclaims 'Fear nothing' to them all." So Lakshman returned to Rāma and informed him, and Rāma sent for the dog to come to him. But the dog would not go in, saying: "We are the vilest born, and we may not enter the houses of gods or kings or Brāhmans." Then Lakshman took this message also to Rāma; but he sent again for the dog and gave him leave to enter, who waited at the gate.

Rāma's Justice

Then the dog went in and stood before Rāma, and praised his truth and asked his pardon; and Rāma inquired: "What shall I do for thee? Do thou speak without fear." Then the dog related how a certain Brāhman mendicant had beaten him without cause, and Rāma sent for the Brāhman, and he came, and asked what Rāma required of him. Then Rāma reasoned with him, saying: "O twice-born one, thou hast hurt this dog, who hurt thee not. Lo, anger is the worst of passions, like a sharp dagger, and steals away all virtue. Greater is the evil that may be wrought by lack of self-control than by the sword, or a serpent, or a foe implacable." The Brāhman answered: "I had been seeking alms and was tired and hungry, and this dog would not move away, although I asked him, so I struck him. But, O king, I am guilty of error, and thou shouldst punish me, that I may escape from the fear of hell."

Rāma considered what was a fitting punishment; but the dog requested: "Do thou appoint this Brāhman head of a family." So Rāma honoured him and sent him away riding on an elephant; but the counsellors were astonished. To them Rāma said: "You do not understand this matter; but the dog knows what it signifies." Then the dog, addressed by Rāma, explained: "I was once the head of a family, and I served the gods and Brāhmans, and fed the very servants before I took my food, and I was gentle and benevolent; yet I have fallen into this sorry state. O king, this Brāhman is cruel and impatient in his nature, and he will fail to discharge the duties of the head of a family, and will fall into Hell." Then Rāma wondered at the dog's words, but the dog went away and betook himself to penance in Benares.

Another time there came a Brāhman to the palace gate bearing the dead body of his son, and wailing: "O my son, thou art but fourteen years of age, and I know not for what sin of mine it is that thou hast died; never have I lied, or hurt an animal, or done any other sin. It must be for some other reason that thou hast gone to Yama's realm. Indeed, it must be that the king has sinned, for else such things may not befall. Therefore, O king, do thou confer life again upon him; or, if not, my wife and I will die here at thy gate, like those that have no king."

Then Rāma summoned a council of eight chief Brāhmans, and Nārada took up the word and explained to Rāma what had been the cause of the boy's premature death. He told him of the four ages. "And now, O king, the Kali age begins already, for a Shudra has begun to practise penances in thy kingdom, and for this cause the boy has died. Do thou search the matter out and put down such misdeeds, so that the virtue of thy subjects may increase and this boy may be restored to life."

So Rāma ordered the body of the boy to be preserved in sweet oil, and he bethought him of the self-coursing car Pushpaka, and it knew his mind and came to him straightway. Then Rāma mounted the car and sought through every quarter; but he found no sin in the west nor in the north, and the east was crystal clear. Only in the south, beside a sacred pool, he found a yogī standing on his head practising the most severe disciplines, and Rāma asked him: "O thou blest and self-devoted, who art thou, and what thy colour, and what dost thou seek to win, whether Heaven or aught else?" And the yogī answered: "O great Rāma, I am of the Shudras, and it is for Heaven that I do this penance." Then Rāma drew his sword and cut off the yogī's head, and the gods rained down flowers and praised the deed; but the Shudra yogī attained to the abode of the heavenly ones. Now Rāma prayed to the gods: "If ye are pleased with me, do ye restore to life the Brāhman's son and so fulfil my promise"; and they granted it, and Rāma returned to Ayodhyā. Meanwhile Sītā, dwelling at Vālmīki's hermitage, gave birth to sons, and they were named Kusha and Lava; and they grew up in the forest hermitage, and Vālmīki taught them wisdom, and he made this book of the Rāmāyana in *shlokas*, and gave them skill in recitation.

Rāma's Sons

In those days Rāma prepared a horse-sacrifice, setting free a jet-black horse with lucky marks to wander where it would, and Lakshman followed it. Then he invited all the bears and monkeys, and Vibhishana and foreign kings, and the rishis and others of the hermits from far and near, to be present at the final ceremony. Countless wealth he gave away throughout the year while the horse wandered, yet the treasure of Rāma was in no way diminished; never before was such an *Ashwamedha* in the world!

Kusha and Lava came with Vālmīki to the ceremony, and Vālmīki told them to recite the Rāmāyana everywhere, and if any questioned them, to name themselves as Vālmīki's disciples. So they went about and sang of Rāma's deeds; and Rāma heard of it, and he called a great assembly of the Brāhmans and all kinds of grammarians and artists and musicians, and the hermit children sang before them all. Wondrous and delightful was their song, and none could hear enough of it; but all men drank up the children with their eyes, and murmured: "They are as like to Rāma as one bubble is like another!" When Rāma would have given them wealth, they answered: "We are dwellers in the forest: what use would money be to us?" And when he asked who had composed that song, they answered: "Vālmīki, who is our teacher. And, O king, if the story of thy feats delights thee, do thou hear it all at leisure."

So Rāma hearkened to the story day by day, and from it he learnt that Kusha and Lava were the sons of Sītā. Then Rāma mentioned Sītā's name before the assembly, and sent a messenger to inquire from the hermits if they would vouch for her faithfulness and to ask herself if she were willing to give proof of her innocence again. "Ask her," he said, "if she will swear before the people to establish her own purity and mine." The hermits sent back the message that she would come, and Rāma was glad thereof, and appointed the next day for the taking of the oath.

When the appointed time had come, and all were seated in the assembly, immovable as mountains, Vālmīki came forward, and Sītā followed him with downcast glance and folded hands and falling tears; and there rose a cry of welcome and a murmuring in the assembly when they saw Sītā following Vālmīki thus, like the *Vedas* following Brahmā. Then Vālmīki spoke before the people and said to Rāma: "O son of Dasharatha, albeit Sītā is pure and doth follow the path of righteousness, thou didst renounce her near my hermitage because of the people's censure. Do thou now permit her to give testimony of her purity. And, O Rāma, I myself, who follow truth, tell thee that these twin children are thy sons. Also I swear before thee that if any sin be found in Sītā I will forgo the fruit of all austerities I have practised for many thousand years." Then Rāma, seeing Sītā standing before the assembly like a goddess, with folded hands, replied: "O great one, thou art ever virtuous, and thy words convince me of the purity of Sītā. I recognize these brothers Kusha and Lava as my sons. Yet Sītā shall give testimony herself, for the sake of those that have come here to witness her avowal."

Sītā taken Home by Earth

Then there blew a sweet, cool, fragrant air, a divine zephyr such as used to blow only in the golden age, and folk were astonished that that air should blow also in the second age. But Sītā, with downcast looks and folded palms, said: "I have never thought of anyone but Rāma even in my heart: as this is true, may the goddess of the earth be my protection. I have always with mind and body and words prayed for Rāma's welfare, and by this I pray Vasundhara to receive me."

Then a heavenly throne rose up from within the earth, borne on the heads of mighty *nāgas*,[1] decked in shining jewels; and the Earth stretched out her arms and welcomed Sītā and placed her on the throne, and the throne sank down again. Thereat the gods cried out in praise of Sītā, and all beings on earth and in the sky were filled with wonder and astonishment, so that one mood for a single moment swayed all the universe at once.

But Rāma sat him down stricken with sorrow and with hanging head, and he was torn by grief and anger that Sītā had disappeared before his very eyes, and he would have destroyed the very Earth if she would not give Sītā back. But Brahmā said: "O Rāma of firm vows, thou shouldst not grieve; rather remember thy essential godhead, and bethink thee thou art Vishnu. Sītā is blameless and pure, and for her virtue she has gone to the abode of *nāgas*;

[1] *Nāgas*, lit. snakes—beings of semi-human, semi-serpent nature inhabiting the waters and underworld.

but thou shalt be with her in Heaven. Hearken now to the ending of Vālmīki's story, and thou shalt know thy future history"; and therewith Brahmā with the gods returned to his own place, and Rāma appointed the morrow for the hearing of the *Uttara Kanda.*

The Last Days of Rāma

But now Rāma was heavy-hearted, and the whole world seemed empty without Sītā, and he knew no peace. He gave the monkeys and the kings and hermits gifts, and sent them back to their own homes, and he made a golden image of Sītā to share with him in the performance of sacred rites, and a thousand years passed, while all things prospered in the kingdom of Ayodhyā. Then Kaushalyā and Kaikeyī died, and were united with King Dasharatha in Heaven. Bharata reigned in Kekaya, and Satrughna was king of Madhu, while the sons of Lakshman founded kingdoms of their own.

At length there came to Rāma's palace the mighty yogī Time, and Rāma honoured him. He named himself Time, begotten by Nārāyana on Māyā, and he reminded Rāma of his godly self and all that he had achieved in Heaven and on earth. "O Lord of the World," he said, "thou wast born on earth for the destruction of the Ten-necked rākshasa, and thou didst undertake to dwell on earth for eleven thousand years. Now that time is ripe and the grandsire sendeth me to tell thee: now wilt thou reign yet longer over men, or wilt thou return to the lordship of the gods?" Then Rāma praised the yogī and said he had spoken truth, and for himself he would return to his own place.

But already Lakshman had left his home and gone to the banks of Sarayu to practise great austerities, and there the gods rained flowers upon him, and Indra lifted him from the earth and returned to his own city, so that all the gods, seeing the fourth part of Vishnu come back to them, were gladdened and began to worship him. Then Rāma would follow the same path, and he sought to crown his brother Bharata as king of Ayodhyā, but he refused and would have the king's sons Kusha and Lava set over North and South Kosala; and Rāma granted it, and they were installed upon the throne and ruled over the new cities of Kushavati and Sravanti; but Ayodhyā was altogether emptied of people, for the folk would all follow after Rāma when he went away. News of these matters was brought to Satrughna also, and he set his two sons on the throne of Mathurā and hastened to return to Rāma. Hearing that Rāma was going away, the monkeys, born of the gods, went to Ayodhyā and beheld him; and Sugriva said: "I have set Angada upon the throne of Kishkindhā, and I will follow thee."

Then Rāma granted the desire of all the monkeys to follow him; but to Hanuman he said: "It is determined already that thou shalt live for ever: do thou be glad on earth so long as the tale of me endures." To Jambavān and some others Rāma appointed life till the end of the Kali age, and other bears and monkeys he gave leave to follow him. To Vibhishana he gave good counsel regarding government, and ever to worship Jagannātha, Lord of the World.

The next day Vāshishtha prepared all due rites for those who go to the other world, and all men following Rāma and the Brāhmans set out for Sarayu. There went Bharata and Lakshman and Satrughna and their wives, and the counsellors and servants; and all the people of Ayodhyā, with the beasts and birds and the least of breathing things; and the bears and rākshasas and monkeys followed Rāma with happy hearts.

When they came to Sarayu, Brahmā, the grandsire, came thither with the godly folk and a hundred thousand goodly cars, and the wind of Heaven blew and flowers rained down from Heaven upon earth. Then Brahmā said to Rāma: "Hail, O Vishnu! Do thou, with thy brothers, enter in again in whatsoever form thou wilt, who art the refuge of all creatures, and beyond the range of thought or speech, unknown of any save thy Māyā." Then Vishnu entered Heaven in his own form, with his brothers, and all the gods bowed down to him and rejoiced. Then said Vishnu to the grandsire: "It behoveth thee to allot their due place to all these people who have followed me for love, renouncing self for my sake." Then Brahmā appointed places in the heavens for all those who had come after Rāma, and the bears and monkeys assumed their godly forms, after the likeness of those who had begotten them. Thus did all beings there assembled, entering the waters of Sarayu, attain to the heavenly state, and Brahmā and the gods returned to their own abode.

Thus ends Rāmāyana, revered by Brahmā and made by Vālmīki. He that hath no sons shall attain a son by reading even a single verse of Rāma's lay. All sin is washed away from those who read or hear it read. He who recites Rāmāyana should have rich gifts of cows and gold. Long shall he live who reads Rāmāyana, and shall be honoured, with his sons and grandsons, in this world and in Heaven.

CHAPTER III : THE MAHĀBHĀRATA RELATED IN FIFTEEN EPISODES

Introduction to the Mahābhārata

THE Indian national saga, beyond all dispute, is the Mahābhārata. This is to the Indian village and the Indian home what the *Iliad* was to the Greek, and, to a certain extent also, what the Scriptures and Gospels are to ourselves. It is the most popular of all the sacred books. It contains, as an interlude, the Bhagavad Gītā, the national gospel. But with this it is also an epic. The story of a divine incarnation, Krishna, as he is called, has been wrought into and upon an immense ballad and military epic of unknown antiquity. Of this epic the main theme is a great battle waged between two families of cousins, the sons of Pāndu and the sons of Dhritarāshtra—or the Pāndavas and the Kauravas, or Kurus—by name. And although, after the fashion of ancient literature, a thousand other tales, some more and some less ancient, have been embedded in its interstices, yet this great drama moves on, full of swiftness and colour, from one end of the poem to the other. It is marked by extraordinary vividness and richness of imagination. But perhaps most of us, remembering that the work is ancient, will be still more impressed by the subtlety and modernness of the social intercourse which it portrays. Here and there we may find an anomalous custom or a curious belief, but in delicacy of character-painting, in the play of personality, and in reflection of all the light and shade of life in society we find ourselves, in the Mahābhārata, fully on a level with the novels and dramas of modern Europe. The fortitude of Karna when his mother embraces him; the low voice in which

Yudhishthira says "elephant" as a concession to his conscience; the laugh of Bhīshma in battle, contenting himself with the slightly emphasized "Shikhandinī?"—these, amongst many others, will occur to the reader as typical instances.

The outstanding fact to be realized about the epic, however, is that from end to end its main interest is held and centred on character. We are witnessing the law that, as the oyster makes its own shell, so the mind of man creates and necessitates his own life and fate. The whole philosophy of India is implicit in this romance, just as it is in the common household life. The Mahābhārata constitutes, and is intended to constitute, a supreme appeal to the heart and conscience of every generation. Far more than the national tradition, it embodies the national morality. In this fact lies the great difference between it and the Greek epics, in which the dominant passion is the conscious quest of ideal beauty.

I. HOW THE PRINCES LEARNED TO SHOOT

Now Bhīshma, the royal grandsire, became eager to find for the princes of the two imperial houses a teacher who might train them thoroughly in the use of arms. And it happened one day about this time that the boys, all in a company, were playing at ball in the forests outside Hastinapura, when their ball rolled away from them and fell into an old well. Try as they would, there was not one of them who could get it back. All kinds of efforts were made by each in turn, but without avail. It seemed as if the ball would never be recovered. Just when their boyish anxiety and vexation were at their height, their glances fell, with one accord, on a Brāhman sitting near, whom they had not at first noticed. He was thin and dark of hue, and appeared to be resting after the performance of his daily worship. "O Brāhman!" cried the lads, surrounding him in a body, "can you show us how to recover our ball?" The Brāhman smiled a little and said: "What? what? Scions of the royal house, and you don't shoot well enough for that! If you'll only promise me my dinner, I will bring up not only your ball but also this ring, which I now throw down, by means of a few blades of grass." And suiting the action to the word, he took a ring off his own finger and threw it into the well. "Why, Brāhman-jī, we'll make you rich for life," cried one of the lads, "if you can really do as you say."

"Is it so?" said the Brāhman. "Then look at this grass," and he plucked a handful of long grass growing near. "I am able by a spell to give to this grass a virtue that weapons might not have. Behold, here I throw"; and as he spoke he took aim and threw a single blade of grass with such deftness and precision that it pierced the ball that lay in the well as if it had been a needle. Then throwing another blade, he pierced the first, and so on and so on, till he had a chain of grass, by which it was easy to draw up the ball.

By this time the interest of the boys was centred more on the skill of the Brāhman than on the recovery of their plaything, and they exclaimed with one accord: "The ring, too, O Brāhman! Show us how you can recover the ring!"

The Recovery of the Ring

Then Drona—for that was the name of the Brāhman—took up his bow, which had been lying beside him, and selecting an arrow from the quiver that he wore, he shot it into the well, and the arrow, returning to his hand, brought up the ring. Taking the jewel, he handed it to the princes, whose astonishment and delight knew no bounds. "What can we do for you? What can we do?" they cried. The Brāhman's face had grown grave again. "Tell Bhīshma, your guardian, that Drona is here," he answered briefly, and relapsed again into the depths of thought.

The lads trooped off, with their enthusiasm fresh upon them, to describe to Bhīshma, the Protector, the extraordinary experience of the morning; and he, struck by the thought that Drona was the very teacher he was seeking, hastened in person to see him and bring him to the palace. Bhīshma had known of Drona formerly as the son of the great sage Bharadwāja, whose *ashrāma* in the mountains, near the source of the Ganges, had been a centre of great learning. To that hermitage had come many illustrious students, who had been playmates and comrades to Drona during childhood and youth. It was also rumoured in the royal and military society of the period that Drona, after his father's death, had performed great austerities and gone through a very determined course of study, in consequence of which he had been mysteriously gifted with divine weapons and the knowledge of how to use them.

It was now the object of the royal grandsire, therefore, to learn how and why the Brāhman should be seeking attention in the capital, and a few adroit questions quickly told him all that he required to know. Drona had married and had a son born to him, Ashvatthāman by name. Moved by the needs of his child, he had for the first time realized his own poverty, and had set out to renew the brilliant friendships of his boyhood. Chief amongst these had been his intimacy with Drupada, now king of the Panchalas, one of the greatest of the minor kingdoms. When Drupada, as a prince, had been a student like himself, they had been inseparable, vowing to each other lifelong friendship. It was natural, therefore, that Drupada, now a sovereign in his own right, should be the first of those to whom in his bitter need he thought of repairing. But when he had appeared before him the king of the Panchalas had laughed him to scorn and repudiated all their ancient friendship. To him it seemed sheer impertinence that the poor Brāhman, in the position of a beggar, though he was the son of a famous scholar, should claim equality and intimacy with one seated on a throne. And then in the heart of Drona had risen a great wrath and wounded pride. The bitterness of his poverty was not now so great as the heat of his resentment. He would do what he would do. But in order to do it he must find pupils of the best. He was desirous, therefore, of placing himself at the disposal of Bhīshma.

The old Protector smiled as he heard the climax of this story. He was far too discreet to inquire as to the purposes of Drona. Instead of this he cut matters short by rising and saying: "Only string thy bow, O Brāhman, and make the princes of my house accomplished in the use of arms. All that we have is at thy disposal. We are indeed fortunate to have obtained thy services!"

The Promise to Drona

One day, soon after Drona had taken the princes as his pupils, he called them together and made them prostrate themselves before him, and having done so he required from them a promise that when they should become skilled in arms they would carry out for him a certain purpose

X

EKALAVYA

NANDA LĀL BOSE

Page 122

that was in his heart. At this demand all the princes fell silent; but one of them, Arjuna, the third of the Pāndavas, vowed eagerly that whatever it might be he would promise to accomplish it. Then Drona embraced Arjuna repeatedly, and from this moment there was a special attachment between the two, and Arjuna was always with his master, with his whole mind bent on the science of arms.

And princes came from the neighbouring kingdoms to learn of Drona. And all the Kurus and all the Pāndavas and the sons of the great nobles were his pupils. And amongst them came that strange and melancholy youth who went by the name of Karna, and was reputed to be the adopted son of a royal charioteer, his actual birth being unknown, though some held, from his auspicious characteristics, that he must be of exalted rank. And young Karna and Arjuna thus early became rivals, each trying to outdo the other in the use of the bow. And Karna tended to mix rather with Duryodhana and his brothers than with the Pāndavas.

Meanwhile Arjuna took every opportunity of learning, and in lightness and skill outdid all his fellows. One evening when he was eating, his lamp went out, and observing that even in the dark his hand carried the food to the mouth, his mind was set on the power of habit, and he began to practise shooting also in the night. And Drona, hearing the twang of the bowstring, came and embraced him, declaring that in the whole world there should not be another equal unto him.

Ekalavya

And amongst those who came to Drona was a low-caste prince of non-Aryan birth known as Ekalavya. But Drona would not accept him as a pupil, lest, as one of the leaders of the lower races, he should come in time to excel all the Aryan princes, and should learn all the secrets of their military science.

Then Ekalavya, retiring to the forest, made a clay image of Drona, and bowed down before it, worshipping it as his teacher. And by reason of his great reverence and devotion to his purpose, it soon came about that there were few archers in the land equal to Ekalavya. And one day, when all the princes were hunting in the forest, a dog ran off alone and found himself suddenly face to face with a man of dark hue wearing matted locks besmeared with mud and with his one piece of raiment black in colour. The dog, in his astonishment at this strange sight, began to bark aloud. But before he could close his mouth the prince Ekalavya had shot into it no less than seven arrows, aiming by the sound alone. The dog, thus pierced with seven arrows and unable to close his mouth, ran back to the princes, and they, fired with jealousy and admiration, began to seek everywhere for the unknown archer. It was not long before they found him, ceaselessly discharging arrows from the bow, and when they asked who and what he was, he replied: "I am the son of the king of the Nishadas. Know me also as a pupil of Drona, struggling for the acquisition of skill in arms!"

But when Drona heard of it he took Arjuna with him and sought out the archer Ekalavya. And when the low-caste prince saw Drona approaching, he prostrated himself and then stood with folded hands awaiting his commands. And Drona said: "If, O hero, thou art really my pupil, give me, then, the teacher's fee!"

"Master," said Ekalavya in his delight, "you have only to name what you will have. I have nothing I would not joyfully give you."

"If you really mean it, Ekalavya," answered Drona coldly, "I should like to have the thumb of your right hand." And the low-born prince, allowing no look of sadness to cross his face, turned without ado and cut off the thumb of his own right hand to lay it at the feet of Drona. But when the Brāhman had gone and he turned again to his archery, he found that his marvellous lightness of hand was for ever vanished.

Thus were the royal princes left without rivals in the use of arms. And two of them, Bhīma, the second of the Pāndavas, and Duryodhana, his cousin, became highly accomplished in the use of the mace. Ashvatthāman, the son of Drona himself, knew most of the theory of warfare. The Pāndava twins, Nakula and Sahadeva, excelled every one in horsemanship and in handling the sword. Yudhishthira, the eldest of the Pāndavas, was greatest as a chariot-soldier and officer. But Arjuna excelled all in every respect. He could use all the weapons, and his intelligence, resourcefulness, strength, and perseverance were admitted on every side. Moreover, he alone amongst the princes became fitted for a general command, being capable of fighting from his chariot with sixty thousand foes at once.

The Triumph of Arjuna

And Drona one day was desirous of testing by open competition the relative excellence of the young men he had trained. So he caused an artificial bird to be made and placed, as their target, on the top of a tree. Then, assembling all his pupils, he said: "Take up your bows and stand practising your aim. When I give the order you will cut off the head of the bird. I shall take you one by one in turn."

Then he called Yudhishthira to him alone. "Now be ready," he said, "to shoot with your arrow when I give the order." And Yudhishthira took up his bow and arrow as he was told, and stood ready at a word to let fly.

"Do you see the bird on the top of that tree?" asked Drona.

"I do," answered Yudhishthira.

"What do you see?" said Drona quickly. "Myself, or your brothers, or the tree?"

"I see yourself, sir," answered Yudhishthira carefully, "my brothers, the tree, and the bird."

Three times Drona repeated his question, and three times Yudhishthira gave the same reply. Then with great sorrow Drona ordered him to one side. It was not by him that the arrow would be shot.

One by one, princes and nobles, the Pāndava brothers and their cousins the Kurus, were all called up, and in each case Yudhishthira's answer was given: "We behold the tree, yourself, our fellow-pupils, and the bird."

One man only remained untried, and Drona made no effort to conceal his disappointment. Now, however, he turned with a smile to the last and called to him Arjuna, his favourite pupil. "By you, if any, must the bolt be sped. So much is clear, O Arjuna!" he said. "Now tell me, with bow bent, what do you see—the bird, the tree, myself, and your friends?"

"No," said Arjuna promptly; "I see the bird alone, neither yourself, sir, nor the tree!"

"Describe the bird to me," said Drona briefly.

"I see only a bird's head," replied Arjuna.

"Then shoot!" said his master with frank delight, and in an instant the bird stood headless on the tree, and Drona, embracing Arjuna, thought of that great tournament in which he would yet see Drupada vanquished before him.

II. THE TRIAL OF THE PRINCES

Then Drona, seeing that his pupils had now completed their education, applied to Dhritarāshtra the king for permission to hold a tournament, in which all would have an opportunity of exhibiting their skill. The request was at once granted, and preparations began for the great occasion. Land was chosen, and the citizens assembled by proclamation to be present at the offering of sacrifices for its consecration on an auspicious day. The lists were levelled and equipped, and a great hall built for the queens and their ladies, while tents and galleries were placed at every advantageous point for the use of the spectators.

And when the day appointed for the tournament arrived the king took his place, surrounded by his ministers and preceded by Bhīshma and the early tutors of the princes. Then Gandhārī, the mother of Duryodhana, and Kuntī, the mother of the Pāndavas, richly robed and jewelled and attended by their retinues, took the places that had been reserved for them. And nobles, Brāhmans, and citizens left the city and came hastening to the spot, till, with the sound of drums and trumpets and the clamour of voices, that great assembly became like the agitated ocean.

At last the white-haired Drona entered the lists dressed all in white and looking as if the moon itself had appeared in an unclouded sky, while beside him his son Ashvatthāman looked like some attendant star.

Ceremonies of propitiation were next performed, and then, as the chanting of the Vedic hymns died away, arms were carried in, the blare of trumpets was heard, and the princes entered in procession with Yudhishthira at their head.

Now began the most marvellous display of skill. The shower of arrows was so thick and constant that few of the spectators could hold their heads up unflinchingly, yet the aim of the knightly archers was so sure that not a single arrow missed its mark. Each, engraved with the name of its owner, was found in that precise spot at which it had been shot. Then they leapt on the backs of spirited horses, and vaulting and careering, turning this way and that, went on shooting at the marks. Then the horses were abandoned for chariots, and driving in and out, racing, turning, soothing their steeds or urging them on, as occasion might demand, the combatants continued to display their agility, their precision, and their resource.

Now leaping from the chariots, and seizing each man his sword and shield, the princes began to fence and exhibit sword-play. Then, like two great mountains and thirsting for battle, Bhīma and Duryodhana entered the arena, clubs in hand, for single combat.

Bracing themselves up, and summoning to their own aid their utmost energy, the two warriors gave a mighty roar, and began careering in due form, right and left, circling the lists, till the moment came for the rush and the mimic onslaught, in which each would strive to defeat his antagonist by right of his superior skill. And so great was the lust of battle in the two princes that the vast assembly caught the infection and became divided in its sympathies, some for Bhīma, some for Duryodhana, till Drona saw that it was necessary to stop the contest if he would not have it degenerate into an actual fight.

Then the master himself stepped into the lists and, silencing the music for a moment, in a voice like that

XI

THE TRIAL OF THE PRINCES

NANDA LĀL BOSE

Page 128

of the thunderstorm, introduced Arjuna, the most beloved of his pupils. The royal Kuntī, mother of the Pāndavas, was transported with delight at the acclamation which she now saw her son receive, and not until it had died down a little could he begin to display his skill in arms. But such were the power and lightness of Arjuna that it seemed as if with one weapon he created fire, with another water, with a third mountains, and as if with a fourth all these were made to disappear. Now he appeared tall and again short. Now he appeared fighting with sword or mace, standing on the pole or the yoke of his chariot; then in a flash he would be seen on the car itself, and in yet another instant he was fighting on the field. And with his arrows he hit all kinds of marks. Now, as if by a single shot, he let fly five arrows into the mouth of a revolving iron boar. Again he discharged twenty-one arrows into the hollow of a cow's horn swaying to and fro from the rope on which it hung. Thus he showed his skill in the use of sword, bow, and mace, walking about the lists in circles.

The Entry of Karna

Just as Arjuna's display was ending a great noise was heard in the direction of the gate, as if some new combatant were about to make his way into the lists. The whole assembly turned as one man, and Duryodhana with his hundred brothers rose hastily and stood with uplifted weapons, while Drona stood in the midst of the five Pāndava princes like the moon in a five-starred constellation.

Then, the centre of all eyes, the hero Karna entered, magnificent in arms and manhood. And far away in the gallery of queens the royal Kuntī trembled to see again the son whom she had long ago abandoned, fearing to own his divine birth. For, all unknown to any, the sun himself had been the father of Karna, and Kuntī—in future to become the mother of the Pāndavas—had been his mother.

And now was he goodly indeed to look upon. Was he not in truth an emanation from the hot-beamed sun? His proportions made him like unto some great cliff. Handsome of feature, he was possessed of innumerable accomplishments. He was tall in stature, like a golden palm-tree, and endued with the vigour of youth, he was capable even of slaying a lion. Bowing quietly to his teacher, he now turned himself towards Arjuna, and in the tones of one challenging declared that he had come to outdo the performance that had just been given. A thrill of excitement passed over the great audience, and Duryodhana openly showed his delight. But, alas! the princely Arjuna flushed crimson with anger and contempt. Then, with the permission of Drona, the mighty Karna, delighting in battle, made good his word and did all that Arjuna had done before him. And when his display of skill was over he was embraced and welcomed by all the sons of Dhritarāshtra, and Duryodhana asked him what he could do for him. "O prince," said Karna in reply, "I have but one wish, and that is to engage in single combat with Arjuna!" Arjuna, meanwhile, hot with resentment at what he deemed the insult put upon him, said quietly to Karna: "The day will yet come, O Karna, when I shall kill you!"

"Speak thou in arrows," answered Karna loudly, "that with arrows I may this very day strike off thy head before our master himself!"

Karna and Arjuna

Thus challenged *à outrance*, Arjuna advanced and took his place for single combat. And Karna likewise advanced and stood facing him.

Now Arjuna was the son of Indra, even as Karna had been born of the sun, and as the heroes confronted one another the spectators were aware that Arjuna was covered by the shadow of the clouds, that over him stretched the rainbow, the bow of Indra, and that rows of wild geese, flying overhead, gave a look of laughter to the sky. But Karna stood illumined by the rays of the sun. And Duryodhana ranged himself near Karna, while Bhīshma and Drona stood close to Arjuna. And up in the royal gallery a woman was heard to moan and fall.

Then the master of the ceremonies advanced and cried out the style and titles of Arjuna, a style and titles that were known to all. And having done this, he waited, and called upon the rival knight to show equal lineage, for sons of kings could not fight with men of inferior birth.

At these words Karna turned pale, and his face was torn with contending emotions. But Duryodhana, eager to see Arjuna defeated, cried out: "If Arjuna desires to fight only with a king, let me at once install Karna king of Anga!"

As if by magic, the priests came forward chanting; a throne of gold was brought forward; rice, flowers, and the sacred water were offered, and over Karna's head was raised the royal umbrella, while yak-tails waved about him on every side. Then, amidst the cheers of the multitude, Karna and Duryodhana embraced each other and pledged each other their eternal friendship.

At that very moment, bent and trembling with age and

weakness, poorly clad, and supporting himself on a staff, an old man was seen to enter the lists. And all present knew him for Adhiratha, one of the charioteers of the royal household. But when the glance of Karna fell upon him he hurriedly left his throne and came and bent himself down before the old man leaning on his staff, and touched his feet with that head that was still wet with the sacred water of coronation. And Adhiratha embraced Karna, and wept for pride that he had been made a king, calling him his son.

And Bhīma, standing amongst the Pāndava heroes, laughed aloud in derision. "What! What hero is this?" he said. "It seems, sir, that the whip is your true weapon. How can he be a king who is the son of a charioteer?"

Karna's lip quivered, but for sole reply he folded his arms and looked upward to the sun. But Duryodhana sprang up in wrath, and said: "The lineage of heroes is ever unknown! What does it matter where a brave man comes from? Who asks for the source of a river? Was a tiger like this ever born of servants? But even if it were so, he is my friend, and well deserves to be king of the whole world. Let him who has any objection to offer bend the bow that Karna bends!"

Loud cheers of approval broke out amongst the spectators, but the sun went down. Then Duryodhana, taking Karna by the hand, led him away from the lamp-lit arena. And the Pāndava brothers, accompanied by Bhīshma and Drona, went back to their own place. Only Yudhishthira carried away the thought that none could defeat Karna. And Kuntī, the queen-mother, having recognized her son, cherished the thought that after all he was king of Anga.

III. THE TEACHER'S FEE

The time had now come when Drona thought he should demand the offering due to the teacher from those he had trained. He therefore assembled together all his pupils, and said: "Seize Drupada, king of Panchala, in battle, and bring him bound unto me. This is the only return I desire as your master and preceptor."

The enterprise was wholly agreeable to the high-spirited youths, and with light hearts they got together an imposing array of chariots, arms, and followers, and set out for the capital of Drupada, not neglecting to strike at the Panchalas on their way. For it was the delight of the princes and nobles who went forth on this raid to display their prowess and skill as they went. And never did they make this more noticeable than when they entered the gates and clattered up the streets of Drupada's capital.

Hearing the clamour, the king himself came to the verandahs of his palace to look down at the sight. But the knights, uttering their war-cry, shot at him a shower of arrows. Then Drupada, accompanied by his brothers, issued from his palace gates in due form on his white chariot, and set himself to encounter the raiding force. But Arjuna held back his brothers and himself from participation in what seemed to him a mere *mêlée*. He realized that the Panchala king, fighting in his own capital, would not be overcome by tactics of this order. But they would have the effect of wearying him, and then would be the opportunity for the Pāndavas to act.

Even as he had predicted, the white chariot of the king was seen, now here, now there, always driving forward, and always hastening toward that point where danger was greatest and the gathering of the raiders thickest, and during these rapid movements he kept pouring into their ranks such a quick and constant shower of arrows that the Kurus showed a tendency to become panic-stricken and to assume that they were fighting not one, but many Drupadas.

By this time the alarm had spread throughout the city, and drums and trumpets began to sound from every house, while the men poured out, ready armed, to the assistance of their king. Now there arose from the great host of the Panchalas a terrible roar, while the twang of their bowstrings seemed to rend the very heavens. A new and answering fierceness blazed up for a moment amongst the invading warriors, but wherever an arrow was shot, there it seemed stood Drupada in person to answer it. He was here, there, and everywhere, and careering over the field of battle like a fiery wheel, he attacked Duryodhana, and even Karna, wounded them, and slaked in right earnest their thirst for battle, till, seeing the host of the citizens to which they were opposed, the Kurus broke and fled with a wail of defeat back to where the Pāndavas were waiting.

The Might of Arjuna

Hastily the Pāndavas now did reverence to Drona and ascended their chariots. To Arjuna fell the leadership, as if by instinct, and he, forbidding Yudhishthira to fight or expose himself, quickly appointed the twins, his youngest brothers, protectors of his chariot-wheels, while Bhīma, ever fighting in the van, ran forward, mace in hand, to lead the attack. Thus, like the figure of Death, Arjuna entered the host of the Panchalas. And Bhīma with his club began to slay the elephants that covered them. And the battle became fierce and terrible to behold. Arjuna singled out the king and his general for his personal attack. Then he succeeded in cutting down the flagstaff, and when that had fallen he leapt from his chariot, and casting aside his bow for his sword, he seized Drupada the king with as much ease as a huge bird seizes a water-snake.

Having thus exhibited his own might in the presence of both hosts, Arjuna gave a loud shout and came forth from amongst the Panchalas, carrying his captive with him. At this sight the Kurus were maddened and would have made to devastate the whole capital of the Panchalas, but Arjuna in a loud voice restrained them. "Drupada," he said, "is our friend and ally. To yield him up personally will satisfy Drona. On no account let us slay his people!"

Then all the princes together, bringing with them their captives, turned to Drona and laid before him Drupada, together with many of his ministers and friends.

The Vengeance of Drona

Drona smiled quietly at the king who had once been his friend. "Fear not, O king," he said; "your life shall be spared. But would you not care to cultivate my friendship?" Then he was silent for a moment. Again opening his lips, he said: "In truth, Drupada, I love you no less to-day than of old in our boyhood. And I still desire your friendship. You told me, alas! that only a king could be the friend of a king, and for that reason shall I restore to you only half of your territory, in order that, being a king myself, I may enjoy your affection on equal terms. You shall be king of all your lands that lie on the south of the river Ganges, and I shall reign over those on the north. And now, Drupada, will it bemean you to grant me your friendship?"

With these words Drona released Drupada, and bestowed on him the sovereignty of half his own kingdom, being those territories that lay south of the Ganges. And Drupada, with many compliments, assured him of his profound admiration and regard. But in his own mind the lesson that the mortified king laid to heart was that of his old friend's superior resources, and from this time forth he in his turn wandered in all directions, even as Drona had wandered to Hastinapura, in the hope of discovering some charm or other means, by devotion or otherwise, to obtain a son who might work out his revenge on the man who had humiliated him. And it came to pass that this enmity to Drona grew in time to be one of the main motives in the life of Drupada, king of the Panchalas.

IV. THE HOUSE OF LAC

It was about a year after the invasion of Drupada's city that Dhritarāshtra, moved by a sense of what was due, and having regard also to the welfare of his subjects, decided to crown Yudhishthira in public as heir-apparent of the empire. For Pandu, the father of Yudhishthira and his brothers, had been the monarch of the realm, and not Dhritarāshtra, whose blindness had been considered to render him incompetent. It was now incumbent upon the blind king, therefore, to nominate Yudhishthira and his brothers as his successors, instead of any of his own children. And this, after the exhibition of knightly prowess that had introduced them to the world, he could no longer refuse to do.

But the Pāndava princes took their new position more seriously than anyone had foreseen. Never contented with mere enjoyment, they went out in all directions for the extension of the suzerainty, and constantly sent back to the royal treasury immense spoils. Duryodhana had been jealous of his cousins from his very childhood, but now, seeing their great superiority and their growing popularity, even his father, Dhritarāshtra, began to be anxious, and at last he, too, could not sleep for jealousy. Feeling in this way, it was easy enough for a king to summon to his side councillors who would give him the advice he craved, and he was assured in due course that the extermination of his enemies was the first duty of a sovereign.

But the Pāndavas also had a watchful friend and adviser in a certain uncle named Vidura, who, though of inferior birth, was a veritable incarnation of the god of justice. Vidura had the gift of reading men's thoughts from their faces, and easily at this juncture did he understand the mind of Dhritarāshtra and his family. But he warned the Pāndavas that while they ought to be on their guard, they must never precipitate the full hatred of those who were in power by allowing it to be seen that they understood their feelings. Rather must they accept everything that was done with an air of cheerfulness, and apparently without suspicion.

About this time Duryodhana openly approached his father, begging him to banish his cousins to the town of Benares, and during their absence confer on himself the sovereignty of the kingdom. The timid Dhritarāshtra could only acknowledge that the suggestion marched well with his own secret wishes, and this being so, his stronger-minded son quickly reassured him as to the difficulties that he foresaw. Theirs was at present, he pointed out, the command of the treasury. Having that, they could buy the popular allegiance, and no critic of their conduct would be strong enough to oppose them. From this time Duryodhana began to win over the people by lavish distribution of wealth and honours.

The Princes are Banished

It was now, under secret instructions from Dhritarāshtra the king, that certain members of the court began to praise the beauties of the city of Benares, in which, they said, the yearly festival of Shiva was already beginning. Presently, as was intended, the Pāndava princes, with others, showed some interest and curiosity as to the beauties of Benares, and said how very much they would like to see it. Suddenly, at the word, the blind Dhritarāshtra turned towards them with apparent kindness. "Then go, my children," he said, "you five brothers together, and satisfy your desire by living for some time in the city of Benares, and you shall take with you from the royal treasury largess for distribution."

There was no mistaking the fact that the words which sounded so friendly were really a sentence of banishment. But Yudhishthira, with his fixed policy, had sufficient presence of mind to bow cheerfully and signify pleasure at the opportunity given him. A day or two later the grey-haired Kuntī set out with her five sons from Hastinapura. Purochanna, the friend and minister of Duryodhana, had, however, left still earlier to make preparations at Benares for receiving the princes. And especially he was instructed to build a house for them of highly inflammable materials and fitted with all the costliest furniture and equipments as close to the public arsenal as possible, that there he might live, as warden of the city, and watch for a suitable opportunity of setting fire to it, as if by accident. The palace, in fact, was to be made of lac.

Meanwhile the watchful Vidura, letting nothing in all this escape him, had made ready on the Ganges a fine ship to which Kuntī and her sons might flee in their hour of peril. Now, also, as the Pāndavas set forth from Hastinapura, Vidura, of all who accompanied them at the beginning of their journey, was the last to leave them; and as they parted he said to Yudhishthira in low tones, and in a language that they two alone understood: "Be always alert! There are weapons not made of steel. One can escape even from fire by having many outlets to one's house, and a deep hole is a wonderful refuge! Make yourselves familiar with the roads through the forest and learn to direct yourselves by the stars. Above all, be ever vigilant!"

"I understand you well," replied Yudhishthira quickly, and without more words they parted.

The Princes arrive at Benares

The Pāndavas were received with great magnificence by the people of Benares, headed by Purochanna, and were lodged for a time in a house outside the city. On the tenth day, however, Purochanna described to them a fair mansion that he had erected for them within the city. His name for it was "the blessed home," but it was of course in reality "the accursed house," and Yudhishthira, judging that course wisest, went forth with his mother and brothers to take up his quarters in it. On reaching the house he inspected it closely, and, indeed, the smell of lac, tar, and oil was strongly perceptible in the new building. Then, turning to Bhīma, he told him that he suspected it to be highly inflammable. "Then ought we not to return at once to our first quarters?" said the simple Bhīma in surprise. "In my opinion it is wiser," answered his brother, "to remain here in seeming contentment, and thus gain time by allaying all their suspicions. If we showed that we understood him, this Purochanna would make an immediate attempt upon us. But we must always have our eyes about us; not for one moment must we allow ourselves to be careless."

No sooner were the princes established in their new abode than there came to them a man who said he was an emissary from Vidura, their uncle, and skilled in mining. It was his opinion that the house in which they now were would be burnt on some moonless night. He therefore proposed to dig for them a wide subterranean passage without delay. And he repeated to them, as password, the last sentence that had been spoken, in a strange tongue, between Yudhishthira and his uncle at the moment of parting. Hearing all this, the Pāndavas accepted him with great joy, and he at once began a careful excavation in the chamber of Yudhishthira, covering up its entrance with planks so as to be level with the rest of the floor. And the princes spent their days hunting and ranging the forests in the neighbourhood, and at night slept always within closed doors, with their arms beside their pillows.

The Escape of the Pāndavas

When a whole year had gone by it appeared to Yudhishthira that Purochanna was completely off his guard. He therefore considered that the time would now be favourable for their escape. On a certain evening, therefore, Kuntī the queen gave a great feast, and hundreds of men and women came to it. And in the dead of the night, as it chanced, when all had gone, a great wind began to blow; and Bhīma at that time, coming out quietly, set fire to that

XII

THE HOUSE OF LAC

NANDA LĀL BOSE

Page 140

part of the house which adjoined Purochanna's own quarters in the arsenal. Then he set fire to various other parts, and leaving it all to blaze up of itself, he, with his mother and brothers, entered the subterranean passage to make their escape. And none knew that a poor low-caste woman had come to the feast, accompanied by her five sons, nor that all six, in the sleep of intoxication, lay within the burning house. And since drowsiness and fear impeded the motion of the Pāndavas, the gigantic Bhīma lifted his mother to his shoulder, and then, taking two brothers under each arm, pushed forward along the secret passage, and came out after a while into the darkness of the forest. And Bhīma, thus loaded, pushed on, breaking the trees with his breast, and pressing the earth deep with the stamping of his feet.

And behind them the citizens of Benares stood all night watching the burning of the house of lac, wailing aloud for the fate of the princes, whom they supposed to be within, and loudly condemning the wicked Purochanna, whose motives they understood thoroughly well; and when morning was come they found the body of Purochanna and the bodies of the innocent low-caste woman and her five sons, and sending word to Dhritarāshtra in the distant capital, they proceeded to render royal honours to the unfortunate victims. But the miner who had been employed by Vidura contrived to help in the moving about of the ashes, and so to cover the entrance to the secret passage as he did so that none suspected its existence.

Meanwhile, when the Pāndavas had emerged from the forest they found in a fair ship on the Ganges a man who seemed to be measuring the river and searching its bed to find a ford. And this was really that captain who had been sent by Vidura to wait for the hour of the Pāndava flight. Seeing the five men, with their mother, reach the river-bank, he now brought up his vessel and said to the grey-haired Kuntī in a low voice: "Escape with thy children from the net that death hath spread around you all!" Kuntī looked up startled, and he turned to the princes and said: "It is the word of Vidura. Be ever alert! I am sent to convey you to the other side of the Ganges!"

Recognizing him by these words as the agent of Vidura, the princes gladly stepped into his boat, and he took them safely to the opposite shore. Then uttering the one word *Jaya* (Victory!), he left them, and returned to the work he had seemed to be doing. And the Pāndavas, with their mother, fled on from forest to forest and town to town. Now they went in one disguise and again in another, till at last they came to the town of Ekachakra, and being there received in the outer rooms of a Brāhman and his family, they settled down to live as learned men by begging. And repeating long passages from the sacred books, it was easy for them to obtain enough food to eat. With their tall forms, their deer-skin garments, their sacred threads, and their matted locks, all men took them for Brāhmans. But returning to Kuntī in the evening with the rice they had gathered during the day, it was always divided by her into two equal portions. One of these was eaten by Bhīma, and the other was divided between the four remaining brothers and herself. And so doing they lived for many months in simplicity and much happiness in the town of Ekachakra.

V. HOW THE PĀNDAVAS WON A BRIDE

Now while the Pāndavas were living with their mother disguised as Brāhmans in the town of Ekachakra, there came one staunch friend and another out of their past life to visit them quietly. And from one of these they heard that Drupada, king of the Panchalas, had announced the *Swayamvara* of his beautiful daughter Draupadī. A few more words passed regarding the extraordinary charms and accomplishments of the princess of the Panchalas, and in the evening, when their guest had gone, Kuntī noticed that her sons had fallen silent and listless. Then, guessing the cause of their changed spirits better than they could have done themselves, she said, with gentle tact, that she was tired of Ekachakra and would be glad to renew their wanderings, if her sons would, in the country of the Panchalas.

The very next day all said good-bye to their host the Brāhman of Ekachakra and set out for Kampilya, the capital of Drupada. And as they went they fell in with certain Brāhmans going by the same road, who told them of the great bridal choice that was about to be held for the princess of the kingdom and of the royal largess to be given to wandering scholars on the occasion. And the princes, making as though they heard of these things now for the first time, joined themselves to their company and announced their intention of witnessing the *Swayamvara*. And when they reached the city they went about it for a time as sightseers and ended by taking up their quarters in the guest-rooms of a certain potter.

Now it happened that ever since the raid of Drona and his pupils Drupada had cherished a secret wish that his daughter Draupadī might be wedded to Arjuna. But this wish he had never mentioned to anyone. Still, not knowing of the reputed death and thinking secretly of him, he caused a very stiff bow to be made and had a ring suspended at a very great height, and announced that he who should string the bow and shoot his arrow through the ring should have the princess for his wife. With these words he proclaimed the *Swayamvara*, and kings, princes, and great sages began to pour in from all sides. Even Duryodhana came with his friend Karna. And all alike Drupada received with lavish hospitality. But the Pāndavas were living as beggars in the house of the potter, and none in all the city recognized them.

The festivities attendant on a royal wedding began, and every day waxed greater and greater, till on the sixteenth day, when everything was at its height, the great moment arrived. The Princess Draupadī, robed and jewelled, stepped into the arena, bearing a golden plate whereon lay a garland of flowers. As she entered, all music was stopped and the royal Brāhmans lighted the sacrificial fire. When all was still, Dhrishtadyumna, her twin-brother, stepped forward beside the princess and said in a voice as deep and rich as thunder itself: "O ye monarchs that are assembled here to-day, behold the bow, and yonder is the ring! He who can shoot five arrows through that ring—having birth, beauty, and strength of person—shall obtain to-day my sister as his bride!"

Then turning to the princess herself, he enumerated all the kings who were candidates for her hand and told her that he who should shoot the mark was to be chosen by her. And Duryodhana's name came first, and Karna was mentioned, but none spoke the names of the five Pāndavas, who, unknown to all, were present in the crowd as Brāhmans.

The Contest

As Dhrishtadyumna finished speaking their names the kings and princes all leapt to their feet, each eager to be first in the stringing of the bow. And as they sprang into the arena and crowded together to the testing-spot, it was said by some that they saw the gods themselves on their heavenly chariots mingling in the concourse. One after another, with hearts beating high, under the eyes of Drupada, in the blaze of the world and covered with glory, the candidates went forward to the shooting-place. And some with swelling lips and straining muscles laboured long to string that bow, and one after another, with crowns loosened and garlands torn, had to desist without success, being tossed to the ground by the resistance of the weapon. Then Karna, seeing the mortification of his friends and eager to show the glory of the knighthood, stepped forward quickly to the place of the bow. And seeing him, five seeming Brāhmans amongst the spectators drew in their breath and gave the princess up for lost, for they had no manner of doubt that Karna could string the bow of Drupada.

But as her eyes fell on the hero the princess exclaimed in cold tones of disdain: "I will not wed the son of a charioteer!" And hearing her, Karna smiled somewhat bitterly, glanced up at the sun, and cast aside the bow, already drawn to a circle.

And now when the last of the monarchs was making his attempt, and their uniform failure was being discussed hotly by the spectators, Arjuna, with his deer-skin rug, his matted locks, and his sacred thread, rose from amongst the crowd of Brāhmans seated as onlookers on the outskirts of the arena and stepped forward to the shooting-dais. Loud murmurs, some of approval and some of disapproval, rose from the Brāhmans to right and left of him as he did so. For, regarding him as one of themselves, they took his movement for the most part as one of mere childish restlessness which would bring disgrace on all of them. Only a few of them, noting his form and bearing, had the courage to cry: "Good, good! Make the attempt!"

But while his friends talked Arjuna walked up to the bow and stood before it like a mountain. Bending his head in prayer, he walked slowly round it. Then in the twinkling of an eye he strung it, and shooting five arrows in quick succession through the ring, he brought down the mark that had been suspended above.

The cheering that followed seemed to come from the heavens as well as from the amphitheatre. The Brāhmans stood up in their excitement waving their scarfs. Flowers rained from the sky in all directions. And the bards immediately burst out into praises of the hero who had won. From the royal seats above the lists Drupada the king beamed approval on the young Brāhman who had shot the mark, and the Princess Draupadī lifted her eyes to Arjuna's and silently signified that she took him as her lord.

But while the uproar was at its height Yudhishthira, with the twins Nakula and Sahadeva, fearing recognition if they remained all in one place, rose and left the assembly, leaving Arjuna and Bhīma together alone. In less time than it takes the clouds to overspread the sky, the whole temper of the assembly seemed to change.

Arjuna had been vested by Draupadī with the white robe and the garland of marriage, and Drupada's approval of the hero was patent to all the beholders. Seeing this, the kings and princes who had failed were suddenly filled with wrath. They had been set at naught. They had been invited to be insulted. They had been openly refused out of contempt, and a Brāhman chosen over their heads. Seizing their maces, the angry warriors made a united rush upon Drupada, who shrank back for the moment amongst the crowd of Brāhmans. But seeing the danger of their host, Arjuna and Bhīma came forward to cover him—Arjuna with the redoubtable bow, and Bhīma, tearing up by the roots a great tree, brandishing it ready for success. Even Arjuna, accustomed as he was to the great feats of his brother, was astonished to see him uproot the tree, while all the monarchs fell back in sheer amazement.

The Pāndavas are Recognized

But one there was in the royal gallery, Krishna by name, a prince of the Vrishnis and cousin by birth of the Pāndava princes, who, seeing that feat, knew suddenly who the two seeming Brāhmans were.

"Look, look!" he said to his brother, who was beside him, "I had heard that the Pāndavas had escaped from the house of lac, and as surely as I am Krishna yonder are two of them, Bhīma and Arjuna!"

Then the Brāhmans, shaking their coco-nut water-vessels and their deer-skins, closed round Drupada for his protection against the onset of the knighthood, while Arjuna and Bhīma took them one by one in single combat. And such was the shooting of arrows between Karna and Arjuna that each was to the other invisible for several minutes at a time, and Karna fainted from loss of blood, but recovered to a greater enthusiasm for battle than before. And all admired the strength and lightness of Bhīma, who could seize a hero and throw him to a distance and yet refrain from hurting him much.

Finally, however, the kings and princes, with all their good humour restored by fighting, surrendered cheerfully to their Brāhman opponents. And when this moment arrived,

Arjuna and Bhīma, leaving the throng and followed by the princess, turned their steps to their mother's house. Kuntī meanwhile had been waiting in great anxiety for the return of her two sons. The day was wearing on, and how many evils might not have befallen them! At last, however, in the midst of a crowd of Brāhmans, she saw Arjuna and Bhīma. Reaching the door, they said: "Ah, mother, behold what we have obtained as alms to-day!" Kuntī, from within the house, not having seen the blushing princess whom they were putting forward as they spoke, answered: "Enjoy ye all what ye have brought!" Then she saw Draupadī and, embracing her warmly, welcomed her as a daughter. Thus the princess of the Panchalas became the bride of the Pāndavas.

But as all sat together in silence in the house of the potter there came two guests—Krishna, the prince of the Vrishnis, and Balarāma, his brother—who laughingly hailed them all as Pāndavas, touching the feet of Yudhishthira in token of their delight that they had escaped from the house of lac. Then, lest any should recognize them and their disguise be penetrated, they hastily withdrew again. And the Princess Draupadī proceeded humbly and lovingly under Kuntī's direction to cook the evening meal for the whole family. And none was aware that her brother, Prince Drishtadyumna, was lying concealed in an adjoining room for the purpose of listening to the secret conversation of the seeming Brāhmans.

And when night came, the Pāndavas, lying awake, discussed with one another of divine weapons and battle chariots and elephants and military matters. And Drishtadyumna set out with the dawn to return to his father and report to him the character of the hero who had bent the bow. But Drupada, running forward, met him, saying: "Tell me! tell me! was it Arjuna who shot the mark?"

Only after the bridal feast had been given, however, at the palace of Drupada, would Yudhishthira admit that he and his brothers were in truth the Pāndava princes. Until Draupadī was duly wedded she knew them only as the shooters-down of the bow, and whatever they might be, kings or Brāhmans, she accepted them on that basis.

But when Drupada knew that he was now in close alliance with the Pāndavas his joy knew no bounds and he feared nothing, even from the gods. And the rumour of their escape from the house of lac and their victory at the *Swayamvara* began to spread through the neighbouring kingdoms, and all men began to look on them as those newly returned from the dead. And Vidura himself carried the news to Dhritarāshtra that the Pāndavas now were alive and well and gifted with many and powerful friends.

VI. THE STORY OF SHISHUPĀLA

When the news reached Dhritarāshtra that the Pāndavas had not after all been burnt in the house of lac, but had escaped and were now at the court of Drupada, accepted in his family and furnished with many and powerful friends, the old king did not know what reply to make. So he called to him his son Duryodhana and all his councillors, and put to them the question of what course he should pursue.

All were for their immediate recall to Hastinapura; every one urged the sending of congratulations on their escape. But Duryodhana was of opinion that after this they should proceed to dispose of them by a series of frauds, dividing their interests and setting them against each other, and so at last deprive them of all resource. Karna, on the other hand, held that they should be fought. Prowess against prowess, knighthood against knighthood, he said. These men could never be divided. Such an attempt would only render ridiculous him who might undertake it. But a fair fight should be the method of a soldier. The Pāndavas were men, they were not gods, and as men they might be defeated in battle.

Bhīshma, on the other hand, supported by Drona and Vidura, pointed out that the right of the Pāndavas to the paternal kingdom was at least as good as that of Duryodhana. They must therefore be recalled and firmly established in half of the kingdom. So strong was the insistence of these good men upon this course that Dhritarāshtra had nothing to do but obey, and an embassy was sent to the court of Drupada, with presents for the princes, to congratulate them on their safety and to invite them again to their ancestral home. By this time not only Drupada, but also, and even more powerfully, Krishna and his brother Balarāma, had become the friends and counsellors of the Pāndavas, and not until they were advised to do so by all of these did they accept the overtures of friendship made by their kinsman Dhritarāshtra. At last, however, they did so, and taking Kuntī, their mother, and Draupadī, their queen, set out for the city of Hastinapura.

The Return of the Pāndavas

Arriving there and staying long enough to rest, they were summoned to the presence of Dhritarāshtra, who told them that in order to prevent any further disturbance his family he was willing to divide the kingdom and give them half, assigning to them a certain desert tract for residence. It had always been the habit of these princes to accept cheerfully what was offered them by the aged sovereign and make the best of it. And on this occasion they did not break their rule. Apparently seeing no flaw in this gift of a barren tract of wilderness for a home, they did homage to Dhritarāshtra and set forth to their new capital.

Once there, however, their energy knew no bounds. Offering the necessary sacrifices of propitiation, they had the ground measured off for a new city, and proceeded to build, fortify, and adorn it till there stood on the plain the famous Indraprastha, a fit abode for the very gods, not to speak of emperors, such were its beauty and magnificence. Not content with building a city, the brothers set about organizing their dominions and their administration, and their subjects, realizing the wisdom and beneficence of these new rulers, felt themselves happy indeed to have passed under their sway. There was no misery in that kingdom caused by arrears of rent. The peasant obtained easy access to his sovereign. Justice was well administered; order was maintained; peace and prosperity were united on all sides. At this time it was suggested to Yudhishthira that he ought to hold a Coronation Sacrifice, and the thought began to cause him some anxiety. On every hand he sought the advice of his ministers, but not until he had obtained that of Krishna, his new and trusted friend, could he be sure of the right course. He was aware of the many motives—kindness, flattery, self-interest, and the rest—that guide men in the giving of counsel, and to his mind there was but one soul that was above all such influence. The Coronation Sacrifice was not a rite to be undertaken lightly. It meant the establishment of the king who performed it as suzerain over all his fellows. To do this it was necessary to bring together an immense concourse of tributary sovereigns, and it was well known that in this great concourse of feudatories lurked immense dangers. It was at such gatherings that revolutions were apt to originate. It behoved him who would offer the sacrifice, therefore, to think well over the state of things, and consider clearly what he was attempting. Successful, he might expect to be regarded as over-lord of the whole empire for life. But the smallest false step might result in supreme disaster, hurling him from the throne and even bringing about a civil war.

The Counsel of Krishna

Even as Yudhishthira had thought, whilst others lightly counselled him to undertake the sacrifice, Krishna alone could point out to him the train of thought that should guide a monarch face to face with so grave an enterprise. Point by point he discussed with him the political state of rival kingdoms and the chances of stability in the country at large. Thus he led him to see what wars must be undertaken and what areas must yet be subjugated before the imperial sacrifice could be offered. But Krishna encouraged Yudhishthira, no less warmly than his own ministers had done, as to his personal fitness and the appropriate condition of the home-kingdom and its government for the proud position that he desired to make his own. Nor did Yudhishthira or any of his brothers suspect that, just as this festival would establish them in the over-lordship, so it was destined to reveal before the eyes of all men, and not only to the trusted few who already knew it, the greatness and power of Krishna himself, who was, indeed, no king, only because he was so far above all earthly kings.

Having taken the advice of this mighty counsellor,

Yudhishthira proceeded to carry it out in every particular, and not until all was finished would he announce his intention of holding the coronation festival. Even after this the preparations for the sacrifice took a long time to make, but finally all was ready, and in every direction invitations were sent out, and kings and heroes began to pour in. And there was one there, Nārada by name, who had the inner sight, and he, looking upon that great assembly and seeing the Lord Krishna as its true centre and occasion, was filled with awe, and where others saw only brilliance and festivity he was all reverence and sat watching, lost in worship.

Now when the last day of the sacrifice was come and the sacred water was about to be sprinkled on the head of Yudhishthira, it was suggested by Bhīshma, head of both the royal houses, that, as a matter of courtesy to the invited guests, homage should first be done to each one of them in turn, according to his rank and precedence. And, added the old grandfather as his eyes dwelt fondly on the face of Krishna, to him first of all, as the incarnation of God, let these royal honours be paid as chief. And Krishna himself consenting also, the honours were paid.

The Quarrel for Precedence

But one there was amongst the assembled kings who grudged the precedence given to Krishna in the midst of sovereigns, as if he also had been a ruling monarch. And this guest, Shishupāla by name, broke out into bitter reproaches against Bhīshma and Yudhishthira for what he regarded as the insult done to the tributary vassals in thus putting before them one who could lay no claim to precedence by right of independence, or long alliance, or age and kinship. Was Krishna, he asked, the oldest who was present? How could such a claim be urged when Vasudev, his own father, was in his proper place? Or was he held as master and teacher? But here was Drona the Brāhman, who had acted as tutor to all the royal princes. Or did the Pāndavas give him precedence because of his treaty-value as an ally in time of war? If so, here was Drupada, who deserved better of them; for he was the father of Draupadī, their queen, and none could be so bound to them as he. But if it was love and reverence that had guided the offering, then surely old Bhīshma, their kinsman, the bond between two lines, had a better right.

At these words of Shishupāla, a certain number of the guests began to manifest disaffection to the sacrifice and its lord, and it became evident that Shishupāla was master of a faction who might take it upon themselves to prevent the proper completion of the ceremonies. Now, if a royal sacrifice were not brought to a proper end, the fact would forbode great disaster for the kingdom and its subjects. Hence Yudhishthira showed great anxiety and did all he could to conciliate the angry king. He, however, like a spoiled child, or like a stern and bitter man, refused by any means to be placated. Seeing this, Yudhishthira looked toward Bhīshma for advice. Bhīshma, however, took no pains to conciliate the angry king. Laughingly he put aside the gravity of Yudhishthira. "Wait," he said, "O king, till the lord Krishna wakes up to the matter! Can the dog slay the lion? Verily this king looks very like a lion, till the lion is roused; then we shall see what we shall see."

But Shishupāla heard the words that Bhīshma spoke, and being deeply galled at the comparison to a dog, he addressed himself to the venerable statesman in words that were openly insulting and unrestrained. He called him an old reprobate, always prating of morality, and as they listened even his own friends and allies were filled with horror and looked to see some judgment fall speedily on the head of one who so forgot the dignity due to his own and equal rank. Bhīshma, however, showed no excitement. Standing calmly there, he held up his hand for silence, and as soon as it was established he spoke to the angry Bhīma, Yudhishthira's brother, whose red eyes showed that he regarded the words that had been spoken to his revered grandfather as a challenge to himself.

Bhīshma's Story

"Softly, O Bhīma," said Bhīshma, "and listen to the story of this very Shishupāla. He was born in the kingly line, having three eyes and four arms, and as soon as he was born he brayed like an ass. And his father and mother, being affrighted by these omens, were making up their minds to abandon the child, when they heard a voice speaking to them out of the air and saying: 'Fear nothing; cherish this boy. His time is not yet come. One is already born who will slay him with weapons when his end arrives. Before that he will be both fortunate and highly placed.'

"Then the queen, his mother, much comforted by these words, took courage, and asked: 'Who is this that shall be the slayer of my son?'

"And the voice answered: 'He on whose lap thy child will be seated when his third eye disappears and his two added arms fall away.'

"And lo, after this, the king and queen of Chedi made a round of royal visits together, and wherever they went they asked the king whose guest they might be at the moment to take their child into his arms. But nowhere did he lose the added arms, nor did his third eye disappear.

"Then, disappointed, they came back to their own city and their own palace. And when they had been some time at home there came to visit them the young Prince Krishna and his elder brother. And they began to play with the baby. But when Krishna took it on his lap, lo, before all, the child's third eye slowly wrinkled up and disappeared, and the two unusual arms withered away. Then the queen of the Chedis knew that this was the destined slayer of her son, and falling on her knees, she said: 'O Lord, grant me one boon!'

"And the Lord Krishna answered: 'Say on!'

"And she said: 'Promise me that when my son offends thee thou wilt forgive him!'

"And he answered: 'Yea, if he offend me even a hundred times, yet a hundred times shall I forgive him.'

"This is that Shishupāla," continued Bhīshma, "who even now, presuming on the mercy of the Lord, summons thee to battle. Truly must he be a portion of the energy of the Creator, and that energy the Almighty would now resume within himself. It is for this that he may bring about his own destruction, that he is provoking so much anger and roaring like a tiger before us, caring nothing for the result."

Now Shishupāla's anger had been mounting higher and higher during Bhīshma's speech, and as it finished he shook his sword threateningly and said, "Dotard! knowest thou not that thou art at this moment alive only by the kindness of myself and these other kings?"

"Whether that be so or not," answered Bhīshma with great haughtiness and calm, "know that I esteem all the kings of the earth but as a straw. Whether I be slain like a beast of the field or burnt to death in the forest fire, whatever be the consequence, here do I place my foot on the heads of you all. Here before us stands the Lord. Him have we worshipped. Let him only who desires a speedy death enter into conflict with him. But such a one may even summon him to battle—him of dark hue, who is the wielder of the discus and the mace—and, falling, he will enter into and mingle with the body of this god!"

The Death of Shishupāla

As the solemn words of Bhīshma ended all present involuntarily turned their eyes toward Krishna. Intent he stood there, looking quietly upon the enraged and anger-inflated Shishupāla, like one whose mind might be summoning the celestial weapons to his aid. And when Shishupāla laughed tauntingly, he merely said: "The cup of thy misdeeds, O sinful one, is now full!" and as he spoke the flaming discus rose from behind him and, passing over the circle of kings, descended upon the helmet of Shishupāla and clove him through from head to foot. Then came forth the soul of that wicked one, as it had been a mass of flame, and, making its own path, bowed itself down and melted away into the feet of Krishna himself. Even as Bhīshma had declared, falling, he entered into and was mingled with the body of that god.

Thus ended Shishupāla, who had sinned to a hundred and one times and been forgiven. For even the enemies of the Lord go to salvation by thinking wholly upon him.

VII. THE FATAL DICE

Now when the imperial sacrifice of Yudhishthira was over, his cousin Duryodhana continued for many days to be his guest in the palace that the brothers had built for such purposes at Indraprastha. And with Duryodhana there stayed as friend and companion a man who was destined to be his evil genius, an uncle of his, Sakuni by name. And together they examined the mansion that the Pāndavas had built. And in one of the rooms, coming upon a crystal floor, Prince Duryodhana took it to be water, and drew aside his garments as if to wade; then, discovering his error, he went about in constant mortification. But next day coming upon a pond, he mistook it for crystal and fell in, whereupon he became a mark for good-natured raillery. But everything affected him with bitterness. Crystal doors appeared to him to be open, and open doors he suspected to be closed, and vexation was added to vexation in his mind. Besides this, the beauty of walls starred with jewels and halls with thousands of carven pillars filled him with jealousy, and in his thoughts he compared Hastinapura with Indraprastha and spoke to himself of the Pāndavas as foes. It was in this mood that his stay with his cousin ended and he returned to Hastinapura.

It was well known that Yudhishthira was sensitive on all points that involved the honour of the knighthood. Now there was one matter that was incumbent upon the true knight: just as he must answer a challenge to battle, so he must comply with a challenge to the dice. But the eldest of the Pāndavas was known to be extremely weak in this matter. He gambled badly, and was subject to the intoxication of the dice. When the stakes were being thrown he would lose his head and throw wildly, and none could at such a time gain his attention to reason with him. For this reason it was the habit of Yudhishthira to avoid gambling, unless it was made imperative by a knightly challenge.

Now Sakuni, the uncle and companion of Duryodhana, in

spite of his high position and associations, was a gambler who carried his skill with the dice to the height of sharp practice. In this there was none living who surpassed him, and like all such men he was ever hungry for new victims. Sakuni now therefore began to harp on the well-known weakness of Yudhishthira, plying Duryodhana with the demand that he should be invited to Hastinapura to play.

The Challenge

The permission of the aged Dhritarāshtra, always like clay in the hands of his eldest son, was not difficult to obtain, and Vidura himself, in spite of his protests, was dispatched to Indraprastha with the challenge to Yudhishthira to come to throw the dice. A large pleasure-house was rapidly erected meanwhile, and every preparation was made to receive the royal guests.

Yudhishthira was very grave when he learned at Indraprastha the errand on which Vidura had been sent. "Gambling is ever productive of dissension," he said; "tell me who are to be the other players?"

One by one Vidura mentioned their names, and at each Yudhishthira and his brothers grew more thoughtful. They were all men known for their skill and for their unscrupulous and greedy methods of play. At last, however, realizing that the invitation was also the king's order, Yudhishthira gave directions that all should be made ready for the journey. "I think," he said, "it is the call of fate. What is a man to fight against destiny?" And with heavy hearts the heroes and Draupadī set forth for Hastinapura, where they were received in right royal fashion, and as soon as their fatigue was gone conducted to the gambling-table.

With manifest reluctance, acceding only in obedience to the royal wish and the honour of his order, Yudhishthira sat down in the presence of the assembled court to play with Sakuni. And Dhritarāshtra himself was present, together with Bhīshma and Drona and Vidura and all the ministers. And it was openly announced, in spite of the irregularity, that Duryodhana would pay the stakes that Sakuni might lose.

But once Yudhishthira had begun to play he became, as all present had known he would, like a man intoxicated. At every throw he was pronounced the loser, and yet each time, with pale face and frenzied hands, he shouted for higher and more precious stakes. And the grave persons present sat with heads bowed and faces hidden in their hands. And the Pāndava brothers held themselves still, with breath indrawn, feeling themselves at the disposal of their brother, who was also their sovereign, though their hearts were bursting with rage and they longed to seize his adversary by the throat and deprive him of life. Only the insolent Duryodhana laughed aloud, and grew flushed with triumph as the madness of Yudhishthira became more and more apparent to the whole of that august assembly. But the weak Dhritarāshtra was full of fear, for he could feel the thoughts of all present and knew well enough, in his timid way, that a storm was here being set in motion that would not end till all the house should be uprooted. And Vidura, sitting beside him, reminded him how asses had brayed when Duryodhana was born. And the monarch shivered, yet had not strength to stop the play.

The Loss of Draupadī

Meanwhile the madness of Yudhishthira progressed. At each cast he lost and Sakuni won. Jewels went, the royal treasures went, chariots, servants, stables, banners—all kinds of possessions followed. Then the play entered on a more dangerous phase. The king staked his kingdom and lost. Yudhishthira was now demented, beyond all hope of reaching by arguments, and one by one, in the passion of the gambler, he staked his brothers, himself, and Draupadī—and lost!

"Aha!" cried the wicked Duryodhana, leaping to his feet in unconcealed delight. "Go, Vidura, and bring us the virtuous Draupadī, that the Pāndava queen may sweep our floors!" But Vidura cursed Duryodhana for the wickedness that would insult a woman and bring a doom upon them all, and a courtier had to be sent for Draupadī. When at last the wife of Yudhishthira stood before them, and was told that she had been made the slave of Duryodhana's faction by her husband, she asked in what condition Yudhishthira had been when he offered such a stake. And when she was told that he had first lost himself to Sakuni, and afterwards staked her, she answered in triumph that she repudiated the transaction. How could one who was himself a slave possess another who was free, and so dispose of her? And all present felt the soundness of her reasoning, yet would not Duryodhana admit himself foiled.

Then when the dispute was at its height, and the lawlessness of Duryodhana in the presence of Draupadī was threatening to provoke Bhīma and Arjuna to his slaughter, at that very instant a jackal was heard to wail in the vicinity of Dhritarāshtra. And in answer to the wail of the jackal there came the braying of an ass from without, and certain birds, also, gave hoarse and terrible cries. Then Bhīshma and Drona and Vidura turned quietly and looked at each other, and Dhritarāshtra grew pale and began to tremble, for he had heard the sounds and understood. "Ask a boon, Draupadī!" he commanded, putting up a shaking hand to still the clamour that was going on around him. "Ask a boon, my daughter. I will grant unto thee whatever thou sayest!"

At those words Draupadī looked up. "I who am free," she said quietly and proudly, "demand the freedom of my son's father, Yudhishthira!"

"Granted," said Dhritarāshtra. "Ask again!"

"And the freedom of all his brothers," continued Draupadī, "with their weapons, their chariots, and their personal belongings!"

"It is given!" said Dhritarāshtra. "Only, O princess, ask more!"

"By no means," said Draupadī firmly and disdainfully. "The Pāndavas, armed and free, can conquer the whole world. They need owe nothing to a boon!"

And Karna, looking on, said to himself: "Was there ever such a woman? The Pāndavas were sinking in an ocean of despair, and the princess of Panchala hath made herself a ship to carry them in safety to the shore!"

Immediately amongst the new-freed princes arose a fiery argument as to whether their first duty was not the slaughter of Duryodhana for the insults done to Draupadī, and it was averred by those who were present that in the heat of his anger smoke issued from the ears of Bhīma. But Yudhishthira, who had regained his habitual calm, pacified them. He turned to Dhritarāshtra to ask what might be the royal wish.

"Oh, go back to your own city and take your wealth with you and rule over your kingdom," entreated the old man, now thoroughly frightened. "You fortunately are open to reason. Leave us for Indraprastha, and that as quickly as possible! I only beg that you will bear no malice against us for what has passed!" And the Pāndavas were glad enough to carry out his instructions. With every formality of courtesy, therefore, they ordered their chariots and escorts and set forth for Indraprastha without delay.

Duryodhana had been absent when his father Dhritarāshtra in his panic had urged the Pāndavas to depart from Hastinapura. Now, however, his evil counsellors crowded round him, exclaiming: "We are undone! All that we had won the old man has given away! He has given their wealth back to the enemy."

Duryodhana hastened to his father's side and, without frightening him by any reproaches, represented to him the danger of allowing the Pāndavas, after the insults showered upon them, again to have access to their friends, their armies, and their stores. Dhritarāshtra listened and wavered, and at this point Duryodhana suggested as a fantastic wager that they should be brought back to throw the dice once more, and whichever side lost should retire into the forest for twelve years to live as ascetics and pass the thirteenth year in some city unrecognized by any, or, if recognized, pass another twelve years in the forest as forfeit. During this time Dhritarāshtra himself, urged his son, could make himself the master of widespread alliances and of a vast standing army, not easily to be conquered by five wandering princes. So might they still retrieve the folly of having allowed them to depart.

The old king listened and, fatally compliant, said: "Then let them return. Bring them back."

"No, no!" cried all the ministers, and even Karna, who surrounded him. "No, no! Let there now be peace!" But Dhritarāshtra said: "My son's desire shall be fulfilled. Let them be recalled!"

Then even Gandhārī, the aged queen, came into the council-chamber and implored the king her husband to cast off Duryodhana, their eldest son, rather than again allow him to have his way.

But Dhritarāshtra's was the obstinacy of a weak intellect. He said: "If our race is about to be destroyed, I am ill able to prevent it. Let my son's desire be fulfilled. Let the Pāndavas return!"

The Renewal of the Contest

Yudhishthira and his brothers had gone far along the road when the royal messenger overtook them with the king's command for their return. There was no great need for compliance. They knew well that the play was false. They might easily have made some courteous excuse and pushed on to their own city. But the mind of a man under the sway of calamity becomes deranged. Yudhishthira, at the words "Return and play!" took on the look of a man under a spell. And in due course, to the despair of all their friends, the Pāndavas once more entered Hastinapura and addressed themselves to play.

Once more the dice were thrown. Again Sakuni cried: "I have won!" And the Pāndavas stood up masters of themselves, but doomed to live twelve years in the forests and a thirteenth year unrecognized in some city; from there, if recognized, to return to the wild woods for another twelve years of exile.

But as they went forth, grim and silent, to their exile, wise men marked the manner of their going and read in it of a terrible return—a return that should be disastrous to all their foes.

VIII. THE KIRAT-ARJUNA

Now while the Pāndavas, in accordance with their defeat at dice, were living in exile in the forest, the mind of Yudhishthira brooded much upon their weakness as compared with the strength and resources of Duryodhana. He clearly foresaw that at some future time the differences between their cousins and themselves would have to be decided by the fortunes of war. And he remembered that Duryodhana was in actual possession of the throne and treasury, and that all the friends of their youth whose prowess on the field they knew were his friends and, he felt sure, devoted to him. Drona and his pupils, above all Karna, would, he feared, fight and die if need be, not for the Pāndavas, but for Duryodhana, son of Dhritarāshtra, the reigning king.

Just at the time when the eldest of the Pāndavas was possessed by these forebodings a holy man came to visit the retreat of the brothers, and the instant he saw Yudhishthira he began to answer the doubt that was in his mind. "Thou art troubled, O king," he said, "about the rival strength of thy friends and thy foes. For that have I come to thee. There is none in the world who can defeat thy brother Arjuna, if once he betakes himself to the mountains and obtains the vision of the Great God. By his hand are all thine enemies destined to be slain. Let Arjuna go to the mountains, and there alone let him fast and pray." Arjuna, therefore, thus selected, took vows of austerity, promising to be turned aside by nothing that he might meet, and set out for the Himālayas. At the foot of the mountains, when he reached them, he found a holy man, seated beneath a tree, and by him he was told that any spiritual gift that he chose might be his with eternal bliss; he had only to name what he wished. But the knight replied disdainfully that he had left his brothers in the forest to the south, and had himself come thither to obtain divine weapons. Was he going to accept bliss and leave them unaided? And the holy man, who was none other than the god Indra in disguise, blessed him and approved his resolution. And Arjuna, passing by this temptation, pushed on to the higher mountains where, if anywhere, he might expect his vision.

Passing through the thick forests, he soon reached the very breast of the mountains and established himself there, amidst trees and streams, listening to the songs of birds, and surrounded by fair blossoms, to practise his vow of prayer, vigil, and fast. Clad in scant clothes made of grass and deer-skin, he lived upon withered leaves and fallen fruits, and month after month he reduced his allowance of these till in the fourth month he was able to live on air alone, taking no other food whatever. And his head looked like lightning because of his constant bathing and purification, and he could stand day after day with arms upraised without support, till the earth began to smoke and the heavenly beings to tremble from the heat of Arjuna's penance.

The Boar

One day, as he performed his morning worship, offering flowers to a little clay image of the Great God, a boar rushed at him, seeking to slay him. And Arjuna, in whom the instincts of the soldier and the sportsman were ever uppermost, seized his bow and arrows and rose from his worship to kill the creature. At that moment the forests

XIII

KIRAT-ARJUNA

NANDA LĀL BOSE

Page 166

had grown strangely and solemnly still. The sound of springs and streams and birds had suddenly stopped. But Arjuna, with his mind still on his half-finished worship, did not notice this. Stringing his bow, he shot an arrow and hit the boar. At the self-same instant the beast was struck by another dart, seemingly as powerful, and with a roar he fell and died. But in Arjuna the wrath of a sportsman had blazed up, and apparently in his unknown rival also, each to find his own shot interfered with at the last moment. For there stood towering above him, as angry as himself, a huntsman, seemingly some king of the mountain tribes, accompanied by his queen and a whole train of merry followers. His form was blazing with energy, and he was saying: "How dared you shoot? The quarry was mine!"

"Let us fight for it!" said Arjuna, and the two began to turn their arrows on each other.

To the mortal's amazement, the body of the huntsman swallowed up his darts without seeming any the worse, and Arjuna could only shoot till his quiver was empty. "Let's wrestle, then!" he cried, and threw himself upon his opponent. He was met by the touch of a hand on his heart, and instead of continuing his combat he turned at once to finish his worship. Taking up a garland of flowers, he threw it about the image, but the next instant it was on the neck of the mountain king.

"Great God! Great God!" cried Arjuna, falling in a rapture at the feet of his unlooked-for guest. "Pardon thou my blows!"

But the Great God, well pleased, put out his hand and blessed his worshipper and granted him the boon of divine weapons, such as could be hurled by the mind, by the eyes, by words, and by the bow. Never should such weapons be used till all others had been exhausted. Never should they be used against feeble foes. For so they might in truth destroy the universe. Then the Great God gave to Arjuna Gāndīva, the divine bow, and, blessing him, turned and left that mountain with its vales and caves and snowy heights, and went up into the sky with all his train.

Such was the *Kirat-Arjuna*, Arjuna's vision of Mahādeva, the Great God, as a *Kirata*, or huntsman.

IX. THE MAIDEN WHO BECAME A KNIGHT

Now it happened that the eldest queen of Drupada, king of the Panchalas, was childless, and had been so for many years. And Drupada worshipped Shiva daily, praying that a son, not a daughter, might be born unto him; and dedicated this son in advance to the task of aiding in the destruction of Drona.

At last, after much prayer and severe austerity, Shiva himself blessed him, saying: "It is enough, O king! Thou shalt in due time have a child who will be first a daughter and then a son. This strange thing is decreed for thee. It will not fail!"

Then Drupada returned home and told his queen of the divine promise that had been made to him. And she, being a woman of strong faith, took the blessing to heart and built her whole mind upon this decree of destiny.

In due time accordingly the queen gave birth to a daughter of great beauty, but from the strength of her belief that the promise of Shiva would be fulfilled she actually gave it out that she had borne a son. And Drupada, concurring in the proclamation, had all the rites performed that were proper on the birth of a son. The mother carefully kept her own counsel and placed her trust firmly in Shiva, and the father everywhere said: "She is a son"; and no one in all the city suspected that that concealed daughter was not a son. And she was called Shikhandin, because that name had a feminine form which was Shikhandinī, and for the education of this Shikhandin-Shikhandinī every care was taken by Drupada. She learned writing and painting and all the arts that were proper to a man. For her parents lived daily in expectation of a miracle, and it behoved them to be ready for it when it should happen. And in shooting and fencing the child became a disciple of the royal *guru* Drona, and was in no way inferior to other princes in the management of weapons.

Then, as she was beginning to grow up, her mother urged her husband to find a wife for their supposed son and marry him in the sight of the whole world to some princess of royal family. Then Drupada sent embassies of betrothal in all directions, and finally selected a maiden to whom marriage was to be proposed on behalf of Shikhandin. And this maiden was a king's daughter.

But now, for the first time, the dread secret began to be whispered, and it came to the ears of the royal father of the princess who was promised to Shikhandin in marriage. And he, thinking he had been purposely insulted in that dearest point, the honour of the names of the women of his house, sent messages of threats and vengeance to Drupada. He would, he declared, destroy his city, and kill both Drupada and his daughter, and place a creature of his own on the throne of the Panchalas.

At this crisis the sense of his own guilt made Drupada somewhat weak. However, the queen publicly took the responsibility of the deception upon herself. She had, she told her husband in the presence of others, had a promise made to her by the god Shiva, and relying on this promise she had deceived him, so that he had publicly advertised the world of the birth of a son. She had been altogether responsible, and even now she believed in the word of the Great God: "Born a daughter, this child would become a son!"

This statement Drupada laid before his councillors, and they conferred all together for the protection of city and subjects against the intended invader. In the first place, they refused to admit that any such insult as was averred had been offered to the brother monarch. The proposals of marriage had been made in all good faith and were perfectly fit and proper proposals. Shikhandin, they repeated, was a man; he was not a woman. Then they refortified the city and strengthened the defences. And last of all, extraordinary ceremonies of worship were instituted, and the king appealed to the gods for help in this crisis, at every temple in his land.

Nevertheless he had his hours of depression, when he would go to talk the situation over with his wife; and she did all she could to encourage him. Every effort was directed to keeping up his courage. Homage to the gods was good, she said, when seconded by human endeavour; no one could tell how good. Hand in hand, these two things were always known to lead to success. Undoubtedly success awaited them. Who could dispute it?

The Resolve of Shikhandinī

While the husband and wife talked thus together their daughter Shikhandinī listened, and her heart grew heavy as she realized the unspoken despair that all this insistent cheerfulness was meant to conceal. It was the sense that they were to blame that so undermined their courage, and the root of trouble and fault alike was in herself. Oh, how worthless she must be! What a good thing it would be if she could wander off and never be heard of again! Even if she died, what matter? Losing her would only rid her unhappy parents of a burden that might possibly cost them, in any case, their lives and kingdom.

Thinking thus in heavy despondency, she rode out of the city and wandered on and on alone till she came to the edge of a dark and lonely forest. Now this forest had the reputation of being haunted. There stood in it an abandoned grange, with high walls and gateway, and rich with fragrance of smoke and grain. But though one might wander through this house day after day, one would never meet the owner of the house, and yet never feel that it had no owner. It was, in fact, the abode of a powerful spirit, a *yaksha*, known as Sthūna. He was full of kindness, and yet the name of the house was a word of dread amongst the peasant folk in the country-side because of the emptiness and mystery that hung about it.

But of all this Shikhandinī had no idea when she entered the place. She was attracted by the open door and the peace and silence; and having entered, she sat down on the floor plunged in sorrow, and remained so for hours and days, forgetting to eat.

The kind-hearted *yaksha* saw her, and grew more and more disturbed at her evident distress. Nothing would distract his visitor from her depth of thought, and her forgetfulness of herself seemed endless. At last the friendly *yaksha*, unable to comfort her, could do nothing but show himself to her, and urged her to tell him what it was she wanted. So he did this, begging her at the same time to tell him her trouble, and encouraging her to trust him by every means in his power. He was a follower, he said, of Kuvera,

God of Wealth. There was nothing that he could not grant if he were asked. He could even bestow the impossible. Let the princess only tell him her trouble. "Oh!" broke out Shikhandinī, unable to resist kindness so overwhelming when her need was so desperate. "Oh! make me a man, a perfect man! My father is about to be destroyed and our country to be invaded; and if I were a man it would not happen! Of thy grace, great *yaksha*, make me a man, and let me keep that manhood till my father is saved!" And poor Shikhandinī began to weep.

Shikhandinī attains her Desire

This was more than her kind-hearted host could bear, and, strange as it may sound, he became eager to do anything in the world, even the absurd thing she asked for, if only it would comfort the unhappy lady. So then and there he made a covenant with her. He would give her his blazing form and his manhood and all his strength, and he would himself become a woman in her place and remain hidden in his house. But when her father should again be safe she was to return and once more make the exchange. She would once more be Shikhandinī the princess, and he would again be Sthūna the *yaksha*.

No words can paint the joy of the knight Shikhandin as he left the presence of the *yaksha* and went forth to save his father and his father's city from the sword. But alas for the poor *yaksha!* It happened within a day or two that his master, the God of Wealth, made a royal progress through those parts and, noticing that Sthūna did not present himself, sent to order him into his presence. And when the poor shrinking *yaksha*, in his altered garb and form, appeared before him in shamefaced fashion, Kuvera his king, between laughter and disgust, hotly declared: "This shall not be undone! You shall remain a woman and she shall remain a man!" And then softening a little, as he saw the look of fright on the *yaksha's* face, he added: "At least, it shall be so until Shikhandin's death. After that this foolish wretch can take back his own form!"

And in due time, all being safe and at peace, the prince Shikhandin returned to Sthūna, as he had promised, to give up his treasured manhood. And when the *yaksha* saw that in the heart of this mortal there was no guile he was much touched and told him the truth—that he had himself been doomed to persist in his newly acquired womanhood. And he comforted the young knight for the injury he had unwittingly done him, saying: "All this was destiny, Shikhandin! It could not have been prevented."

Thus was fulfilled the blessing of Shiva, spoken over Drupada: "The child that thou shalt have, O king, shall first be a daughter and then a son!" And thus it came about that there was amongst the princes and soldiers of that period one who, though he had been born a woman, was actually a man and known as Shikhandin, maiden and knight.

But to Bhīshma only was it revealed that this Shikhandin was no other than Ambā, who had been born a second time for the very purpose of his destruction.

X. THE STORY OF THE LADY AMBĀ

Now Bhīshma, the great knight, was guardian of the imperial house of the Kurus. And this Bhīshma had made a vow in his youth that he would never marry, and never, though he was heir-apparent, seat himself on his father's throne. And this vow he made in order to enable his father to marry a certain fisher-maid, Satyavatī by name, on whom he had set his heart. And it came to pass that when Bhīshma's father, Shāmtanu, was dead, Bhīshma set on the throne his own half-brother, Vichitravīrya. And it was necessary that he should find a suitable marriage for this brother in order that the royal succession might be duly secured. And he heard that the bridal choice of the three daughters of the king of Benares—Ambā, Ambikā, and Ambālikā—was about to take place, and that all the kings and princes of the earth were bidden, their father having announced that his daughters should have for their dowry the courage of the bravest knight. So they were to be borne away by that prince whose unaided might should win them from all the rest. Nor did the king of Benares dream, when he made this announcement, that his eldest daughter Ambā was already secretly betrothed to a certain king, Shālwa by name; nor did the princess think it necessary to speak to her father of the matter, for she made sure that her true love, strengthened by her faith and the sure prospect of immediate happiness, would overbear all obstacles and, displaying his prowess before the whole assembled world, would carry her off as the prize of victory. But alas! when Bhīshma heard of this bridal tournament he decided that the opportunity was an excellent one to secure suitable queens for the young Vichitravīrya, and he determined to seize the three maidens and do combat for them against all comers.

In accordance with this purpose, therefore, Bhīshma set out for the city of Benares as a simple gentleman without a retinue. Arriving at the royal lists, he beheld the three maidens, all unrivalled for beauty and richly robed and ornamented, and before them, ranged on thrones and in cars, under royal umbrellas and pearl-embroidered canopies, each with his proper cognizance blazoned on his banner, all the greatest of the earth.

For a moment the prince paused to survey the scene; then, with a voice that was like the roaring of a lion, he sounded three times the great battle-cry that was to summon his rivals to mortal combat.

The Challenge

"Bhīshma, son of Shāmtanu, seizes these maidens. Let who will rescue them! By force do I seize them, from amongst men before your very eyes!"

No one could stir while the challenge was being sounded, and as for the third time the cry died away Bhīshma's charioteer, in the twinkling of an eye, turned his battle-chariot and swiftly drove down upon that part of the lists where the three princesses waited surrounded by their ladies. It was not a moment before their attendants had been made to place them on Bhīshma's car, with a line of his servants drawn up in front of them, and even while the great counter-challenge was ringing out on all sides, and angry kings had risen, with swords unsheathed, to leap to chariot or elephant or horseback, as the case might be, he stood alert and smiling, with bow drawn and his back to the royal maidens, ready to do battle for his prize against a world in arms. Never had there been an archer like Bhīshma. With a shower of arrows he stopped the rush that came upon him from all sides at once. His part was like that of Indra fighting against the crowds of asuras. Laughingly with his blazing darts did he cut down the magnificent standards, all decked with gold, of the advancing kings. In that combat he overthrew their horses, their elephants, and their charioteers, each with a single arrow, till, seeing how light was the hand and how true was the aim of Bhīshma, son of Shāmtanu, all the kings of the earth broke ranks and accepted their defeat. And he, having vanquished so many sovereigns, retained his royal prize of three princesses, and escorted them back to Hastinapura, the royal city, to the queen-mother Satyavatī, that they might become the brides of her son Vichitravīrya the king. Well might it be told henceforth amongst men that Ambā, Ambikā, and Ambālikā had had knightly prowess itself for their dower.

But as the wedding-day itself drew near, Ambā, the eldest of the three princesses, sought an audience of Bhīshma, the guardian of the imperial house, and with much shyness and delicacy disclosed to him the fact of her prior betrothal to the king of the Shālwas. It seemed to her a far from noble deed that she should marry one man while secretly longing, she said, for another. She therefore asked Bhīshma to decide for her whether she might be allowed to depart from the Kuru court.

The matter was quickly laid by Bhīshma before his mother, the council of state, and the priests both of the realm and of the royal household. And all these persons judged it with kindly judgment, as if Ambā had been some tenderly guarded daughter of their own. Secretly, then, before the time arranged for the Kuru wedding, she was allowed to leave Hastinapura and proceed to the capital of the king of the Shālwas. And her escort was carefully chosen, being made up of a number of old Brāhmans. And besides these, her own waiting-woman, who had from childhood been her nurse, travelled with her.

And when she reached the city of the Shālwas, she came before the king and said simply to him: "I have come, O king. Here I am."

Ambā is Rejected

But some blindness and perversity had come upon the king of the Shālwas. Perhaps he was really angry and mortified by his defeat at the hands of Bhīshma. Perhaps at first his attitude was taken half in play and gradually grew more and more bitter and earnest. Or perhaps—and this seems the most likely—he was indeed an unknightly man, and the girl had done ill to trust him. In any case, he proved utterly unworthy of the great and faithful love of the Lady Ambā.

At first, with lightness and laughter, he declared that he did not want a wife who had once been carried off by Bhīshma and intended for another's bride. Then he taunted the princess with having gone to Hastinapura cheerfully. But she, poor girl, could truthfully urge that she had wept all the way.

Finally, he showed himself simply indifferent, and though she made her feeling clear over and over again with a sincerity that all her life after it made her hot to remember, he showed not the slightest affection for her, but turned away from her, casting her off, say the chronicles, as a snake discards his old skin, with no more feeling of honour or of affection. And when the maiden, eldest daughter of the king of Benares, at last understood that this was King Shālwa's intention, her heart was filled with anger, and in the midst of her tears of sorrow and pride she rose and said: "Though thou dost cast me off, O king, righteousness itself will be my protection, for truth cannot be defeated!" And with these words she turned, crying softly, and haughtily went forth from the city.

Suffering the deepest humiliation as she was, and scarcely

knowing where to turn, the royal maiden for that night took refuge in one of the great forest-hermitages of the time, known as *ashrāmas*, of which her own grandfather happened to be the head. Her heart was full of pain and her whole mind was in confusion. She had been scorned and refused, but whose was the fault? Had it been Shālwa or Bhīshma who was more to blame? Sometimes she would reproach herself that she had not publicly refused, in the tournament-ground, to go with her sisters, under Bhīshma's protection, to Hastinapura. Then she would make her father responsible for the rashness that had announced that prowess should be the dower of his daughters. Again, her mind would turn upon Bhīshma. If he had not captured her, if he had not taken her to Hastinapura, and, again, if he had not arranged for her expedition to the king of the Shālwas, this trouble would not have come upon her. Thus she blamed herself, her father, and Bhīshma all by turns, but never did this princess of Benares turn in her heart to blame the king of the Shālwas, whom she would fain have had for her lord. Even in the insult he had inflicted upon her she made endless excuses for him. She could not see his lightness and vanity. She saw only the trial to which he had been put. Her own mind was set to give up the world. Rejected on two sides—for she could not now return to Hastinapura—and too proud to ask shelter in the home of her childhood, there was nothing before the royal maiden save a life of austerity and penance. And gradually, as she grew calm and took the help and advice of the old sages of the *ashrāma*, her mind began to settle on Bhīshma as the source and root of her woes, and the destruction of Bhīshma gradually became the motive to which all her self-severities were to be directed.

Ambā and Bhīshma

Religion itself took the part of Ambā, for the hermits, headed by her grandfather, loved and pitied the mortified girl. And in after ages a story was current of a great mythical combat waged against Bhīshma on her behalf by Parashu-Rāma, who had been his early teacher, and was even as God himself. And this combat lasted, it was said, many days, being fought with all the splendour and power of warring divinities, till at last it was brought to an end by the intervention of the gods, surrounded by all the celestial hosts. For they feared to see the exhaustion of mighty beings who owed each other reverence and affection and could by no means kill one another. But when Ambā was called into the presence of Parashu-Rāma to hear the news of the cessation of the conflict, she merely bowed and thanked the old warrior with great sweetness for his energy on her behalf. She would not again, she said, seek the protection of Bhīshma in the city of Hastinapura, and she added that it now lay with herself to find the means of slaying Bhīshma.

Parashu-Rāma, who was almost the deity of fighting men, must have smiled to hear a girl, with her soft voice, promise herself the glory of killing the knight whom even he had not been able to defeat. But Ambā rose and left his presence with her head high and despair on her face. There was now no help for her even in the gods. She must depend upon herself.

From this time her course of conduct became extraordinary. Month after month she would fast and undergo penances. Beauty and charm became nothing in her eyes. Her hair became matted and she grew thinner and thinner. For hours and days she would stand in stillness and silence as if she had been made of stone. In this way she did more than was human and "made heaven itself hot" with her austerities.

Every one begged her to desist. The old saints near whom she lived, and embassies constantly sent by her father, all begged her to surrender her resolve and live a life of greater ease. But to none of these would she listen, and only went on with redoubled energy practising her asceticisms. Then she began to seek out pilgrimages, and went from one sacred river to another, performing the while the most difficult of vows. On one occasion as she bathed, Mother Ganges herself, who was known to have been the mother of Bhīshma, addressed her, and asked her the cause of all these penances. But when the poor lady replied that all her efforts were bent toward the destruction of Bhīshma the spirit of the Ganges rebuked her severely, and told her the terrible consequences of vows of hatred. Yet still the Princess Ambā did not desist. Until he was slain through whom she had come to be "neither woman nor man," she would not know peace and she would not stop.

At last Shiva, the Great God, appeared before her, drawn by the power of her prayers and penances, and standing over her with the trident in his hand, he questioned her as to the boon she sought.

"The defeat of Bhīshma!" answered Ambā, bowing joyfully at his feet, for she knew that this was the end of the first stage in the execution of her purpose.

"Thou shalt slay him," said the Great God. Then Ambā, filled with joy, and yet overcome with amazement, said: "But how, being a woman, can I achieve victory in battle? It is true that my woman's heart is entirely stilled. Yet I beg of thee, O thou who hast the bull for thy cognizance, to give me the promise that I myself shall be able to slay Bhīshma in battle!"

Then answered Shiva: "My words can never be false. Thou shalt take a new birth and some time afterwards thou shalt obtain manhood. Then thou shalt become a fierce warrior, well skilled in battle, and remembering the whole of thy present life, thou thyself, with thine own hands, shalt be the slayer of Bhīshma."

And having so said, the form of Shiva disappeared from before the eyes of the assembled ascetics and the Lady Ambā there in the midst of the forest *ashrāma*. But Ambā proceeded to gather wood with her own hands, and made a great funeral pyre on the banks of the Jamna, and then, setting a light to it, she herself entered into it, and as she took her place upon the throne of flame she said over and over again: "I do this for the destruction of Bhīshma! To obtain a new body for the destruction of Bhīshma do I enter this fire!"

XI. KURUKSHETRA

The thirteen years' exile was over, and the Pāndavas once more, by their prowess in battle, had revealed themselves to their friends. Now was held a great council of kings at the court of one of those allies, and Dhritarāshtra, hearing of it, sent to it an ambassador charged with vague words of peace and friendship to the Pāndavas, but not empowered to make any definite proposal for giving them back their kingdom and property. To this embassy all agreed with Yudhishthira that there was only one answer to be given: "Either render us back Indraprastha or prepare to fight!"

It was now clear indeed to all men that nothing remained for either family but war. The aggressions of Duryodhana had been too many and too persistent. The insults offered at the gambling party had been too personal and too offensive. Duryodhana, moreover, had had all the opportunity he craved. For thirteen years, while his cousins were in exile, he had enjoyed the power of making alliances and dispensing benefits. It was now for him to test the faithfulness and the courage of the friends he had won. The clouds of war hung thick and black above the rival houses, and both knew now that the contest must be to the death. And Duryodhana put the command of the Kaurava forces into the hands of Bhīshma, while Karna, in order that he might not create a separate faction in the army, pledged himself not to fight till after the grandsire should be slain. And the Pāndava forces were put under the command of the Panchala prince, Draupadī's brother, Dhrishtadyumna. And Hastinapura, at the approach of battle, crowded with kings and men-at-arms, with elephants and chariots and thousands of foot-soldiers, looked like the ocean at the moment of moonrise. And the Pāndavas also gathered their forces in the capital of Drupada, and both sides marched down on the great plain of Kurukshetra, which was to form the scene of action. Thus entered both parties into that mansion where the play was to be war, where the gamblers were men and their own lives the stakes, and where the dice-board was the battle-field, filled with its armies, chariots, and elephants. From the beginning Duryodhana had given orders that Bhīṣhma, as commander, was to be protected at all hazards, and having heard vaguely from Bhīshma himself that through Shikhandin alone could his death come, he commanded that every effort was to be made throughout the battle to kill Shikhandin.

And the smaller army that marched beneath the banners

of the Pāndavas and Panchalas was full of joy and spirit. Their minds soared to the combat. They seemed like men intoxicated with delight at the thought of battle. But terrible omens were seen by Bhīshma, and whenever Duryodhana sat down to think of battle he was heard to sigh.

The Battle

When the sun rose on the fatal day the two great armies stood face to face with one another, with their chariots and steeds and splendid standards, looking like two rival cities. Then sounded the conch shells and battle trumpets, and with a vast movement, as of a tidal wave passing over the ocean or a tempest sweeping over the forests, the two forces threw themselves upon one another, and the air was filled with the neighs of the chargers and the noise and groans of combatants. With leonine roars and clamorous shouting, with the blare of trumpets and cow-horns and the din of drums and cymbals, the warriors of both sides rushed upon each other. For a while the spectacle was beautiful, then it became furious, and, hidden in its own dust and confusion, there was nothing to be seen. The Pāndavas and the Kurus fought as if they were possessed by demons. Father and son, brother and brother forgot each other. Elephants rent each other with their tusks. Horses fell slain and great chariots lay crushed up on the earth. Banners were torn to pieces. Arrows flew in all directions, and wherever the darkness was rent for a moment was seen the flashing of swords and weapons in deadly encounter.

But wherever the combat was thickest, there at its heart might be seen Bhīshma, the leader of the Kurus, standing in white armour on his silver car, like unto the full moon in a cloudless sky. Over him waved his standard, a golden palm-tree wrought on a white ground. And no warrior whom he marked for his aim could survive the shooting of his deadly arrow. And the whole host of those who were opposed to him trembled, as one after another he shot down trusted officers. And as darkness began to fall the rival commanders withdrew their forces for their nightly rest. But there was sorrow in both camps for those that had fallen in the combat of the day.

Day after day went by, and amidst growing ruin and carnage it became clear to the Pāndavas that so long as Bhīshma, their beloved grandsire, lived they themselves could not conquer. On the tenth day, therefore, the fatal combat was undertaken. Bhīshma was mortally wounded, and the command of the Kurus made over to Drona in his stead.

Under Drona the Kurus once more enjoyed a blaze of victory. The science of the old preceptor had its value in enabling him to dispose of his forces to advantage and teaching him where was the point to attack. After a time it became evident that under his direction all the strength of the Kurus was being concentrated on the seizure of Yudhishthira's person, for Drona was known to have made a vow to capture the Pāndava king. The enemy, on the other hand, had aimed from the beginning at the personal defeat of Drona; only it was the dearest wish of Arjuna that his old master should be taken alive.

The Deception of Bhīma

This wish was not realized. As long as Ashvatthāman, the son of Drona, lived it came to be believed that his father would never be conquered, for his love and hope for his son were sufficient to keep him filled with courage and energy. Bhīma, therefore, being bent on the defeat of Drona, selected an elephant named Ashvatthāman and slew it with his own hands, and then threw himself in his might on the Kuru front in the neighbourhood of Drona, shouting: "Ashvatthāman is dead! Ashvatthāman is dead!"

Drona heard the words, and for the first time his stout heart sank. Yet not easily would he accept the news that was to be his death-blow. Unless it was confirmed by Yudhishthira, who was, he said, incapable of untruth, even for the sovereignty of the three worlds, he would never believe that Ashvatthāman was dead. Making his way then to Yudhishthira, Drona asked him for the truth, and Yudhishthira answered in a clear voice: "Yes, O Drona! Ashvatthāman is dead!" And this he said three times. But after the word Ashvatthāman he said indistinctly each time the words "the elephant." These words, however, Drona did not hear. And up to this time the horses and wheels of Yudhishthira's chariot had never touched the earth. But after this untruth they came down a hand's-breadth and drove along the ground. Then Drona, in his despair for the loss of his son, became unable to think of his divine weapons. Seeing, then, that the time had come, he charged the great bowmen who were about him as to how they were to conduct the battle, and laying down his own weapons, he sat down on the front of his chariot fixing his mind on itself. At that very moment Dhrishtadyumna, the Pāndava general, had seized his sword and leapt to the ground in order to attack Drona in personal combat. But before he touched him the soul of the Kuru general had gone forth, and to the few who had vision it appeared for a moment as if the sky held two suns at once. But none parried the blow of Dhrishtadyumna. The uplifted sword fell and cut off Drona's head, which was at once raised from the ground by his supposed slayer and tossed like a ball into the midst of the Kuru hosts. For a moment it seemed as if the army would break and flee. Then darkness came on, and wearily and mournfully all departed to their quarters. Still a few days were left, and Karna took command. But with his death two days later it became clear that the Pāndavas were to be the victors. Yet still Duryodhana remained with unabated courage, determined neither to give nor to take quarter; and not until he had been vanquished in single combat with Bhīma, and all their schoolboy enmities fulfilled in death, could the Pāndavas be finally acclaimed as victors.

Then at last the eighteen days' battle was ended with the victory of Yudhishthira and his brothers, and Duryodhana and all the sons of Dhritarāshtra had vanished in death, even as a lamp that is extinguished at midday.

The Bhagavad Gītā

The *Bhagavad Gītā* is a partly philosophic, partly devotional inspired utterance of Krishna immediately before the great battle between the Kurus and the Pāndavas—spoken in reply to Arjuna's protest that he has no will to slay his friends and kinsmen. This *Gītā*, or song, has become a gospel universally acceptable among all Indian sects. No single work of equal length so well expresses the characteristic trend of Indian thought, or so completely depicts the Indian ideals of character.

It speaks of diverse ways of salvation—that is, escaping from self and knowing God: by love, by works, and by learning. God has two modes of being, the unmanifest and unconditioned, and the manifest and conditioned. There are, indeed, some who seek direct experience of the unconditioned; but, as Shrī Krishna says: "Exceeding great is the toil of these whose mind is attached to the unshown, for the unshown way is painfully won by them that wear the body." For all those who are not yet ripe for such supreme effort Shrī Krishna teaches passionate devotion to himself and the strenuous *sva-dharma*—that is, action according to the duty of each individual. We have already seen (Rāmāyana, p. 10) that morality or rules of conduct are not the same for all individuals: the morality of a yogī is different from that of a knight. Shrī Krishna teaches that the doing of such action as a man is called to, without attachment to the fruits of action—that is, indifferent to failure or success, or to any advantages or disadvantages resulting to oneself—is a certain means of progress toward the knowledge of God. And to those whom the problem of suffering dismays he says: "Do not grieve for the life and death of individuals, for this is inevitable; the bodies indeed come and go, but the life that manifests in all is undying and unhurt, this neither slayeth nor is slain"—*nāyam hanti na hanyate.* Therefore, when Arjuna protests that he has no desire to slay his kinsmen in battle, Krishna answers, like Brynhild to Sigurd:

Wilt thou do the deed and repent it? thou hadst better never been born:
Wilt thou do the deed and exalt it? then thy fame shall be outworn:
Thou shalt do the deed and abide it, and sit on thy throne on high,
And look on to-day and to-morrow as those that never die.

The extract following expresses these ideas in the words of the *Gītā* itself:

Arjuna spake:

"O Krishna, when I see my kinsmen thus arrayed for battle, Gāndīva falls from my hand, and my mind is all awhirl,
"For I do not long for victory, O Krishna, nor kingdoms, nor delights; what is kingship, what is pleasure, or even life itself, O Lord of Herds,
"When they for whose sake kingship, pleasure, and delight are dear, stand here arrayed for battle, abandoning life and wealth?
"These I would not slay, though they should seek to slay myself; no, not for the lordship of the three worlds, much less for the kingdom of the earth.
"What pleasure can we find, O Troubler of the People, in slaying Dhritarāshtra's folk? We shall be stained by sin if we kill these heroes.
"It were better that the sons of Dhritarāshtra, weapon in hand, should slay me unresisting and unarmed."
Thus did the Wearer of the Hair-knot speak with the Lord of Herds, saying: "I will not fight."

Krishna answered:

"Thou speakest words of seeming wisdom, yet thou dost grieve for those for whose sake grief is all unmeet. The wise grieve not at all, either for the living or the dead.
"Never at any time have I not been, nor thou, nor any of these princes of men, nor verily shall we ever cease to be in time to come.
"As the Dweller-in-the-Body endureth childhood, youth, and age, even so he passeth on to other bodies. The steadfast grieve not because of this.

XIV

KRISHNA INSTRUCTING ARJUNA

SURENDRA NĀTH KAR

Page 188

"It is but the touchings of the instruments of sense, O son of Kuntī, that bring cold and heat, pleasure and pain; it is they that come and go, enduring not; do thou bear with them, O son of Bharata.

"But know that That is indestructible by which all this is interpenetrated; none can destroy that changeless Being.

"It is but these bodies of the Body-Dweller, everlasting, infinite, undying, that have an end; therefore do thou fight, O son of Bharata."

Then, still speaking of that imperishable Life, which life and death do not touch, Krishna continued:

"That is not born, nor doth it die; nor, having been, doth it ever cease to be; unborn, everlasting, eternal, and ancient, this is not slain when a body is slain.

"Knowing That to be undying, everlasting, unborn, and undiminished, who or what may it be that a man can slay, or whereby can he be slain?

"As a man casting off worn garments taketh new, so the Body-Dweller, casting off a worn-out body, enters into another that is new.

"Unmanifest, unthinkable, unchangeable is That. Knowing it so, thou shouldst not grieve.

"For this Body-Dweller may never in any body be wounded, O son of Bharata; therefore thou shouldst not grieve for any creature.

"But, looking upon thine own appointed task [*sva-dharma*], fear not; for there is nothing more to be welcomed by a knight than a righteous war."

In later passages Shrī Krishna proclaimed his own immanence:

"Hear thou, O child of Prithā, how thou mayst verily

know Me to the uttermost, practising *yoga*, and thy mind attached to Me:

"Eightfold is my nature—of earth, of water, fire and wind; of ether, mind and understanding, and the sense of I-hood.

"That is the lower; do thou also know my other nature, the higher—of elemental soul that holdeth up the universe, thou great-armed hero.

"Know that from these twain are sprung all beings; in Me is the evolution of the universe, and in Me its dissolution.

"There is naught whatsoever higher than I, O wealth-winner; all this universe is strung on Me like rows of gems upon a thread.

"I am the savour in the waters, O son of Kuntī, and the light in sun and moon; in the *Vedas* I am the *Om*, in the ether I am sound, in men I am their manhood.

"The pure fragrance of the earth am I, and the light in fire; the life in all born beings I, and the asceticism of ascetics.

"Know, child of Prithā, that I am the eternal seed of beings one and all; I am the reason of the rational, the splendour of the splendid.

"The strength of the strong am I, void of longing and of passion; in creatures I am the desire that is not against the law, O Bharata lord.

"Know that from Me are sprung the moods of goodness, fieriness and gloom; I am not in them, but they in Me.

"Bewildered by these threefold moods, all this world knows Me not, who am above the moods and imperishable.

"For this my divine illusion, born of the moods, is hard to pierce. They come to Me who pass beyond this glamour.

"I know the beings that are past and present and to come, Arjuna; but none knoweth Me."

XII. THE BED OF ARROWS

We have seen that Bhīshma was struck down with mortal wounds on the tenth day of the great battle. This was the manner of his death:

Long, long ago, in the youth of Bhīshma, when as heir-apparent to the kingdom he had taken the vow never to marry, in order that the throne might be left to the sons of the fisher-maid queen, his father had pronounced over him a great blessing, saying that death should never be able to approach him till he himself should give permission. For this reason, to Bhīshma personally, war had all his life been only play. And now, in the battle of Kurukshetra, day after day went by because of this without any decisive victory. Bhīshma believed that the cause of the Pāndavas was just and they could not be defeated, and yet he fought with a skill and gaiety that nothing could approach. He constantly, with his shower of arrows, cut down whoever was opposed to him at the head of Yudhishthira's army. Even as the sun with his rays sucks up the energies of all things during summer, so did Bhīshma take the lives of the hostile warriors. And the soldiers who faced him, hopeless and heartless, were unable even to look at him in that great battle—him who resembled the midday sun blazing in his own splendour!

Things being at this pass on the ninth day of the battle, night fell, and the Pāndavas and their friends assembled with Krishna to hold a council of war. There the stern necessities of war battled in their minds with the feelings of reverence and affection with which, from their very babyhood, Yudhishthira and his brothers regarded Bhīshma. Still, they repeated constantly that as long as Bhīshma remained undefeated the victory could not be theirs. It was necessary, therefore, to kill Bhīshma, and this must be done by Arjuna, who had long ago promised, half laughingly, that he would bring to the grandsire his means of escape from life. Yet how was it to be done? None present could offer a suggestion. Bhīshma was personally invincible. Death himself could not approach him without permission. Who, therefore, was competent to slay him?

Suddenly Yudhishthira raised his head. "I have it!" he cried. "When we were preparing for war the grandsire promised me that, though he could not fight for us, he would always be ready to give us counsel. Let us go and ask him for the means by which he should be slain! There can be no doubt but he will aid us!"

The thought was worthy of the knightly counsellors, and putting off armour and weapons, they left the tent and proceeded unarmed toward the quarters of the Kuru general. Warm and loving was the welcome that Bhīshma gave his grandchildren as they entered his tent, and eagerly he inquired what he could possibly do for them.

The brothers and Krishna stood moodily before him in a row. At last, however, Yudhishthira broke the silence. "O thou," he cried, "whose bow is ever in a circle, tell us how we may slay thee and protect our troops from constant slaughter!"

Bhīshma's face lighted up with sudden understanding and then grew grave. "You must indeed slay me," he said gently, "if you are to have the victory in this battle. As long as I am alive it cannot be yours. There is nothing for you but to slay me as quickly as may be!"

"But the means!" said Yudhishthira. "Tell us the means! To us it seems that Indra himself would be easier to defeat!"

The Answer of Bhīshma

"I see, I see," said Bhīshma thoughtfully. "Yet there are certain persons whom I shall never fight. Against a man unarmed, against the vulgar, or against one born a woman I never take aim. And if covered by one of these, anyone may kill me easily. Yet I warn you that only by the hand of Krishna or of Arjuna can the arrow be shot by which I consent to die."

Then Arjuna, his face burning in grief and shame, broke out. "Oh, oh, how am I to kill him who has been my own grandfather? When I was a child I climbed in play upon thy knee, O Bhīshma, and called thee 'father.' 'Nay, nay,' thou didst reply, 'I am not thy father, little one, but thy father's father!' Oh, let my army perish! Whether victory or death be mine, how can I ever fight with him who has been this to us?"

But Krishna reminded Arjuna of the eternal duty of the knightly order, that without any malice they should fight, protect their subjects, and offer sacrifice. The death of Bhīshma was ordained from of old by the hand of Arjuna. Even thus should he go to the abode of the gods. And thus soothed and braced to the thought of the morrow, the princes reverently saluted Bhīshma and withdrew from his presence.

Even before sunrise, on the tenth day, the great host was astir. And in the very van of the Pāndava troops was the knight Shikhandin, while Bhīma and Arjuna to right and left were the protectors of his wheels. And similarly, in the front of the Kurus was Bhīshma himself, protected by the sons of Dhritarāshtra.

The energy of the Pāndavas, inspired as they now were by certain hope of victory, was immense, and they slaughtered the troops of the Kurus mercilessly. But this sight Bhīshma, their commander, could not brook. His one duty was the protection of his soldiers, and he shot a rain of arrows into the hostile force. In all directions under his mighty arrows fell officers, soldiers, elephants, and horses. His bow seemed to be ever in a circle, and to the Pāndava princes he looked like the Destroyer himself devouring the world. In spite of the courage and violence with which Bhīma and Arjuna confronted him everywhere, and centred their whole attack and onslaught on Bhīshma himself, the old grandsire succeeded in cutting to pieces the whole division of Shikhandin. Then that officer, transported with anger, succeeded in piercing Bhīshma with no less than three arrows in the centre of the breast. Bhīshma looked up to retaliate, but, seeing that the blow had come from Shikhandin, he laughed instead, and said: "What! Shikhandinī?" These words were too much for the younger knight.

Shikhandin and Bhīshma

"By my troth," he cried, "I will slay thee! Look thy last on the world!" And even as he spoke he sent five arrows straight into the heart of Bhīshma.

Then careering like death himself on the field of battle, Arjuna rushed forward, and Shikhandin sped another five arrows at Bhīshma. And all saw that Bhīshma laughed and answered not, but Shikhandin himself, carried away by the fury of battle, was not aware. And Arjuna as protector of his wheel scattered death in the Kuru ranks on every side.

Then Bhīshma, thinking of a certain divine weapon, made to rush upon Arjuna with it in his hand. But Shikhandin threw himself between, and Bhīshma immediately withdrew the weapon. Then the grandsire took up an arrow that was capable of clearing a mountain, and hurled it like a blazing bolt on the chariot of Arjuna; but Arjuna with lightning speed fixed on his bow five arrows and cut the dart as it coursed towards him into five great fragments. Again and again struck Shikhandin, and still the grandsire answered not, either by look or blow; but Arjuna, drawing Gāndīva, sped hundreds of arrows and struck Bhīshma in his vital parts. And whenever the old general shot, the prince cut off his arrow in its course; but his own arrows Bhīshma could not escape. Then smiling he turned to one near him and said: "These darts coursing toward me in the long line, like the messenger of Wrath, are not Shikhandin's!" Then he took sword and shield and made to jump from his car to close with Arjuna in single combat. But even at this moment the arrows of Arjuna cut his shield as he seized it into a thousand pieces. And even his car was struck, and for the first time the mighty bowman trembled.

Then seeing this, like a vortex in the river the tides of battle closed over and around him, and when again there was a break in the struggling mass Bhīshma was seen, like a broken standard, to have fallen to the ground.

Then it was seen that, pierced all over with arrows, his body touched not the ground. And a divine nature took possession of the great bowman, lying thus on that thorny bed. He permitted not his senses for one moment to falter. All round him he heard heavenly voices. A cool shower fell for his refreshment, and he remembered that this was not an auspicious moment for the flight of the soul. Then there swept down upon him from the distant Himālayas messengers from Mother Ganges, a flock of swans which circled round and round him, bringing celestial memories. And Bhīshma, indifferent to the pains of the body, and having death in his own control, determined to lie there on his bed of arrows till the sun should have entered once more on his northern path and the way be open to the region of the gods. And the battle was hushed, while the princes of both houses stood around their beloved guardian. And he, giving them a cheerful welcome, asked for a pillow. Then all kinds of soft and beautiful pillows were brought. But he waved them aside as not fit for the bed of a hero, and turned to Arjuna. And Arjuna, stringing Gāndīva, shot three arrows into the earth for the support of Bhīshma's head. "Thus should the hero sleep," said Bhīshma, "on the field of battle. Here, when the sun turns again to the north, shall I part from life, like one dear friend from another. And now blessings be with you and peace! I spend my time in adoration!"

With these words he motioned all to withdraw, and he, Bhīshma, was left alone for the night, lying on his bed of arrows.

XIII. KARNA

The birth of the warrior Karna had been on a strange fashion. Having the sun for his father, he was born of Kuntī, or Prithā, the mother of the Pāndavas, before her marriage, and she had prayed that if the child were indeed the son of a god he should be born with natural ear-rings and a natural coat of armour as the signs of his immortality. And it was even so, and these things were the tokens that he could not be slain by mortal foe. And Kuntī, coming with her maid, put the child at dead of night into a box made of wicker-work and, weeping bitterly, floated it out with many tender farewells upon the current of the river.

And carried by the waves, and bearing with him the signs of his divine origin, the babe came to the city of Champa, on the Ganges, and there he was found by Ādiratha the charioteer and Rādhā his wife, and they took him and adopted him as their eldest son. And years went by, and Ādiratha left Champa for Hastinapura, and there Karna grew up amongst the pupils of Drona; and he contracted a friendship for Duryodhana and became the rival of Arjuna. Now all the sons of Prithā had had gods for their fathers, and Arjuna's father was Indra. And Indra, seeing that Karna wore natural mail and ear-rings, became anxious for the protection of Arjuna. For it was ordained in the nature of things that one of these two must slay the other.

And it was known of Karna that, at the moment when after bathing he performed his morning worship of the sun, there was nothing that he would not, if asked, give away to a mendicant. Indra, therefore, one day, taking the form of a Brāhman, stood before him at this hour and boldly demanded his mail and ear-rings.

But Karna would not easily part with the tokens of invincibility. Smiling he told the Brāhman again and again that these things were part of himself. It was impossible, therefore, for him to part with them. But when the suppliant refused to be satisfied with any other boon, Karna turned suddenly upon him and said: "Indra, I know thee! From the first I recognized thee! Give me something in exchange, and thou shalt have my mail and ear-rings!"

And Indra answered: "Except only the thunderbolt, ask what thou wilt!"

Then said Karna: "One invincible dart! In exchange I give thee my mail and ear-rings!"

The Arrow of Death

And Indra answered: "Done! I give thee, O Karna, this dart called Vāsava. It is incapable of being baffled, and thrown by me returns to my hand to slay hundreds of enemies. Hurled by thee, however, it will slay but one powerful foe. And if, maddened by anger, while there still remain other weapons or while thy life is not in deadly peril, thou shoot this arrow, it will rebound and fall upon thyself!"

Then taking the blazing dart, Karna, without wincing, began to cut off his own coat of natural armour and his own living ear-rings, and handed them to the Brāhman. And Indra, taking them, ascended with a smile to Heaven. And news went about on all hands that Karna was no longer invincible. But none knew of the arrow of death that he treasured, to be used once upon a single deadly foe.

The Mission of Krishna

Now it happened before the outbreak of hostilities that Krishna had gone himself to Hastinapura to see if it were not possible to persuade Dhritarāshtra to restore Indraprastha peacefully, and thus to avoid war. Finding, however, that this plan could not be carried out, and turning to leave the Kuru capital, he had still tried one more device to make the fratricidal contest impossible. Taking Karna aside, he privately told him the secret of his birth, and begged him to announce himself to the whole world as the son of Prithā, and therefore the elder brother of Yudhishthira himself; not only a prince of blood as proud as the Pāndavas' own, but even, if the truth were known, their actual leader and sovereign.

Karna listened with his usual courtesy, not untouched with sadness. He had long known, he said in reply, the nature of his own origin, that Prithā, the mother of the Pāndavas, had been his mother and the sun his father, and he also knew that it was by command of the god that she had then abandoned him and floated him out on the river beside which he was born. But he could not forget that all the love and devotion of parents had actually been shown him by the old charioteer and his wife. Nor could he forget that they had no other child, and that if he gave them up there would be none to make for them the ancestral offerings. He had married, moreover, in the caste of the charioteer, and his children and grandchildren were all of that rank. How could he, out of mere desire for empire, cut loose his heart from bonds so sweet? There was the gratitude, moreover, that he owed to Duryodhana. Because of his fearless and heroic friendship he had enjoyed a kingdom for thirteen years without a care. His one desire in life had been the right of single combat with Arjuna, and undoubtedly it was the knowledge of this that had made Duryodhana bold to declare war. Were he now to withdraw, it would be treachery to his friend.

Above all, it was important that Krishna should tell no one the secret of this conversation. If Yudhishthira came to know that his place was by right Karna's, it was not to be believed that he would consent to retain it. And if the Pāndava sovereignty were to come into the hands of Karna, he himself could do nothing save hand it over to Duryodhana. It was best, therefore, for all parties that the secret should be as though never told, and that he should act as he would have acted had it remained unknown.

And then, swept away on the current of his own melancholy into a mood of prophecy, the charioteer's son said: "Ah, why should you tempt me? Have I not seen in a vision the kingly hall entered by Yudhishthira and his brothers all in white? Do I not know as well as another that victory must always follow the right? This is no battle, but a great sacrifice of arms that is about to be celebrated, and Krishna himself is to be the high priest. When Drona and Bhīshma are overthrown, then will this sacrifice be suspended for an interval. When I am slain by Arjuna will the end begin, and when Duryodhana is killed by Bhīma all will be concluded. This is the great offering of the son of Dhritarāshtra. Let it not be defeated! Rather let us die by the touch of noble weapons there on the sacred field of Kurukshetra!" Remaining silent for a moment or two, Karna looked up again with a smile, and then, with the words: "Beyond death we meet again!" he bade a silent farewell to Krishna, and, alighting from his chariot, entered his own and was driven in silence back to Hastinapura.

Prithā and Karna

But Krishna was not the only person who could see the importance of Karna to the Kuru cause. It was the next morning, by the river-side, as he ended his devotions after bathing, that Karna, turning round, was surprised to find the aged Prithā, mother of the Pāndavas, waiting behind him. Dwelling in the household of Dhritarāshtra, and hearing constantly of preparations for war against her own sons, it had occurred to her distracted heart that if she could induce Duryodhana's ally to fight on their side, instead of against them, she would greatly increase for them the chances of victory.

Karna was standing with arms uplifted, facing the east, when she crept up behind him and waited trembling in his shadow till, when from very weariness she looked like a fading lotus, he at last turned round. Karna was startled at the encounter, but controlling himself he bowed gravely and said: "I, O Lady, am Karna, the son of Ādiratha the charioteer. Tell me what I can do for you!"

The little aged woman, in spite of her royal dignity, quivered at his words. "No, no!" she exclaimed eagerly. "Thou art my own child, and no son of a charioteer! Oh, be reconciled, I beg of thee, and make thyself known to thy brothers the Pāndavas! Do not, I entreat, engage in war against them!" And as she spoke a voice came from the sun itself, saying: "Listen, O Karna, to the words of thy mother!"

But Karna's heart was devoted to righteousness, and even the gods could not draw him away from it. He did not waver now, though entreated by his mother and father at once.

"Alas, my mother!" he said, "how should you now demand my obedience who were contented in my babyhood to leave me to die? Not even for my mother can I abandon Duryodhana, to whom I owe all I have. Yet one thing I promise. With Arjuna only will I fight. The number of your sons shall always be five, whether with me and without Arjuna, or with Arjuna and me slain!"

Then Prithā embraced Karna, whose fortitude kept him unmoved. "Remember," she said, "you have granted to four of your brothers the pledge of safety. Let that pledge be remembered in the heat of battle!" And giving him her blessing, she glided quietly away.

Karna leads the Host

Fifteen days of battle had gone by, ending with the death of the aged Drona, and before dawn on the sixteenth Duryodhana and his officers met together and installed Karna as commander-in-chief of the Kuru host. This was a war in which victory depended on slaughtering the rival commander, and now that he had lost two generals Duryodhana could not but be tempted to despondency regarding his own ultimate triumph. With each great defeat death crept nearer and nearer to himself, and he truly felt now that the command of Karna was his last stake, and that all depended for him on its success. Bhīshma might have been accused of undue partiality towards the men whom he had loved as children. Drona might have had a secret tenderness for his favourite pupils. But Karna's whole life had been bent towards the single end of combat with Arjuna to the death. Here was one who would on no account shirk the ordeal. And Karna, in truth, was repeating his vow for the slaughter of the Pāndavas when he took his place in battle. No man can see always clearly into the future, and from him now, the hour of his vision being past, the event was hidden as completely as from any other. He could only hope, like Arjuna, that he, and he alone, was destined to succeed.

The sixteenth day of battle opened and passed. Karna had arranged the Kurus in the form of a great bird, and Arjuna spread out the Pāndavas to oppose them as a crescent. But though he sought him earnestly all that day throughout the length and breadth of the battle-field, Karna was never able to encounter Arjuna face to face. Then night fell, and the two armies rested.

At dawn the next morning Karna sought out Duryodhana.

This, he declared, was to be the great day of destiny. At nightfall without doubt the Pāndavas would sleep amongst the slain and Duryodhana stand undisputed monarch of the earth. Only he must recapitulate the points of superiority on each side. And then he proceeded to tell the king of the divine weapons that he and Arjuna possessed. If Arjuna had Gāndīva, he himself had Vijaya. In respect of their bows they were not unequal. It was true that Arjuna's quivers were inexhaustible, but Karna could be followed by supplies of arrows in such abundance that this advantage would not tell. Finally, Arjuna had Krishna himself for his charioteer. And Karna desired to have a certain king who was famous throughout the world for the knowledge of horses for his.

This was readily arranged, and with a king for his charioteer Karna went out to lead the battle on the day of destiny.

Hither and thither on the field sped Karna that day, constantly seeking for the deadly encounter. But though he met one and another of the Pāndavas, held him at his mercy, and then, perhaps remembering his promise to Prithā, allowed him to depart, he and Arjuna nowhere met. It was not till noon was past that Arjuna, stringing his bow and speeding a shaft, while Karna, though in sight, was yet too far off to intervene, slew Vrishasena, the son of his rival. At this sight, filled with wrath and grief, Karna advanced in his chariot upon Arjuna, looking as he came like the surging sea, and shooting arrows like torrents of rain to right and left. Behind him waved his standard with its device of the elephant rope. His steeds were white, and his car was decked with rows of little bells. He himself stood out against the sky with all the splendour of the rainbow itself. At the sound of his great bowstring Vijaya all things broke and fled from him in fear. On, on he came, with his royal charioteer, toward the point where Arjuna awaited the onset. "Be cool! Be cool!" whispered Krishna to the Pāndava; "now, verily, have you need of all your divine weapons!"

The Supreme Struggle

A moment later the two heroes, resembling each other so remarkably in person and accoutrements, like angry elephants, like infuriated bulls, had closed in mortal combat. And all the spectators held their breath, and for a moment the battle itself stood still, while involuntarily the question rose in every mind which of these two would emerge the victor. Karna was like a stake cast by the Kurus, and Arjuna by the Pāndavas. It was only for a moment, and then on both sides the air rang with trumpets and drums and acclamations, all sounded for the encouraging of one or other of the combatants.

Fiercely they challenged each other and fiercely joined in fight. And it was even said that their two standards fell upon each other and closed in conflict.

Then each of the two heroes, raining arrows upon the other, darkened the whole sky. And each baffled the other's weapons with his own, like the east and west winds struggling against each other. Wound upon wound they dealt each other, but as long as they were not mortal neither seemed to feel. Then the arrows of Arjuna covered the chariot of Karna like a flock of birds darkening the sky as they flew to roost. But each one of those shots was deflected by an arrow of Karna. Then Arjuna shot a dart of fire. And as he did so he himself stood illuminated in the blaze, and the garments of the soldiers about him were in danger of burning. But even that arrow was quenched by Karna shooting one of water.

Then Gāndīva poured forth arrows like razors, arrows like crescents, arrows like joined hands and like boars' ears. And these pierced the limbs, the chariot, and the standard of Karna. Then Karna in his turn called laughingly to mind the divine weapon Bhargava, and with it cut off all the arrows of Arjuna and began to afflict the whole Pāndava host. And showering innumerable darts, the son of the charioteer stood in the midst, with all the beauty of a thunder-cloud pouring down rain. And urged on by the shouts of those about them, both put forth redoubled energy.

Suddenly the string of Gāndīva with a loud noise broke, and Karna poured out his arrows in swift succession, taking advantage of the interval thus given. By this time the troops of the Kurus, thinking the victory was already theirs, began to cheer and shout. This only drew forth greater energy from Arjuna, and he succeeded in wounding Karna again and again. Then Karna shot five golden arrows which were in truth five mighty snakes, followers of one Ashwasena, whose mother Arjuna had slain. And these arrows passed each one through the mark and would have returned to Karna's hand that had sent them forth. Then Arjuna shot at them and cut them to pieces on the way, and perceived that they had been snakes. And his wrath so blazed that he shouted in his anger, and so deeply pierced Karna with his darts that the son of the charioteer trembled with pain. At the same moment all the Kurus deserted their leader and fled, uttering a wail of defeat. But Karna, when he saw himself left alone, felt no fear or bitterness, and threw himself only the more cheerfully upon his foe.

And now the mighty snake Ashwasena, beholding the point that the contest had reached, and desiring to gratify his own hatred of Arjuna, entered into the quiver of Karna. And he, eager at any cost to prevail over his enemy, and unaware that Ashwasena had entered into the shaft, set his heart upon that one particular arrow that he had kept in his quiver for the fatal blow.

Then said his charioteer: "This arrow, O Karna, will not succeed. Find thou another that will strike off his head!" But the warrior answered haughtily: "Karna never changes his arrow. Seek not to stain a soldier's honour!"

Having said these words, he drew his bow and sped that arrow which he had worshipped to this end for many a long year. And it made a straight line across the firmament as it sped toward Arjuna through the air.

But Krishna, understanding the nature of the arrow, pressed down his foot so that Arjuna's car sank a cubit's depth into the earth. The horses also instantly knelt down, and that arrow carried away the diadem of Arjuna, but injured not his person.

Then the arrow returned to the hand of Karna and said in a low voice: "Speed me once more, and I will slay thy foe!"

But Karna answered: "Not by the strength of another does Karna conquer. Never shall I use the same arrow twice!"

Then, the hour of his death having come, the earth itself began to swallow the wheel of Karna's car, and the son of the charioteer, reeling with pain and weariness, bethought him of another divine weapon. But Arjuna, seeing this speed forth, cut it off with another; and when Karna began to aim at his bowstring, not knowing that he had a hundred ready, the ease with which he replaced the broken strings seemed to his enemy like magic.

At this moment the earth swallowed up one of Karna's wheels completely, and he called out: "In the name of honour, cease shooting while I lift my chariot!"

But Arjuna replied: "Where was honour, O Karna, when the queen was insulted?" and would not stop even for an instant.

Then Karna shot an arrow that pierced Arjuna and caused him to reel and drop the bow Gāndīva. Taking advantage of the opportunity, Karna leapt from his chariot and strove without avail to extricate the wheel. While he was doing this Arjuna, recovering, aimed a sharp arrow and brought down the standard of his foe—that splendid standard wrought in gold with the cognizance of the elephant rope. As they saw the banner of the commander fall despair seized the watching Kurus, and the cry of defeat rose loudly on the wind. Then, hastening to act before Karna could regain his place on his chariot, Arjuna swiftly took out Anjalikā, the greatest of all his arrows, and, fixing it on Gāndīva, shot it straight at the throat of his enemy, and the head of Karna was severed at the stroke. And the rays of the setting sun lighted up that fair face with their beauty as it fell and rested, like a lotus of a thousand petals, on the blood-stained earth. And all the Pāndavas broke out into shouts of victory. But Duryodhana wept for the son of the charioteer, saying: "Oh, Karna! Oh, Karna!" And when Karna fell the rivers stood still, the sun set in pallor, the mountains with their forests began to tremble, all creatures were in pain; but evil things and the wanderers of the night were filled with joy.

XIV. THE GREAT HOST OF THE DEAD

That was a terrible hour for the Pāndavas in which, with their own hearts full of grief for the bereavements of battle, they had to meet with the aged Dhritarāshtra and Gandhārī his queen, deprived as they now were of their whole century of sons. The victory of Kurukshetra had made Yudhishthira king of the whole country, and this fact Dhritarāshtra recognized by announcing his intention of giving up the world and retiring with Gandhārī and Prithā to the Ganges side, there to live out their lives in piety and prayer. For the first month the Pāndava princes accompanied them and stayed with them in order to pray with them for their own illustrious dead. And at the close of the month they were visited by Vyāsa, the chief of the royal chaplains, a man famous for his gifts of spirituality and learning. Seated with Vyāsa, Gandhārī, Kuntī, and Dhritarāshtra talked out many an old grief and sought the explanation of mysteries that had long puzzled them.

Then turning to Gandhārī in reverence for the sorrow that was greater than any borne by woman, and speaking to the heart that had no words to utter, Vyāsa said: "Listen, O queen! I have a blessing to bestow. To-night ye shall all see again your children and kinsmen, like men risen out of sleep. Thus shall your sorrow be lightened and your heart set at rest."

Then the whole party, scarcely able to believe that the words of Vyāsa would be fulfilled, took up their position in expectation on the banks of the Ganges. The day went by, seeming to them, in their eagerness to look again upon the deceased princes, like a year. But at last the sun set, and all ended their evening bathing together with their worship. When night came and all were seated in groups and in lonely and sheltered places along the banks of the Ganges, Vyāsa went forward and summoned in a clear voice the dead of both sides to grant themselves once more to mortal vision that hearts aching with sorrow might be comforted a space.

The Procession

Then a strange sound was heard from within the waters, and gradually, in their ranks and companies, with splendour of shining forms and banners and cars, rose all the kings, and with them all their troops. There were Duryodhana and all the sons of Gandhārī and Dhritarāshtra. There were Bhīshma and Drona and Karna. There was Shikhandin and there was Drupada, and there were a thousand others. All were robed in heavenly vesture and brilliantly adorned. They were free from pride and anger and divested of all jealousy. The scene was like some high festival of happiness, or it looked like a picture painted on the canvas. And Dhritarāshtra the king, blind all his life, saw his sons for the first time, with the eye of a quickened vision, and knew in all its keenness the joy of fatherhood.

And the dead came forward and mingled with the living. There was no grief, no fear, no suspicion, and no discontent on that hallowed night. Karna accepted Kuntī as his mother and became reconciled with the Pāndavas as his brothers. And the aching sorrow of Gandhārī for Duryodhana and the rest of her children was appeased.

And when dawn approached, those shades of the mighty dead plunged once more into the Ganges and went each to his own abode, and the living, with sorrow lightened, turned to the duties of life and set about the tasks that lay before them.

XV. YUDHISHTHIRA AND HIS DOG

A time came in the development of Hinduism when religion turned its back on all the deities of power and worldly good. The god, like his worshipper, must eschew wealth and material benefits. Since five hundred years before the Christian era the Buddhist orders had been going up and down amongst the people popularizing certain great conceptions of renunciation and personal development as the true end of religion. About the time of the Christian era the volume of these ideas was becoming ripe for the taking of organized shape, in India itself, as a new faith. But the evolution did not cease at this point with the emergence of the worship of Shiva. Some few centuries later a new phase of this higher Hinduism was again elaborated, and the worship of Satya-Nārāyana appeared in his embodiment as Krishna. This religion was laid down and promulgated in the form of a great epic—the Indian national epic *par excellence*—which was now cast into its final form, the Mahābhārata.

In the opinion of some amongst the learned we have here in the Mahābhārata a recapitulation of all the old wonder-world of the early sky-gazer. Gods, heroes, and demigods jostle each other through its pages, and whence they came and what has been their previous history we have only a name here or a sidelight there to help us to discover. As in some marvellous tapestry, they are here gathered together, in one case for a battle, in another for a life; and out of the clash of the foemen's steel, out of the loyalty of vassal and comrade, out of warring loves and conflicting ideals, is made one of the noblest of the scriptures of the world. Is it true that, with the exception of what has been added and remoulded by a supreme poet, fusing into a single molten mass the images of æons past, most of the characters that move with such ease across these inspiring pages have stepped down from the stage of the midnight sky? However this may be, one thing is certain: the very last scene that ends the long panorama is that of a man climbing a mountain, followed by a dog, and finally, with his dog, translated to Heaven in the flesh.

The Pilgrimage of Death

The five royal heroes for whose sake the battle of their prime was fought and won have held the empire of India for some thirty-six years, and now, recognizing that the time for the end has come, they, with Draupadī their queen, resign their throne to their successors and set forth on their last solemn journey—the pilgrimage of death—followed by a dog who will not leave them. First circling their great realm in the last act of kingly worship, they proceed to climb the heights of the Himālayas, evidently by way of ascending to their rightful places amongst the stars. He who has lived in the world without flaw may hope for translation at the last. But, great as is the glory of the Pāndava brothers, only one of them, Yudhishthira, the eldest, is so unstained by life as to merit this, the honour of reaching Heaven in the flesh. One by one the others, Bhīma, Arjuna, and the twins Nakula and Sahādev, together with Draupadī the queen, faint and fall and die. And still without once looking back, without groan or sigh, Yudhishthira and the dog proceed alone.

Suddenly a clap of thunder arrests their steps, and in the midst of a mass of brightness they see the god Indra, King of Heaven, standing in his chariot. He is there to carry Yudhishthira back with him to Heaven, and immediately begs him to enter the chariot.

It is here, in the emperor's answer, that we are able to measure how very far the Hindu people have gone since the early worship of purely cosmic deities, in the moralizing and spiritualizing of their deities and demi-gods. Yudhishthira refuses to enter the chariot unless his dead brothers are all first recalled to enter it with him, and adds, on their behalf, that they will none of them accept the invitation even then unless with them be their queen, Draupadī, who was the first to fall. Only when he is assured by Indra that his brothers and wife have preceded him and will meet him again on his arrival in the state of eternal felicity does he consent to enter the divine chariot, and stand aside to let the dog go first.

The Dog

But here Indra objected. To the Hindu the dog is unholy. It was impossible to contemplate the idea of a dog in Heaven! Yudhishthira is begged, therefore, to send away the dog. Strange to say, he refuses. To him the dog appears as one who has been devoted, loyal in time of loss and disaster, loving and faithful in the hour of entire solitude. He cannot imagine happiness, even in Heaven, if it were to be haunted by the thought of one so true who had been cast off.

The god pleads and argues, but each word only makes the sovereign more determined. His idea of manliness is involved. "To cast off one who has loved us is infinitely sinful." But also his personal pride and honour as a king are roused. He has never yet failed the terrified or the devoted, or such as have sought sanctuary with him, nor one who has begged mercy, nor any who

XV

YUDHISHTHIRA

NANDA LĀL BOSE

Page 212

was too weak to protect himself. He will certainly not infringe his own honour merely out of a desire for personal happiness.

Then the most sacred considerations are brought to bear on the situation. It must be remembered that the Hindu eats on the floor, and the dread of a dog entering the room is therefore easy to understand. There is evidently an equal dislike of the same thing in Heaven. "Thou knowest," urges Indra, "that by the presence of a dog Heaven itself would be defiled." His mere glance deprives the sacraments of their consecration. Why, then, should one who has renounced his very family so strenuously object to giving up a dog?

Yudhishthira answers bitterly that he had perforce to abandon those who did not live to accompany him further, and, admitting that his resolution has probably been growing in the course of the debate, finally declares that he cannot now conceive of a crime that would be more heinous than to leave the dog.

The test is finished. Yudhishthira has refused Heaven for the sake of a dog, and the dog stands transformed into a shining god, Dharma himself, the God of Righteousness. The mortal is acclaimed by radiant multitudes, and seated in the chariot of glory, he enters Heaven in his mortal form.

Even now, however, the poet has not made clear all that is to be required of a perfect man elevated alone to a position of great glory. Yudhishthira, entering Heaven, beholds his enemies, the heroes with whom he has contended, seated on thrones and blazing with light. At this the soul of the emperor is mightily offended. Are the mere joys of the senses to be accepted by him, he argues in effect, as any equivalent for the delight of good company? Where his comrades are will be Heaven for him—a place inhabited by the personages he sees before him deserves a very different name.

Yudhishthira, therefore, is conducted to a region of another quality. Here, amidst horrors of darkness and anguish, his energy is exhausted and he orders his guide angrily to lead him away. At this moment sighing voices are heard in all directions begging him to stay. With him comes a moment of relief for all the souls imprisoned in this living pain of sight and sound and touch.

Yudhishthira in Hell

Involuntarily the emperor paused. And then as he stood and listened he realized with dismay that the voices to which he was listening were familiar. Here, in Hell, were his kinsmen and comrades. There, in Heaven, he had seen the great amongst his foes. Anger blazed up within him. Turning to the messenger, who had not yet left him—"Go!" he thundered in his wrath, "return to the high gods, whence thou camest, and make it known to them that never shall I look upon their faces again. What! evil men with them, and these my kinsfolk fallen into Hell! This is a crime! Never shall I return to them that wrought it. Here with my friends, in Hell, where my presence aids them, shall I abide for ever. Go!"

Swiftly the messenger departed, and Yudhishthira remained alone, with head sunk on his breast, brooding in Hell on the fate of all he loved.

Only a moment passed, and suddenly the scene was changed. The sky above them became bright. Sweet airs began to blow. All that had been foul and repulsive disappeared. And Yudhishthira, looking up, found himself surrounded by the gods. "Well done!" they cried.

"O lord of men, thy trials are ended and thou hast fought and won. All kings must see Hell as well as Heaven. Happy are they who see it first. For thee and these thy kin nothing remains save happiness and glory. Then plunge thou into the heavenly Ganges and put away in it thy mortal enmity and grief. Here, in the Milky Way, put on the body of immortality and then ascend thy throne. Be seated amongst the gods, great thou as Indra, alone of mortal men raised to Heaven in this thine earthly form!"

The Greatness of Self-Conquest

That process of spiritualizing which we see at its moment of inception in the story of Daksha and Shiva is here seen at its flowering-point. Thoroughly emancipated from the early worship of cosmic impressiveness and power, the Hero of the Sky appears no longer as a great Prajāpati, or Lord of Creation, nor even as the Wild Huntsman, slaying the winter sun, but entirely as a man, one of ourselves, only nobler. The Hindu imagination has now reached a point where it can conceive of nothing in the universe transcending in greatness man's conquest of himself. Yudhishthira shone amongst men in royal clemency and manly faithfulness and truth, even as now he shines amongst the stars. Whatever came to him he first renounced, and finally accepted on his own terms only. This was the demand that Buddhism, with the exaltation of character and detachment, had taught the Indian people to make of manly men. Greatest of all was the renunciation of the monk; but next to this, and a different expression of the same greatness, was the acceptance of life and the world as their master, not as their slave.

It cannot be denied that this story of Yudhishthira, with

its subtlety of incident and of character-drawing, is thoroughly modern in tone and grasp. The particular conception of loyalty which it embodies is one that is deeply characteristic of the Indian people. To them loyalty is a social rather than a military or political virtue, and it is carried to great lengths. We must remember that this tale of Yudhishthira will be in part the offspring and in part the parent of that quality which it embodies and extols. Because this standard was characteristic of the nation, it found expression in the epic. Because the epic has preached it in every village, in song and sermon and drama, these fifteen centuries past, it has moulded Indian character and institutions with increased momentum, and gone far to realize and democratize the form of nobility it praises. Would the Greek myths, if left to develop freely, have passed eventually through the same process of ethicizing and spiritualizing as the Indian? Is India, in fact, to be regarded as the sole member of the circle of classical civilizations which has been given its normal and perfect growth? Or must we consider that the early emergence of the idea of beauty and conscious effort after poetic effect supersedes in the Hellenic genius all that becomes in the Indian high moral interpretation? A certain aroma of poetry there cannot fail to be in productions that have engaged the noblest powers of man; but this in the Indian seems always to be unconscious, the result of beauty of thought and nobility of significance, while in the Greek we are keenly aware of the desire of a supreme craftsman for beauty as an end in itself.

CHAPTER IV : KRISHNA

Notes on Krishna

KRISHNA, son of Devakī, is barely mentioned in the *Chhāndogya Upanishad* (*c.* 500 B.C.). In the Mahābhārata (300 B.C.–200 A.D.) he is a prominent figure; in the *Bhagavad Gītā*, which is a late addition, there is first put forward the doctrine of *bhakti*, loving devotion to him as a means of salvation, additional to the ways of work and knowledge. No mention is made of his youthful gestes. He is represented as the friend and adviser of princes; he is essentially Dwārkānāth, the Lord of Dwārakā; he is identified with Vishnu in many passages, although in his human form he worships Mahādeva and Umā and receives gifts from them.

At a subsequent period, between the time of the compilation of the Gītā and that of the Vishnu and Bhāgavata Purānas, probably in the tenth or eleventh century, arose the worship of the boy-Krishna, the chief element in the modern cult. The boy-Krishna no doubt represents the local god of a Rājput clan. The names of Govinda and Gopāla (herdsman) indicate his origin as a god of flocks and herds.

A summary of the Mahābhārata has already been given; in the following pages, therefore, are related the more modern legends of Krishna's youth, with brief reference only to his doings in the Great War. What is given is essentially a condensed translation, compiled from various sources, particularly the *Vishnu Purāna*, the *Bhāgavata Purāna*, and the *Prem Sāgara*. At the close of the Third Age a Rājput clan, the Yādavas, descendants of Yadu, a prince of the Lunar dynasty, dwelt beside the Jamna, with Mathurā for their capital. Ugrasena, at the time of the beginning of the story, though the rightful king, had been deposed by his son Kans, a cruel and tyrannical ruler—in fact, a rākshasa begotten by violence on Ugrasena's wife Pavanarekhā. We thus find the rākshasas in possession of Mathurā, where some of the Yaduvamsīs also still dwell; but most of the latter reside with their flocks and herds at Gokula, or Braj, in the country, and are represented as paying annual tribute to Mathurā. There is thus, as in the Rāmāyana, a state of opposition between two ideal societies, a moral society wherein the gods become incarnate in heroic individuals, and an immoral society which it is their object to destroy. It is in response to the prayer of the outraged earth, wasted by the tyranny of Kans, and at the request of the gods, that Vishnu takes birth amongst the Yaduvamsīs at the same time with other heavenly beings—gods, rishis, kinnaras, gandharvas, and the like.

Such is the pseudo-historical legend of Krishna. This story, whatever its origins, has sunk deep into the heart and imagination of India. For this there are many reasons. It is the chief scripture of the doctrine of *bhakti* (devotion) as a way of salvation. This is a way that all may tread, of whatever rank or humble state. The *gopīs*[1] are the great type and symbol of those who find God by devotion (*bhakti*), without learning (*jnānam*). It is for Krishna that they forsake the illusion of family and all that their world accounts as duty; they leave all and follow him. The call of his flute is the irresistible call of the Infinite; Krishna is God, and Rādhā the human soul. It matters not that the Jamna and Brindāban are to be found on the map: to the Vaishnava lover Brindāban is the heart of man, where the eternal play of the love of God continues.

[1] *Gopīs*, herd-girls.

The Birth of Krishna

Vasudev was a descendant of Yadu, of the Lunar dynasty; he was married to Rohinī, daughter of King Rohan, and to him Kans also gave his own sister Devakī. Immediately after the marriage a heavenly voice was heard announcing: "O Kans, thy death will come to pass at the hand of her eighth son." Kans therefore resolved to slay Vasudev at once, and dissuaded from this, he did actually slay the sons one by one till six were dead. In Devakī's seventh pregnancy the serpent Shesh, or Ananta, on whom Nārāyana rests, took on a human birth. To save this child from Kans, Vishnu created a thought-form of himself and sent it to Mathurā. It took the babe from Devakī's womb and gave it to Rohinī, who had taken refuge with the herdsmen at Gokula, and was cared for by Nand and Yasodā, good people dwelling there, who had as yet no son of their own. The child born of Rohinī was afterwards called Balarāma. After transferring the child, the Sending of Vishnu returned to Devakī and revealed the matter in a dream, and Vasudev and Devakī gave Kans to understand that the child had miscarried.

Then Shrī Krishna himself took birth in Devakī's womb, and the Sending of Vishnu in Yasodā's, so that both were with child. Kans, when he learnt that Devakī was again pregnant, set a strong guard about the house of Vasudev to slay the child the moment it was born; for, much as he feared the prophecy, he dared not incur the sin of slaying a woman. At last Krishna was born, and all the heavens and earth were filled with signs of gladness—trees and forests blossomed and fruited, pools were filled, the gods rained down flowers, and gandharvas played on drums and pipes. But Krishna stood up before his father and mother, and this was the likeness of him—cloudy grey, moon-faced, lotus-eyed, wearing a crown and jewels and a robe of yellow silk, with four arms holding conch and disc and mace and lotus-flower. Vasudev and Devakī bowed down to him, and Shrī Krishna said to them: "Do not fear, for I have come to put away your fear. Take me to Yasodā, and bring her daughter and deliver her to Kans." Then he became again a human child, and the memory of his Godhead left both father and mother, and they thought only, "We have a son," and how they might save him from Kans.

Devakī, with folded palms, said to her husband: "Let us take him to Gokula, where dwell our friends Nand and Yasodā and your wife Rohinī." At that very moment the fetters fell from their limbs, the gateways opened, and the guards fell fast asleep. Then Vasudev placed Krishna in a basket on his head and set out for Gokula. He knew not how to cross the Jamna, but with thought intent on Vishnu he entered the water. It rose higher and higher till it reached his nose; but then Krishna saw his distress and stretched down his foot, and the water sank. So Vasudeva crossed the river and came to Nand's house, where a girl had been born to Yasodā; but Devī had put forgetfulness upon her so that she remembered nothing of it. Vasudeva exchanged the children and returned to Mathurā; and when he was back again with Devakī the fetters and the doors closed, the guards awoke, and the baby cried. Word was sent to Kans, and he went in terror, sword in hand, to his sister's house. A voice announced to him: "Thy enemy is born, and thy death is certain"; but finding that a girl had been born, he released Vasudeva and Devakī, and prayed their pardon for the past slayings and treated them well. But Kans was more than ever enraged against the gods forasmuch as they had deceived him and his guard-

XVI

THE BIRTH OF KRISHNA

NANDA LĀL BOSE

Page 220

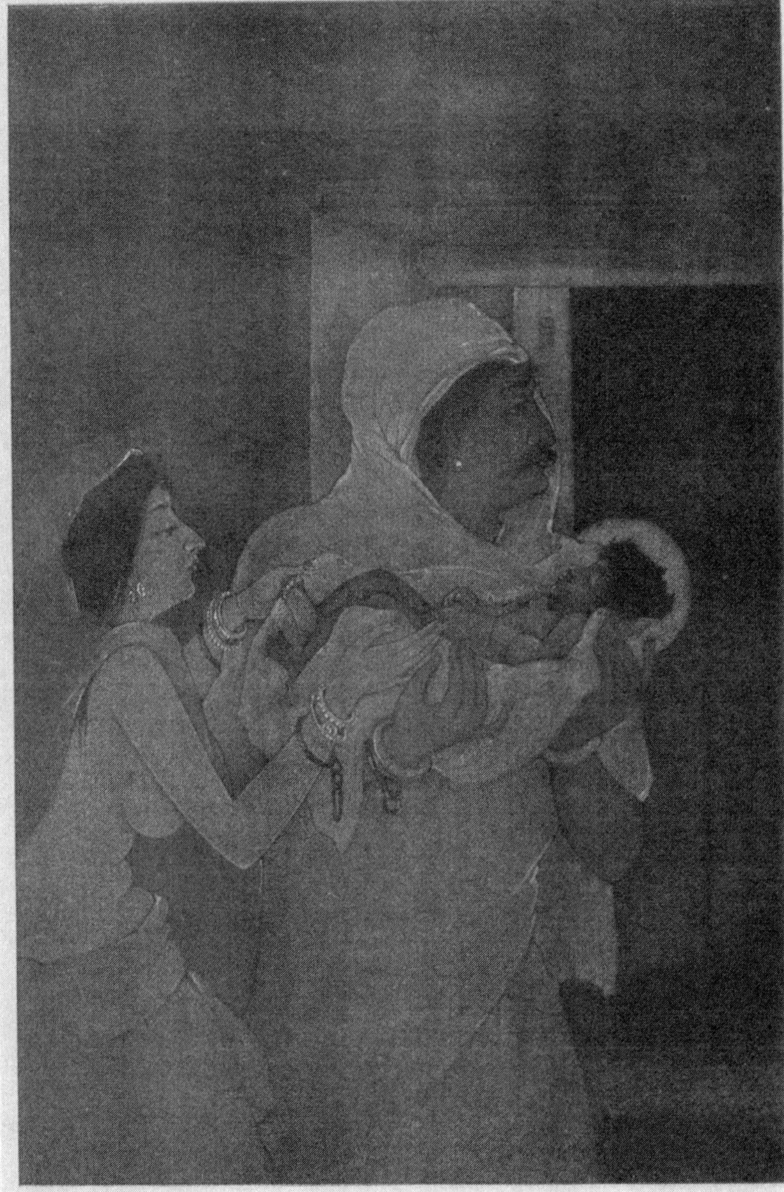

ing of Devakī had been in vain, and especially he longed to slay Nārāyana—that is, Vishnu. To this end his ministers counselled him to slay all those who served Vishnu, Brāhmans, yogīs, sannyāsis, and all holy men. Kans gave orders accordingly, and sent forth his rākshasas to kill cows and Brāhmans and all worshippers of Hari.

The Feats of Krishna's Youth

Meanwhile there were great rejoicings in Gokula for the birth of a son to Nand and Yasodā: the astrologers prophesied that the child would slay the demons and should be called Lord of the Herd-girls, the gopīs, and his glory should be sung throughout the world. But Kans knew not where Shrī Krishna had been born, and he sent out murderers to slay all children. Among his followers there was a rākshasī named Putana, who knew of the birth of Nand's son, and she went to Gokula for his destruction, taking the shape of a beautiful woman, but she had poison in her breasts. She went to Yasodā's house and made herself very friendly, and presently she took the boy on her lap and gave him her breast. But he held her tightly and drew hard, so that with the milk he took away her life. She fled away, but Krishna would not let her escape, and she fell dead, assuming her own hideous and huge form. Just then Nand returned from Mathurā, where he had gone for paying tribute; he found the rākshasī lying dead, and all the folk of Braj standing about her. They told him what had taken place, and then they burnt and buried her enormous body. But her body gave out a most sweet fragrance when it was burnt, and the reason for that was that Shrī Krishna had given her salvation when he drank her milk; blessed are all those whom Vishnu slays.

It was not long after this that a feast was held for rejoicings at the birth of Krishna; but he was forgotten in the general merry-making, and lay by himself under a cart. Now another rākshasī, passing by, saw that he lay there sucking his toes, and to avenge Putana she sat on the cart as if to crush it; but Krishna gave a kick and broke the cart and killed the demoness. All the pots of milk and curds in the cart were broken, and the noise of the broken cart and flowing milk brought all the herd-boys and herd-girls to the spot, and they found Krishna safe and sound. When Shrī Krishna was five months old another fiend came in the shape of a whirlwind to sweep him away from Yasodā's lap where he lay; but at once he grew so heavy that Yasodā had to lay him down. Then the storm became a cyclone, but no harm came to Krishna, for none could even lift him. But at last he allowed the whirlwind to take him up into the sky, and then, while the people of Braj were weeping and lamenting, Krishna dashed the rākshasa down and killed him, and the storm was over.

Krishna's Mischief

Krishna and Balarām grew up together in Gokula; their friends were the gopas and gopīs, the herd-boys and herd-girls; their hair was curly, they wore blue and yellow tunics, and crawled about and played with toys and used to catch hold of the calves' tails and tumble down; and Rohinī and Yasodā followed them about lest any accident should happen to them. But Krishna was very mischievous. He used to take away the pots of curds when the gopīs were asleep; when he saw anything on a high shelf he would climb up and pull it down and eat some of it, and spill or hide the rest. The gopīs used to go and complain of him to Yasodā, calling him a butter-thief;

and she found him, and told him he must not take the food from other people's houses. But he made up a plausible story, and said the gopīs had fed him themselves or asked him to do some work for them; and now, he said, "they are telling tales of me." So Krishna always got the best of it.

One day he was playing with Balarām in the courtyard and ate some clay, and one of his comrades told Yasodā, and she came with a switch to beat him. But he had wiped his mouth and denied all knowledge of the matter. However, Yasodā insisted on looking inside his mouth; but when he opened his mouth what she saw there was the whole universe, the "Three Worlds." Then she said to herself: "How silly am I to think that the Lord of the Three Worlds could be my son." But Vishnu again veiled his Godhead, and Yasodā fondled the child and took him home.

Another time, when he had been stealing butter and Yasodā was going to beat him, she found him with his comrades sitting in a circle, and Krishna was eating and giving others to eat. Then Krishna, seeing his mother, ran up to her, saying: "O mother, I don't know who upset the buttermilk; let me go." So she could only laugh; but she took him home and tied him to a big wooden mortar to keep him out of mischief. But he just then remembered that two men had once been cursed by Nārada to remain in the form of trees till Krishna should release them, and he dragged the mortar after him and went to the grove where the trees were, and pulled the trees up by the roots. Two men appeared in their place: Krishna promised them a boon, and they prayed that their hearts might always be attached to him. This Krishna granted, and dismissed them. Presently

Yasodā came and found that Krishna was gone, and she ran everywhere to seek him; but when the gopīs found him by the fallen trees and heard what had happened they wondered how such things could be, and asked each other: "Who can comprehend the doings of Hari?" Not long after this Nand and Yasodā removed their goods and chattels from Gokula, where they suffered from constant dangers and oppression, and crossed the river to Brindāban and began to live there in peace and ease.

More Miracles of Krishna

When Krishna was five years old he took the cattle out into the woods to graze; that day Kans sent a demon in the shape of a crane, and he came to Brindāban and sat on the river-bank like a mountain. All the herd-boys were frightened; but Krishna went up to the crane and allowed it to take him up in its huge beak. Then Krishna made himself so hot that the crane was glad to put him out, and then he held open the crane's jaws and tore them apart; and collecting the calves, the herd-boys all went home with Krishna, laughing and playing.

Another time Kans sent a dragon named Aghāsur; he came and hid himself in the woods with his mouth open. The herd-boys thought this open hole was a mountain cave, and they all went near and looked in. Just then the dragon drew in his breath, and all the gopas and calves were swept into his mouth and felt the poisonous hot vapour, and cried out in distress. Krishna heard that and jumped into the dragon's mouth too, and then the mouth was shut. But Krishna made himself bigger and bigger till the dragon's stomach burst, and all the herd-boys and calves fell out unhurt.

More Miracles of Krishna

Another time Krishna and all the gopas were feasting and laughing and talking in the woods, leaving the calves to graze, when Brahmā came and stole away the calves. Krishna went to look for them and did not find them, but he created another herd just like them. Then he came back to the feasting-place and found the boys gone too, and he made others in their likeness and went home in the evening with the changeling boys and calves, and nobody but Krishna knew that the real children and calves had been hidden by Brahmā in a mountain cave. Meanwhile a year went by; it was only a moment of time as it seemed to Brahmā, but it was a year for men. Brahmā remembered his doings and went to see what had happened. He found the boys and the calves asleep in the cave; then he went to Brindāban, and found the boys and the calves there too. And Krishna made all the herd-boys into the likeness of gods, with four arms and the shape of Brahmā and Rudra and Indra. Seeing this, the Creator was struck with astonishment; still as a picture, he forgot himself, and his thoughts wandered away. He was afflicted like an unworshipped, unhonoured stone image. But Krishna, when he saw that Brahmā was thus afraid, drew back all those illusory forms into himself, and Brahmā fell at Krishna's feet and prayed his pardon, saying: "All things are enchanted by thy illusion; but who can bewilder thee? Thou art the creator of all, in whose every hair are many such Brahmās as I. Thou compassionate to the humble, forgive my fault." Then Krishna smiled, and Brahmā restored all the herd-boys and calves. When they awoke they knew nothing of the time that had passed, but only praised Krishna for finding the calves so quickly; then they all went home.

The Quelling of Kālīya

One day the cowherds started out very early, and wandered through the woods and along the river-bank till they came to the place called Kālīya. They drank some of the water, and so did the cows; but all at once they rolled over and over and were dying of poison. Then Krishna cast a life-giving look upon them, and they revived.

Now there was living in that part of the Jamna a poisonous hydra or naga named Kālīya, and for four leagues all about him the water boiled and bubbled with poison. No bird or beast could go near, and only one solitary tree grew on the river-bank. The proper home of Kālīya was Ramanaka Dwīpa, but he had been driven away from there by fear of Garuda, the foe of all serpents. Garuda had been cursed by a yogī dwelling at Brindāban, so that he could not come to Brindāban without meeting his death. Therefore Kālīya lived at Brindāban, the only place where Garuda could not come.

Presently Krishna began to play at ball with the herd-boys, and while they were playing he climbed up the *kadamb* tree that hung over the river-bank, and when the ball was thrown to him it fell into the river, and Shrī Krishna jumped after it. Kālīya rose up with his hundred and ten hoods vomiting poison, and Krishna's friends stretched out their hands and wept and cried, and the cows ran about lowing and snorting. Meanwhile some one ran back to Brindāban and brought Rohinī and Yasodā and Nand and all the gopas and gopīs, and they came running and stumbling to the edge of Kālīya's whirlpool; but they could not see Krishna. Only Balarām comforted every one, saying: "Krishna will come back very soon. He cannot be slain."

XVII

KĀLĪYA DAMANA

KHITINDRA NĀTH MAZUMDAR

Page 226

The Quelling of Kālīya

Meanwhile Kālīya wrapped himself round about Krishna's body, but Krishna became so huge that Kālīya had to release him. So Krishna saved himself from every attack, and when he saw the Braj folk were so much afraid he suddenly sprang into Kālīya's head and assumed the weight of the whole universe, and danced on the nāga's heads, beating time with his feet. Then Kālīya began to die. He dashed his hoods about, putting forth his tongues, and streams of blood poured from his mouths. When he was quite overcome the thought arose in his heart: "This must be the Primal Male, for none other could resist my venom"; so thinking, he gave up all hope and remained still. But then the nāga's wives came and stood round Krishna, and some stretched out their folded hands toward him and some bent to kiss his feet, worshipping Krishna and praying for their husband. "Be pleased to release this one," they said, "or slay us with him, for death itself is good to a woman without a husband. Moreover, please consider that it is the nature of a serpent to be venomous, and pardon him." Shrī Krishna stepped from Kālīya's head, and Kālīya worshipped him and prayed forgiveness for not recognizing the Lord. So Krishna pardoned him, and sent him away home to Ramanaka Dwīpa. But he was afraid to go there because of Garuda. When he told Krishna this he answered: "Go without fear. When Garuda sees the mark of my feet on your head he will not touch you." So Kālīya with his family went to Ramanaka Dwīpa, and Krishna came out of the water.

All the people of Braj were glad when Krishna came out safe; but they were too weary to go home that day, so they spent the night in the woods near Kālīya's whirlpool. But about midnight a terrible forest fire broke out, and would have destroyed the trees and the cows and the people had not Shrī Krishna risen and drunk up the fire and saved them. In the morning every one returned to their homes rejoicing and singing.

Krishna's Flute

Now the hot season came on, but because of Krishna there was only perpetual spring in Brindāban. One day a rākshasa came in the form of a cowherd, and played with the others; but Krishna made a sign to Balarām and told him to kill the demon, but not in his cowherd shape. So Balarām let the demon carry him off on his back as if in play, and when they were some distance off, and the rākshasa took his own form to kill Balarām, suddenly Balarām knocked him down and slew him. While this had been going on the cows had wandered away, and the cowherds could not find them in the woods; but Krishna climbed up a kadamb tree and played his flute, and at once the cows and the boys came running to him, like the waters of a river that meets the sea.

Krishna used often to play his flute in the woods; all the herd-girls in Braj, when they heard it, would go out and look for him; but they could not find him, and had to wait till he came back again in the evening. So they sat down together in the road and talked of the flute. One said: "Just see how that bamboo tube is honoured; drinking the nectar of Krishna's lips all day, it resounds like a cloud and pours out delight. Why is it more beloved than we? This thing made before our very eyes has become like a rival wife! Even the gods attend when Krishna plays his flute. What discipline has it performed that all things are obedient to it?" Another gopī replied: "First, when it grew in the bamboo stem, it remembered Hari; then it endured heat and cold and water; and lastly, cut to pieces, it breathed the smoke of its own burning. Who else performs such mortifications? The flute was made perfect and has its reward." Then another Braj woman exclaimed: "Why did not the lord of Braj make flutes of us, to remain with him day and night?"

Once in the winter-time, when it was cold and frosty, the Braj girls went down to bathe in the Jamna together. They made an image of Devī and worshipped it with flowers and fruit and incense, and prayed: "O goddess, do thou grant that Shrī Krishna may be our lord." Then they fasted all day and bathed, and when night came they slept by the river-side, to the end that Devī would grant their prayer.

Krishna steals the Gopīs' Clothes

Another day they went to a lonely place to bathe and laid all their clothes on the bank, and played in the water and sang their songs in praise of Hari. But Shrī Krishna himself was sitting near by in a tree watching his cows. Hearing their songs, he came near very quietly and looked on; then he saw the clothes, and a thought came into his mind, and he took the clothes and climbed up a kadamb tree. Presently the gopīs came out of the water, and could not find their clothes. They looked everywhere to find them, till at last one girl looked up and saw Shrī Krishna sitting in the tree with the bundle of clothes. He was wearing a crown and yellow robes, and had a staff in his hand, and he had a garland of flowers. So she called out to the others: "There he is, who steals our hearts and our clothes, up in the kadamb tree." Then all the girls were ashamed and jumped into the water to hide themselves, and stood there praying Krishna to give them their clothes. But he would not give them; and, "by Nand," he said, "you must come out and fetch them."

The Braj girls were not very pleased at that, and they said: "That is a nice thing for you to ask; but we shall go and tell our fathers and friends and Nand and Yasodā, and they will punish you. Thou it is that shouldst protect our husbands' honour. And it is for thy sake we are bathing and keeping our vows."

Then Krishna answered: "If you are really and truly bathing for my sake, then cast away shame and receive your clothes." Then the gopīs said to themselves: "What Hari says, that alone we ought to respect; he knows all our body and mind; what shame in this?" And they came up out of the water with downcast looks.

But Krishna laughed and said: "Now with joined hands come forward and take the clothes." The gopīs answered: "Darling of Nand, why dost thou deceive us? We are simple Braj girls"; but they joined hands, and Krishna gave them the clothes.

Then the gopīs went home, and Krishna followed with the herd-boys and cows. But as he went he looked again and again at the deep forest all round about, and began to tell of the glory of trees. "Behold," he said, "these that have come into the world, what burdens they bear and what shelter they give to others. It is good that such kindly folk are here."

Krishna lifts a Mountain

The people of Braj had been wont to worship Indra, king of heaven and lord of rain. Once, when they had made an offering to Indra, Krishna came and persuaded them to give up his worship. "Indra is no supreme deity," said he, "though he is king in heaven; he is afraid of the asuras. And the rain that you pray for, and prosperity, these depend on the sun, that draws up the waters and makes them fall again. What can Indra do? What virtue and fate determine, alone comes to pass." Then Krishna taught them to worship the woods and streams and hills, and especially Mount Govardhan. So they brought offerings of flowers and fruits and sweetmeats for the mountain, and when Nand and Yasodā stood before the mountain, with minds intent on him, Krishna assumed a second form, like that of the mountain god, and received the offerings. In his own form he still remained with Nand and worshipped the mountain king. That mountain received the offerings and ate them up, so that all the people of Braj were glad.

But Indra was greatly enraged at the loss of his honour and gifts; he sent for the King of the Clouds, and ordered him to rain over Braj and Govardhan till both were swept away. So an army of clouds surrounded the district of Braj and began to pour down sheets of water, so that it seemed that the end of the world was at hand. Then all the Braj folk, with Nand and Yasodā, came to Krishna and said: "You persuaded us to give up the worship of Indra; now bring the mountain here to protect us." So Krishna filled Govardhan with the burning heat of his energy and lifted him up on his little finger, and all the people of Braj, with the cows, took shelter under the mountain, looking at Krishna in utter astonishment. Meanwhile the rain that fell on the mountain hissed and evaporated, and although torrents of water rained for seven days, not even a drop fell in Braj. Then Indra gave up the conflict, for he knew that none but an incarnation of the Primal Male could have thus withstood him. Next day when Krishna and Balarām went out to graze the cows, with music of flute and song, Indra came down from heaven upon his elephant Airavata and fell at the feet of Krishna and made submission.

The Dance of Love

The time Krishna had stolen the gopīs' clothes he made a promise to dance with them in the month of Kārttik, and they had ever since been eagerly waiting for the appointed time. At last the autumn came, when heat and cold and rain were finished and all the country was full of delight; and Krishna went out on the night of full moon in Kārttik. A gentle air was blowing, the stars shone bright and clear, and all the woods and meadows were bathed in moonlight; so Krishna determined to fulfil his promise, and went toward the forest playing his flute. The Braj girls were restless and disturbed at the sound of the flute, calling them away from their homes, till at last they cast off the illusion of family, put off their shame, and left their household duties, decked themselves hurriedly, and ran out to Krishna. One as she went was stopped by her husband and brought back to her house and bound; but she set her mind only on Hari, and so left her body and came to him first, before all the others, and Krishna, because of her love, gave her full salvation.

Now she did not think that Krishna was God when she died for his love; it was as a man she desired him. How, then, could she come by salvation? Even if one should drink the water of life unknowingly, still he will be immortal; just such is the fruit of worshipping Hari. There were many that won salvation through him, howsoever diverse their will toward him. Nand and Yasodā deemed him their son; the gopīs thought him their lover;

Kans did him honour by fear; the Pāndavas found him a friend; Shishupāl honoured him as a foe; the Yaduvamsīs thought he was one of themselves; the yogīs and rishis pondered upon him as God; but all these alike attained salvation. What wonder, then, if one herd-girl, fixing her heart upon him, should reach the farther shore of existence?

At last the gopīs, following the sound of the flute, came upon Krishna deep in the forest, and stood gazing upon his loveliness, astonished and abashed. Then Krishna inquired of their welfare and blamed them for leaving their husbands; and he said: "As it is, you have seen the dense forest, the silvery moonlight, the beautiful banks of the Jamna; so now go home to your husbands." All the gopīs, when they heard these cruel words, were stricken senseless and sank in a boundless ocean of thought, and the tears fell from their eyes like a broken necklace of pearls. At last they found words to reproach him. "O Krishna," they said, "you are a great deceiver. You led us away by your flute and stole our hearts and minds and wealth, and now you are cold and unkind and would put an end to our lives. We have abandoned clan and home and husband, and despised the reproach of the world; now there is none to protect us but you, O Lord of Braj. Where shall we go and make our home, for we are enwrapped in love of you?"

Then Shrī Krishna smiled and called them near, and asked them to dance with him, and made them glad. Then by his skill he formed a golden terrace in a circle on the Jamna bank, and it was planted all about with plantain-trees hung with wreaths and garlands of all manner of flowers. Then the gopīs went to a pool named Māna-sarowar, and decked themselves from head to foot, and were well apparelled in robes and jewels. They brought lutes and cymbals and began to play and sing and dance, while Govinda stood amidst them like a moon in a starry sky. So they altogether gave up restraint and shame and were intoxicate with love, and they thought of Krishna as now entirely their own.

But he saw their pride and left them alone; he took only Rādhā with him and vanished. Then all the gopīs were frightened and sad, and began to ask each other where Krishna had gone, and they began to search for him here and there, crying out: "Why have you left us, O Lord of Braj, who have surrendered all to thee?" At last they began to ask the trees and birds and beasts, as the fig-trees, the cuckoo, and the deer: "Has the Darling of Nand gone here or there?" At last they found the marks of his lotus feet, and near them the footprints of a woman; and then they came on a bed of leaves and a jewelled mirror beside it. They asked the mirror where he had gone, and when there was no reply the pain of separation overwhelmed them altogether. Thus for their part the gopīs were miserably searching for Krishna; but Rādhā was full of delight and fancied herself the greatest of all, and grew so proud that she asked Shrī Krishna to carry her on his shoulders. But just when she would have climbed up he vanished away, and she stood there alone with hands outstretched, like moonlight without the moon or lightning without its clouds; so fair she was that her radiance streamed upon the ground and made it shine like gold. She stood there and wept, and all the birds and beasts and trees and creepers were crying with her.

The gopīs found her standing there, and they were as glad to see her as anyone would be who had lost a great treasure and found the half of it. They embraced her

XVIII

RĀDHĀ AND KRISHNA

KHITINDRA NĀTH MAZUMDAR

Page 234

again and again, and then entered the forest with her to search for Krishna. As far as there was any moonlight they went; but when they could find no path in the dark forest, they had to come back. They sat them down on Jamna bank, and talked of Krishna and cried out for him till they were faint and tired; but still he did not come.

Now when Krishna saw that the gopīs were dying for love he appeared again in their midst, so that they all came up out of the ocean of loneliness and were glad, for he said to them: "This I have done to try you. How can I now reward you enough? For like a *vairāgī* leaving his home and giving his heart to God, you have come to me." Then Krishna played and danced with the gopīs. He made his appearance manifold and danced with them in a ring, so that each one thought that Krishna himself was by her side and held her hands; so they whirled round in a circle, the dark Krishna and fair Braj girls, like a gold and sapphire necklace. Then some of them played on their lutes and sang in many modes; so rapt were they that mind and body were both forgotten. When one of them stopped the sound of flute with her hand and sang the notes of the flute herself, then Krishna forgot all else, as a child, seeing its face in a mirror, forgets everything else in its wonder. So they spent the time, and even the gods came down from heaven to see the dancing, and wind and water stood still to hearken. But when four watches yet remained of the night Krishna said it was time for the gopīs to go to their homes, and to comfort them he said: "Do you ever meditate upon me, as yogīs do, that I may always be near you." So they were satisfied and returned to their homes, and no one knew they had been away.

The Journey to Mathurā

When all other plans for slaying Krishna had failed Kans determined to lure him to Mathurā. He sent a messenger to Nand to invite the cowherds, with Krishna and Balarām, to a sacrifice to Shiva and sports and festivities to take place in Mathurā. This invitation was accepted, and all the Braj folk, with their flocks and herds and carts, set out for the city; only the herd-girls remained behind weeping, and stood with Yasodā watching to catch the last glimpse of Krishna and begging him to come back again soon.

The Braj folk, when they arrived at Mathurā, sent offerings to Kans, and made their camp outside the city. Krishna and Balarām went in to see the wonders of the town, with its great walls and palaces and gardens and groves. On the way they met a washerman and asked him for fine clothes, and when he laughed and refused they took them by force and made themselves very gay. Soon after they met a humpbacked woman, who prayed that Krishna would let her rub sandal-paste on his body; and he, for her deep devotion, went up to her, placing foot on foot, and with two fingers under her chin, lifted her up and made her straight and fair, and he said: "When I have slain Kans I will come and be with you."

The Tournament at Mathurā

Presently the brothers came to the lists where Shiva's bow was set up, huge as three palm-trees, and great and heavy; and Krishna went up to the bow and pulled it, and broke it in two with a great noise. When Kans heard that, he was terrified and saw death approaching; but he sent men out to kill the brothers. But they slew all the soldiers that Kans sent out against them, and returned to the cowherds' camp and said they had seen the city and had good sport, and now were tired and hungry; so Nand gave them food and they went to sleep. But Kans had evil dreams, and when he woke he gave orders to have the lists prepared for the tournament and the trumpets blown for assembly. Shrī Krishna and Balarām went to the tournament disguised as jugglers, and all the cowherds followed them. When they came to the gate of the lists there was a furious elephant, as strong as ten thousand common elephants, waiting, and the driver rode it at Krishna to crush him; but Balarām gave it such a blow with his fist that it turned back, and when it was driven against them again the two brothers killed it easily. Then they entered the lists, and to each Krishna appeared as their own nature revealed him: the wrestlers thought him a wrestler, the gods knew him as their lord, the herd-boys as a friend, the women of Mathurā thought him the treasure of beauty, and Kans and the rākshasas thought he was Death himself.

Soon Krishna had fought with all the king's wrestlers and slain the strongest; then he sprang up on the royal dais and dragged the king by his hair and killed him then and there, so that men and gods and saints were delighted. When the king's wives heard of this they came forth and mourned over him inconsolably, till Krishna comforted them with deep wisdom. "O Mother, grieve not," he said; "none may live and not die. He is mistaken who thinks that anything is his own. No one is father or mother or son; there is only the constant succession of birth and death." Then Kans' funeral rites were done by Jamna bank, and Krishna himself set light to the pyre. Then Krishna and Balarām went to Vasudeva and Devakī and set them free; and they, perceiving his form, knew him for God, till again he hid his Godhead, so that they thought him their son, and they embraced the two brothers gladly. Then Krishna established his grandfather Ugrasena upon the throne, and asking Nand to return to Brindāban, Krishna began to dwell with his friends in Mathurā. The Braj girls were always mourning for Krishna, for he did not return to Brindāban; but he sent a messenger, saying: "Do you now give up the hope of delight, and practise only devotion: I shall never be absent from you." Little did such a message comfort them when they thought of his flute and the dance, for they thought that prayer and vows and self-restraint more fitting for widows than for devoted hearts, and they thought the reason he stayed in Mathurā was that more beautiful women had won his love, or he preferred the court life to dwelling with cowherds. They sent a message back to say: "O Lord, you have spoken of spiritual union, while all the time there is disunion between us; but rather come back to us who are dying for love and save our lives." Yet there was no help for it, for that which had been could not be again as it had been.

About this time news came of the Kurus and Pāndavas, how the latter were sorely oppressed, and Krishna sent messengers to find out news of the matter; and the messenger went to Hastinapur and came again with the tale.

The Migration to Dwārakā

Meanwhile a rākshasa named Jurāsindhu, father-in-law of Kans, invaded Mathurā with a vast army; and though Krishna destroyed his army of demons, another asura, Kālayavan by name, surrounded Mathurā with another army of thirty million monstrous fiends. Then Krishna thought it well to depart; and he summoned Vishvakarmā and bade him prepare a great city amidst the sea, twelve leagues in extent, and to convey all the Yaduvamsīs thither without their being aware of it. So Vishvakarmā transported them all to the city in the sea, and when they awoke they marvelled how the sea had surrounded Mathurā, for they did not know what had happened.

Then leaving the people in Dwārakā, Krishna returned to Mathurā and slew Kālayavan; and Jurāsindhu gave him chase, but he escaped, and returned secretly with Balarām to Dwārakā, while Jurāsindhu possessed the city of Mathurā.

Now at that time there was born in Kundalpur a daughter of Rāja Bhīshmak, and she was most beautiful and gentle. When Shrī Krishna heard of this his heart was set upon her night and day. She also heard of Krishna, in this wise: there had come to Kundalpur some wandering yogīs, who sang the praise and high deeds of him, and they came also to court and recited their tales, and Rukminī heard as she sat in her high balcony, so that the vine of love sprang up in her breast. Thereafter night and day she thought of nothing but Krishna; sleeping and waking, or eating or playing, her mind was set upon him. She made an image of Gaurī, and prayed her to give her the Lord of the Yadus for husband. By this time Rukminī was of age to be married, and her father and brothers sought for a bridegroom. The eldest brother, Rukma, suggested Shishupāla, king of Chanderi; but the old king was for betrothing her to Shrī Krishna. But the brothers laughed and called him a cowherd, and settled the affair for Shishupāla and sent him the bridal gift; and a day for the wedding was fixed. All the city people were very sad, for they would have liked Rukminī to marry Shrī Krishna. Rukminī herself was told of what was settled; but she answered: "The Lord of the World is mine, in thought and word and deed." Then she wrote a letter to Krishna, and sent a Brāhman to Dwārakā. This was the letter: "Thou art a Searcher of Hearts and knowest the thoughts of all; what need I say? Thou art my refuge; my honour is in thy hands. Do thou act so as to guard it, and come and reveal thyself to thy servant." When Shrī Krishna received this note he set out at once for Kundalpur. Shishupāla was there already, and the wedding about to take place. Krishna, however, succeeded in carrying Rukminī off and took her away on his car, followed by Balarām and all his army. Shishupāla pursued them with Jurāsindhu, but Krishna beat them off, and defeated and bound Rukma, and carried his bride home: their son was Pradyumna, a rebirth of Kāmadev. Pradyumna's son was Aniruddha, a rebirth of Satrughna; he married Charumatī, though this alliance did not suffice to heal the family feuds, and her grandfather Rukma was slain by Balarām. Afterwards Aniruddha also married Ūshā, daughter of Vanāsur; Krishna waged war with Vanāsur to rescue his grandson, whom Vanāsur had imprisoned. In this war Shiva fought on the side of Vanāsur, but was defeated and made his submission to Krishna; then Krishna welcomed him with the words: "Shiva-jī, there is no difference between thee and me, and whoever thinks of us as diverse he falls into Hell and is not saved; but he that meditates upon thee obtaineth me also."

Krishna married Mitrabindā, Satibhāma, and others, winning each by great deeds; and another time, when a demon named Bhaumāsur carried off and concealed many thousand princesses, Krishna pursued and slew him, and received these also into his house. Each of his wives had ten sons and one daughter, all cloudy of hue and moon-faced and lotus-eyed, and wearing yellow and blue. The people of Dwārakā were known as the Vrishnis.

Krishna marries Kālindī

While Krishna was ruling at Dwārakā, Duryodhana was oppressing the Pāndavas at Hastinapur and sought to compass their death. Krishna and Balarāma went to give them help, and it was while Krishna was the Pāndavas' guest that he married Kālindī, daughter of the Sun.

Balarām was married to Rewatī, daughter of Rāja Rewat of Arntā. Once Balarām paid a visit to Braj, and related the doings of Hari to Nand and Yasodā, and delighted the gopīs with dancing and music. Krishna's son Sambu sought to marry Lakshmanā, daughter of Duryodhana; but he was taken and kept a prisoner till Balarām went to his rescue and dragged the city of Hastinapur down to the Ganges bank before he could be persuaded to spare the people. He brought away Sambu safe with his bride to Dwārakā.

Once Nārada visited Krishna at Dwārakā to see how he dwelt as a householder with all his thousands of wives. He went in turn to the palace of Rukminī, Satibhāma, Mitrabindā, and others, and in every one he found Krishna, and marvelled at the power of his *yoga-māyā*, the magic illusion of manifestation. Another time Nārada came and invited Krishna to a great sacrifice held in his honour by the Pāndavas. At this glorious ceremony Shishupāla was present, and was slain by Krishna.[1]

[1] For this episode see p. 157.

Hiranyakashipu's Choice

It has also been related how Rāma overcame Rāvana in the battle for the recovery of Sītā. This Shishupāla and this Rāvana were one with Hiranyakashipu, an impious Daitya king, who nursed an implacable hatred for Vishnu. He met his death when blaspheming against God. Vishnu himself sprang from a pillar of his palace in the form of a man-lion (Narasimha) and tore him to pieces. It is said that he had been once of high estate in Vishnu's heaven, but had committed a great fault; and given the choice of expiation by three births on earth as the enemy of Vishnu, or seven births as his friend, chose the former as leading to the soonest return.

It should be noticed that Rāvana before the battle in a brief moment of recollection admits Rāma's divinity, and says: "I am to be slain by him, and therefore I have carried off this daughter of Janaka. It is not from passion or anger that I retain her. I desire, being slain, to reach that highest home of Vishnu." Of Shishupāla it is said that he more than any other creature hated Vishnu in his incarnation as Krishna, and for this reason met death at his hands; "but inasmuch as his thoughts were ever concentred on the Lord, albeit in hatred, Shishupāla was united with him after death, for the Lord bestows a heavenly and exalted station upon those he slayeth, even in wrath."

The End of Krishna

After this Krishna again went to join the Pāndavas, and remained with them during the Great War as Arjuna's charioteer. On the field of Kurukshetra he uttered the *Bhagavad Gītā*. He was present at the death of Bhīshma, and after Duryodhana's death he received the curse of his mother. She bewailed the death of her son and of friend and foe; then, recognizing Hari as the Prime Mover, the One behind All, she cursed him for letting such things befall. This was her curse: that after thirty-six years Krishna should perish alone and miserably, and his people, the Vrishnis, should be destroyed. These things in due time came to pass. A madness seized the people of Dwārakā so that they fell upon one another and were slain, together with all the sons and grandsons of Krishna. Only the women and Krishna and Balarāma remained alive. Then Balarāma went to the forest, and Krishna first sent a messenger to the Kuru city, to place the city and women of Dwārakā under the Pāndavas' protection, and then took leave of his father; afterward he himself sought the forest, where Balarām awaited him. Krishna discovered his brother seated under a mighty tree on the edge of the forest; he sat like a yogī, and behold, there came forth from his mouth a mighty snake, the thousand-headed nāga Ananta, and glided away to the ocean. Ocean himself and the sacred rivers and many divine nāgas came to meet him. Thus Krishna beheld his brother depart from the human world, and he wandered alone in the forest. He that was full of energy sat down on the bare earth and thought of Gandhārī's curse and all that had befallen, and he knew that the time had come for his own departure. He restrained his senses in yoga and laid himself down. Then there came a hunter that way and thought him a deer, and loosed a shaft and pierced his foot; but when he came close the hunter beheld a man wrapped in yellow robes practising yoga. Thinking himself an offender, he touched his feet. Then Krishna rose and gave him comfort, and himself ascended to Heaven, filling the whole sky with glory; passing through Indra's paradise, he went to his own place.

Arjuna went to Dwārakā and brought away the women and children of the Vrishnis, and set out for Kurukshetra. On the way a band of warriors attacked the cavalcade and carried away a great part of the women. Arjuna established the others with the remnant of Krishna's descendants in new cities; but Rukminī and many others of Krishna's wives became Satī, burning themselves on a pyre, and others became ascetics and nuns. The waters of the ocean advanced and overwhelmed Dwārakā so that no trace remained.

CHAPTER V : BUDDHA

The Historical Foundation

THE history of Buddha, it may be said, is not a myth. It is true that it is possible to disentangle from the Buddha legend, as from the Christ story, a nucleus of historical fact. To do this, and to clearly set forth his own teaching, has been one great achievement of Oriental scholarship during the last half-century. Here, however, we shall be concerned with the whole mythical history of the Buddha as related in various works which are not, strictly speaking, historical, but have a quite distinct literary and spiritual value of their own. But before proceeding to set forth the Buddha myth, it will be useful to briefly summarize its historical nucleus so far as we can determine it, and to give some account of the Buddha's doctrines.

The Life of Buddha

By the fifth century before Christ the Aryan invaders of India had already pushed beyond the Panjāb far into the plains, and were settled in villages and little kingdoms along the valley of the Ganges. One of the Aryan tribes, the Shākyas, was established at Kapilavastu, about one hundred miles north-east of the city of Benāres and thirty or forty miles south of the Himālayas. They were an agricultural people, whose livelihood depended mainly on rice and cattle. The rāja of the Shākyas was Suddhodana, to whom were married the two daughters of the rāja of a neighbouring tribe, the Koliyans. Both were childless until in her forty-fifth year (about 563 B.C.) the elder became the mother of a boy, herself dying seven days afterward. The boy's family name was Gautama, and the name of Siddhārtha was afterward given to him. Gautama was early married to his cousin Yashodharā, the daughter of the rāja of Koli, and lived happily with her, free from the knowledge of care or want. In his twenty-ninth year, as the result of four visions, of age, illness, death, and, lastly, of dignified retreat from the world or in some more normal way, the problem of suffering was suddenly and impressively set before him. Filled with the thought of the insecurity of all happiness and with grief at the sufferings of others, he felt a growing unrest and dissatisfaction with the vanity of life; and when, ten years after his marriage, a son was born to him, he only felt that there was one more tie to be broken before he could leave his guarded world to seek a solution for the deep problems of life and a way of escape from the suffering that seemed inevitably associated with it.

The same night, when all were asleep, he left the palace, taking only his horse with him, and attended only by his charioteer, Channa. He had hoped for the last time to hold his son in his arms, but, finding him asleep with Yashodharā, feared to wake the mother, and so turned away for ever from all that he loved most to become a homeless wanderer. Truly, it is danger and hardship, and not safety or happiness, that lure men to great deeds!

Gautama attached himself in turn to various Brāhman hermits at Rājagriha in the Vindhyan hills; then, dissatisfied with their teaching, he endeavoured by solitary penance in the forest, after the manner of Brāhman ascetics, to attain superhuman power and insight. But after enduring the most severe privations and practising self-mortification with the greatest determination for a long period, he found himself no nearer to enlightenment, though he acquired great reputation as a saint. Then he abandoned this life and again took regular food; he sacrificed this reputation, and his disciples deserted him.

The Temptation

In this time of loneliness and failure there came to him the great temptation, symbolically described as presented to him by Māra, the evil one, in the form of material temptation and assault. Unvanquished, however, Gautama wandered along the banks of the river Nairanjara and took his seat under a bo-tree (*Ficus religiosa*), and there received a simple meal from the hands of Sujāta, daughter of a neighbouring villager, who at first mistook him for a sylvan deity. During the day he sat there, still assailed by doubt and the temptation to return to his home. But as the day wore on his mind seemed to grow clearer and clearer, his doubts vanished, a great peace came over him as the significance of all things made itself apparent. So day and night passed till by the dawn came perfect knowledge; Gautama became Buddha, the enlightened.

With perfect enlightenment there came upon the Buddha a sense of great isolation; how could it be possible to share this wisdom with men less wise, less earnest than himself? Was it likely that he could persuade any of the truth of a doctrine of self-salvation by self-restraint and love, without any reliance upon such rituals or theologies as men everywhere and at all times lean upon? Such isolation comes to all great leaders; but love and pity for humanity determined the Buddha at all hazard of misunderstanding or failure to preach the truth he had seen.

The Buddha accordingly proceeded to Benāres to "turn the wheel of the Law," *i.e.* to set rolling the chariot wheel of a universal empire of truth and righteousness. He established himself in the "Deer Park" near Benāres, and though at first his doctrine was not well received, it was not long before it was accepted by his old disciples and many others. Some became his personal followers; others became lay disciples without leaving the household life. Amongst those who accepted his teaching were his father and mother and wife and son. After a ministry lasting forty-five years, during which he preached the new doctrines in Kapilavastu and the neighbouring states, and established an order of Buddhist monks, and also, though reluctantly, an order of nuns, the Buddha passed away or entered into Nirvāna (about 483 B.C.), surrounded by his mournful disciples.

The Teaching of Buddha

If we know comparatively little about the life of Buddha, we have, on the other hand, a trustworthy knowledge of his teaching. Conceptions of the personality of the Buddha himself have indeed changed, but the substance of his teaching has been preserved intact since about 250 B.C., and there is every reason to believe that the works then accepted formally as canonical include the essential part of his own doctrine.

It is necessary, in the first place, to realize that though a reformer, and perhaps from a priestly point of view a heretic (if such a word can be used in connexion with a system permitting absolute freedom of speculation), the Buddha was brought up and lived and died as a Hindu. Comparatively little of his system whether of doctrine or ethics, was original, or calculated to deprive him of the support and sympathy of the best among the Brāhmans, many of whom became his disciples. The success of his system was due to various causes: the wonderful personality and sweet reasonableness of the man himself, his courageous and constant insistence upon a few fundamental principles, and to the way in which he made his teaching accessible to all without respect to aristocracy of birth or intellect.

The idea of impermanence, of the inevitable connexion of sorrow with life and of life with desire, the doctrine of rebirth, of *karma* (every man must reap what he himself sows), and a complex formal psychology—all these belong to the intellectual atmosphere of the Buddha's own time. Where he differed most profoundly from the Brāhmans was in his denial of soul, of any enduring entity in man apart from temporary associations producing the illusion of a person, an *ego*.

Yet even this difference is more apparent than real, and we find in later times that it became almost impossible to distinguish between the Buddhist "Void" and the Brāhman "Self." For the distinguishing characteristic of each is the absence of any characteristics at all; each is other than Being, and other than non-Being. Even the word "Nirvāna" is common to Buddhism and Hinduism, and controversy turns upon whether Nirvāna is or is not equivalent to extinction. The question is really improper, for the meaning of Nirvāna is no more than a freeing from the fetters of individuality —as the space enclosed in an earthen pot is freed from its limitation and becomes one with infinite space when the pot is broken. Whether we call that infinite space a Void or a Whole is more a matter of temperament than of fact; what is important is to realize that the apparent separateness of any portion of it is temporary and unreal, and is the cause of all pain.

The heresy of individuality, then, is the first great delusion which the one who would set out on the Buddhist road to salvation must abandon. Desire to maintain this illusory, individual self is the source of all sorrow and evil in our experience. The idea of soul or self is illusory, because there is, in fact, no being, only an everlasting becoming. Those free from these delusions could enter on the path which leads to peace of mind, to wisdom, to Nirvāna (Release). Most briefly, this Path is summed up in the celebrated verse:

To cease from all sin,
To get virtue,
To cleanse one's own heart—
This is the religion of the Buddhas.

So much for history. Now let us see what legends the race imagination has woven around this story of the Enlightened One. We have to begin with his resolve in a long previous life to become a Buddha, and with his subsequent incarnations in many forms, till at last he was born as the Shākya prince of whom we have spoken.

How Sumedha became a Buddha-Elect

A hundred thousand ages past, a wealthy, learned, and righteous Brāhman dwelt in the great city of Amara. One day he sat him down, reflecting on the misery of rebirth, old age, and disease, exclaiming:

There is, there must be, an escape!
Impossible there should not be!
I'll make the search and find the way,
Which from existence shall release!

Accordingly he retired to the Himālayas and dwelt as a hermit in a leaf-hut, where he attained to great wisdom. While he was sunk in trance there was born One-who-overcame, Dīpankara. It happened that this Buddha was proceeding on his way near where Sumedha lived, and men were preparing a path for his feet to tread. Sumedha joined in this work, and when the Buddha approached lay down in the mud, saying to himself:

Can I but keep him from the mire,
To me great merit shall accrue.

As he lay there the thought came to his mind: "Why should I not now cast off all remaining evil in myself and enter into Nirvāna? But let me not do so all for myself alone; rather let me also some day achieve omniscience and convey a multitude of beings in the ship of doctrine over the ocean of rebirth safely to the farther shore?" Dīpankara, all-knowing, paused by his side and proclaimed him to the multitude as one who ages after should likewise become a Buddha, and named the place of his birth, his family, his disciples, and his tree. At this the people rejoiced; for they thought, if we attain not to Nirvāna now, in another life, taught by this other Buddha, they would have again a good opportunity to learn the truth; for the doctrine of all Buddhas is the same. All nature then showed signs and presages in witness of Sumedha's undertaking and dedication: each tree bore fruit, the rivers stood still, a rain of flowers fell down from Heaven, the fires of Hell died down. "Do not turn back," Dīpankara said. "Go on! Advance! Most certainly we know this thing; surely a Buddha shalt thou be!" Sumedha determined then to fulfil the conditions of a Buddha—perfection in alms, in keeping the precepts, in renunciation, in wisdom, in courage, in patience, in truth, in resolution, in goodwill, and in indifference. Beginning, then, to fulfil these ten conditions of the quest, Sumedha returned to the forest and dwelt there till he passed away.

Thereafter was he reborn in countless forms—as a man, as a *deva*,[1] as an animal, and in all these forms he adhered to the path marked out, so that it is said there exists not a particle of earth where the Buddha has not sacrificed his life for the sake of creatures. The story of these rebirths is given in the *Jātaka* book, where 550 births are related. Out of these we shall select a few typical examples.

The Six-tusked Elephant

Once upon a time the Buddha-elect was born as the son of the elephant chief of a herd of eight thousand royal elephants, who lived near to a great lake in the Himālayas. In the middle of this lake was clear water, and round this grew sheets of white and coloured water-lilies, and fields of rice and gourds and sugar-cane and plantains; it was surrounded by a bamboo grove and a ring of great mountains. In the north-east corner of the lake grew a huge banyan-tree, and on the west side there was an enormous golden cave. In the rainy season the elephants lived in the cave, and in the hot weather they gathered under the branches of the banyan to enjoy the cool shade. One day the Buddha-elect with his two wives went to a grove of sāl-trees, and while there he struck one of the trees with his head so that a shower of dry leaves, twigs, and red ants fell on the windward side, where his wife Chullasubhadda happened to be standing, and a shower of green leaves and flowers on the other side, where his other wife, Mahasubhadda, was. On another occasion one of the elephants brought a beautiful seven-sprayed lotus to the Buddha-elect, and he received it and gave it to Mahasubhadda. Because of these things Chullasubhadda was offended and conceived a grudge against the Great Being. So one day when he had

[1] *Deva*, lit. a shining one, *i.e.* a god, other than the Supreme God.

prepared an offering of fruits and flowers, and was entertaining five hundred private buddhas, Chullasubhadda also made offerings to them, and made a prayer that she might be reborn as the daughter of a king and become the queen-consort of the king of Benāres, and so have power to move the king to send a hunter with a poisoned arrow to wound and slay this elephant. Then she pined away and died. In due course her wicked wishes were fulfilled, and she became the favourite wife of the king of Benāres, dear and pleasing in his eyes. She remembered her past lives, and said to herself that now she would have the elephant's tusks brought to her. So she went to bed and pretended to be very ill. When the king heard of this he went to her room and sat on the bed and asked her: "Why are you pining away, like a wreath of withered flowers trampled under foot?" She answered: "It is because of an unattainable wish"; whereupon he promised her whatever she desired. So she had all the hunters of the kingdom called together, amounting to sixty thousand, and told them that she had had a dream of a magnificent six-tusked white elephant, and that if her longing for the tusks could not be satisfied she would die. She chose one of the hunters, who was a coarse, ill-favoured man, to do her work, and showed him the way to the lake where the Great Being lived, and promised him a reward of five villages when she received the tusks. He was very much afraid of the task, but finally consented when she told him that she had also dreamt that her desire would be fulfilled. She fitted him out with weapons and necessaries for the journey, giving him a leather parachute to descend from the hills to the lake.

Deeper and deeper he penetrated into the Himālayan jungle, far beyond the haunts of men, overcoming incredible difficulties, until after seven years, seven months, and seven days' weary travelling he stood by the great banyan-tree where the Buddha-elect and the other elephants lived so peacefully and unsuspectingly. He dug a hole in the ground and, putting on the yellow robe of a hermit, hid in it, covering it over except a little space for his arrow. When the Great Being passed by he shot him with a poisoned arrow, which drove him nearly mad with anger and pain. Just when he would have killed the wicked hunter he noticed his yellow robe—

Emblem of sainthood, priestly guise,
And deemed inviolate by the wise.

Seeing this robe, the wounded elephant recovered his self-control and asked the hunter what reason he had for slaying him. The hunter told him his story of the dream of the queen of Benāres. The Great Being understood the whole matter very well and suffered the hunter to take his tusks. But so great was he, and the hunter so clumsy, that he could not cut them away; he only gave the Great Being unbearable pain and filled his mouth with blood. Then he took the saw in his own trunk, and cut them off and gave them to the hunter, saying: "The tusks of wisdom are a hundred times dearer to me than these, and may this good act be the reason of my attaining omniscience." He also gave the hunter magic power to return to Benāres in seven days, and so died and was burned on a pyre by the other elephants. The hunter took back the tusks to the queen and, evidently disapproving of her wickedness now that he knew its full significance, announced that the elephant against whom she had felt a grudge for a trifling offence had been slain by him. "Is he dead?" she cried; and, giving her the tusks, "Rest assured he is dead," the hunter replied. Taking

XIX

THE BODHISATTVA'S TUSKS

ABANINDRO NĀTH TAGORE

Page 254

the beautiful tusks on her lap, she gazed at these tokens of one that had been her dear lord in another life, and as she gazed she was filled with inconsolable grief, and her heart broke and she died the same day.

Long ages afterward she was born at Savatthi, and became a nun. She went one day with other Sisters to hear the Buddha's doctrine. Gazing upon him, so peaceful and radiant, it came into her heart that she had once been his wife, when he had been lord of a herd of elephants, and she was glad. But then there came to her also the remembrance of her wickedness—how she had been the cause of his death only because of a fancied slight—and her heart grew hot within her, and she burst into tears and sobbed aloud. Then the Master smiled, and when the brethren asked him why he smiled, he told this story, which hearing, many men entered on the Path, and the Sister herself afterward attained to sainthood.

The Tree-God

Long ago, when Brahmadatta was king of Benāres, there came this thought into his mind: "Everywhere in India there are kings whose palaces have many columns; what if I build a palace supported by a single column only? Then shall I be the first and singular king among all other kings." So he summoned his craftsmen, and ordered them to build him a magnificent palace supported by a single pillar. "It shall be done," they said; and away they went into the forest.

There they found a tree, tall and straight, worthy to be the single pillar of such a palace. But the road was too rough and the distance too great for them to take the trunk to the city, so they returned to the king and asked him what was to be done. "Somehow or other," he said, "you must bring it, and that without delay." But they answered that neither somehow nor anyhow could it be done. "Then," said the king, "you must select a tree in my own park."

There they found a lordly sāl-tree, straight and beautiful, worshipped alike by village and town and royal family. They told the king, and he said to them: "Good, go and fell the tree at once." But they could not do this without making the customary offerings to the tree-god living there, and asking him to depart. So they made offerings of flowers and branches and lighted lamps, and said to the tree: "On the seventh day from this we shall fell the tree, by the king's command. Let any deva that may be dwelling in the tree depart elsewhere, and not unto us be the blame!" The god that dwelt in the tree heard what they said, and considered thus: "These craftsmen are agreed to fell my tree. I myself shall perish when my home is destroyed. All the young sāl-trees round me will be destroyed as well, in which many devas of my kith and kin are living. My own death touches me not so nearly as the destruction of my children, so let me, if possible, save their lives at least." So at the hour of midnight the tree-god, divinely radiant, entered the king's resplendent chamber, his glory lighting up the whole room. The king was startled, and stammered out: "What being art thou, so god-like and so full of grief?" The deva-prince replied: "I am called in thy realm, O king, the Lucky-tree; for sixty thousand years all men have loved and worshipped me. Many a house and many a town, many a palace, too, they made, yet never did me wrong; honour thou me, even as did they, O king!" But the king answered that such a tree was just what he needed for his palace, a trunk so fine and tall and straight; and in that palace, said he, "thou shalt long endure, admired of all who behold thee." The tree-god answered: "If it must be so, then I have one boon to ask: Cut first the top, the middle next, and then the root of me." The king protested that this was a more painful death than to be felled entire. "O forest lord," he said, "what gain is thine thus to be cut limb from limb and piece by piece?" To which the Lucky-tree replied: "There is a good reason for my wish: my kith and kin have grown up round me, beneath my shade, and I should crush them if I fall entire upon them, and they would grieve exceedingly."

At this the king was deeply moved, and wondered at the tree-god's noble thought, and lifting his hands in salutation, he said: "O Lucky-tree, O forest lord, as thou wouldst save thy kindred, so shall I spare thee; so fear nothing."

Then the tree-god gave the king good counsel and went his way; and the king next day gave generous alms, and ruled as became a king until the time came for his departure to the heavenly world.

The Hare-Mark on the Moon

Once upon a time, when Brahmadatta was king of Benāres, the future Buddha was born as a hare and lived in a wood. He had three friends, a monkey, a jackal, and an otter; all these animals were very wise. The hare used to preach to the others, exhorting them to give alms and keep the fast-days. On one of these fast-days the hare and his friends were seeking their food as usual; the otter found some fish, the jackal some meat, the monkey some mangoes. But the hare, as he lay in his form before going out to eat his grass, reflected that if anyone should ask him for a gift of food, grass would be useless. As he had no grain or meat he made up his mind to give up his own body if anyone asked him for food.

Now when any wonderful thing such as this takes place on earth, the throne of Sakra in Heaven grows hot. Sakra looked down to see what was happening, and perceiving the hare, determined to test his virtue. He took the shape of a Brāhman, and went first to the otter and asked for food. The otter offered him fish. The jackal and the monkey in turn offered him meat and fruit. Sakra declined all these offers and said that he would return next day. Then he went to the hare, who was overjoyed at the chance of giving himself in alms. "Brāhman," said he, "to-day I will give such alms as I never gave before; gather wood and prepare a fire and tell me when it is ready." When Sakra heard this he made a heap of live coals and told the hare that all was ready; then the hare, who would some day be a Buddha, came and sprang into the fire, as happy as a royal flamingo alighting in a bed of water-lilies. But the fire did not burn—it seemed as cold as the air above the clouds. At once he inquired of the disguised Sakra what this might mean. Sakra replied that he was indeed no Brāhman, but had come down from Heaven to test the hare's generosity. The hare replied: "Sakra, your efforts are wasted; every creature alive might try me in turn, and none could find in me any unwillingness to give."

Then Sakra answered: "Wise hare, let your virtue be proclaimed to the end of this world-cycle." Taking a mountain, he squeezed it, and holding the hare under his arm, he drew an outline picture of him on the moon, using the juice of the mountain for his ink. Then he put down the hare on some tender grass in the wood and departed to his own heaven. And that is why there is now a hare in the moon.

Santusita

The last incarnation of the Buddha-elect of this age was as King Vessantara, concerning whose perfection in almsgiving a long *Jātaka* is related. After reigning for many years the Buddha-elect passed away to the *Tusita* heaven, to await his final birth amongst men. It should be understood that a Buddha-elect shortens his stay in the god-world between each incarnation as much as possible, though his merit, of course, entitles him to lengthy residence there; indeed, he might have attained Nirvāna at the time of his first assurance of future Buddhahood had he not chosen constant rebirth in this world for the sake of creatures. But for these sacrifices the *Bodhisattva* (Buddha-elect) has some compensations; in itself the attainment of Buddhahood is a great incentive, a feat likened to the difficult ascent of a man to the top of a tree to pluck its fruit. Again, a Bodhisattva is never born in any hell nor in a degraded or deformed shape. Above all, the pain of constant sacrifice is overpowered by the joy of looking forward to the greatness of the reward, the attainment of power to enlighten others.

When born in any heaven the Buddha-elect can exercise his peculiar power of incarnation at will; he lies down upon a couch and "dies," being reborn on earth in such place and manner as he determines. Previous to his last incarnation, contrary to custom he lingered for a long time in the *Tusita* heaven, where he was known as Santusita; and when at last the devas perceived that he was about to be reborn, they gathered round him with congratulations. Vanishing from there, he was conceived in the womb of Mahāmāyā, wife of Suddhodana, the Shākya king of Kapilavastu. His conception was miraculous, taking place in a dream. Mahāmāyā was translated by the devas of the four quarters to the Himālayas, and there bathed and ceremonially purified by their four queens. Then the Bodhisattva appeared to her, like a moonlit cloud, coming from the north, holding a lotus in his hand, or, as some say, in the form of a white elephant. This appearance approached the queen and circumambulated her thrice; at that moment, Santusita, who had followed the course of the dream, disappeared from the presence of the devas and entered the womb of Mahāmāyā. At this moment great wonders took place: the ten thousand spheres thrilled at once, the fires of Hell were quenched, instruments of music played untouched, the flowing of rivers ceased (as if to stand and behold the Bodhisattva), and trees and herbs burst into flower, even beams of dry wood bore lotus blooms. Next day the queen's dream was interpreted by sixty-four Brāhmans, who announced that she would have a son who would become either a Universal Emperor or a Supreme Buddha. For nine months Mahāmāyā was guarded by the devas of the four quarters and forty thousand devas of other worlds. Meanwhile her body was transparent, so that the child could be distinctly seen, like an image enclosed in a crystal casket. At the conclusion of ten lunar months Mahāmāyā set out to visit her parents, riding in a golden litter. On the way she stopped to rest in a garden of sāl-trees, called Lumbini; and while resting there the Buddha was born, without pain or suffering. The child was received by Brahmā, and from him by the four devas, and from them by the nobles attendant on the queen; but at once he stepped to the ground, and on the spot first touched by his feet there sprang up a lotus. On the same day were born Yashodharā Devī, who afterwards became his wife; the horse Kantaka, upon which he fled from the city when he went forth to seek for wisdom; his charioteer, Channa, who accompanied him on that occasion; Ānanda, his favourite disciple; and the bo-tree under which he attained enlightenment.

The Guarding of Siddhārtha

Five days after his birth the young prince was named Siddhārtha, and on the seventh his mother died. When he was twelve years old the king took counsel with his Brāhmans, who informed him that the prince would become an ascetic, as the result of seeing old age, sickness, death, and a hermit. The king desired to avoid this event, saying to himself: "I do not wish my son to become a Buddha, as in so doing he will be exposed to great danger from the attacks of Māra; let him rather become a Universal Emperor." The king therefore took every precaution to keep him far away from the "four signs," having three guarded palaces built, where every delight abounded, and sorrow and death might not even be mentioned.

The rāja, moreover, thought that a sure way to attach the prince to his royal estate would be to find him a wife. In order to discover secretly some princess who might awaken his love the king had made a number of splendid jewels, and announced that on a certain day the prince would bestow these one by one upon the noble ladies of the land. When all the gifts had been bestowed, there came one lady more, whose name was Yashodharā, daughter of the minister Mahānāma. She asked the prince if he had no gift for her, and he, meeting her eyes, gave her his own costly signet-ring. The king was duly informed of the glances exchanged, and he sent to Mahānāma to ask his daughter in marriage for the prince. It was, however, a rule amongst the Shākya nobles that the fairest maidens could be given only to those who proved themselves victors in martial exercises. "And I fear," he said, "that this delicately nurtured prince may not be expert in archery or wrestling." However, a day was appointed for the trial, and the young nobles came with the prince to compete for the hand of Yashodharā. There was first a competition in literary and mathematical lore, and then in archery. Each of the young nobles did well; but the prince, using a sacred bow handed down from his grandfather's time, which none else could string, much less draw, easily surpassed them, and he excelled in turn in riding, swordsmanship, and wrestling. Thus he won Yashodharā, and he lived with her in the beautiful palace made by his father, guarded from all knowledge of suffering and death. About the palace was a great garden with a triple wall, each wall with a single gate, well guarded by many soldiers.

Meanwhile the devas reflected that time was passing, and the Great One ought no longer to linger amid the pleasures of the palace, but must go forth on his mission. They therefore filled all space with this thought, "It is time to go forth," so that it reached the mind of the prince; and at the same time the music of the singers and the gestures of the dancers assumed a new meaning, and seemed to tell no more of sensuous delights, but of the impermanence and vanity of every object of desire. The songs of the musicians seemed to call to the prince to leave the palace and see the world; so he sent for his charioteer, and announced that he wished to visit the city. When the rāja heard this he ordered the city to be swept and garnished and made ready for the prince's visit, and no old or infirm person nor any inauspicious object was to be left in view. But all these precautions were in vain; for a deva appeared before him as he drove through the streets, in the form of a tottering old man, bent with sickness and age, short of breath, and wrinkled. The prince inquired the meaning of this strange sight, and his charioteer replied: "This is an old man." The prince again asked: "What is the meaning of this word 'old'?" and the charioteer explained that the man's bodily powers were now impaired by long years, and he might die at any moment. Then the prince asked again: "Is this man one only, or does this fate come to all alike, and must I also become old?" And when he was informed that it was even so, he would see no more that day, but returned to the palace to reflect on so strange a thing and to bethink him if there were no way of escape.

Another day the prince drove out again, and in the same way beheld a man very ill; and still another day he beheld a corpse. "Must I also die?" he asked, and learnt that it was even so. On another day still, the prince drove out and beheld a begging monk, and conversed with him; the yogī explained that he had left the world to seek equanimity, to have done with hatred and love, to attain freedom for self. The prince was deeply affected and worshipped the wandering beggar, and returning home, prayed his father's leave to go forth alone in the same fashion, for, he said: "All worldly things, O king, are changeable and impermanent." The old king was thunderstruck and could but weep bitterly; and when the prince had retired he redoubled the guard about the palace and the delights within it, and, indeed, the whole city strove to prevent the prince from leaving his home.

The Departure of Siddhārtha

About this time Yashodharā bore a son to Prince Siddhārtha, and he was named Rāhula. But not even this new tie could dissuade the prince from his purpose, and there came a night when the devas called upon him to depart. He beheld for the last time Yashodharā sleeping, with one hand resting on the baby's head, so that he could not even lift it in his arms for fear of waking her; leaving them both, he lifted the jewelled net that divided the chamber from the outer hall, and passing slowly through the outer rooms, he paused at the eastern door, and invoked all the Buddhas and stood with lifted head surveying the sky with its countless stars. Then Sakra and the guardian devas of the four quarters, and innumerable devas from the heavens, surrounded him and chanted: "Holy Prince, the time has come to seek the Highest Law of Life." Then he reflected: "Now all the devas have come down to earth to confirm my resolution. I will go: the time has come." Then he sent for Channa, his charioteer, and for his horse, born the same day as himself. So Channa brought the horse, splendidly caparisoned, and he neighed with joy; then the prince mounted him, making a vow that it should be for the last time. The devas lifted Kantaka's feet from the ground that he might make no noise, and when they came to the gates each opened silently of itself. Thus Prince Siddhārtha left the palace and the city, followed by hosts of angels lighting up the path and scattering flowers before him.

Channa strove continually to dissuade the prince from his purpose, praying him rather to become a Universal Emperor. But the prince knew that he would attain Perfect Enlightenment, and would have preferred any

XX

DEPARTURE OF PRINCE SIDDHĀRTHA

ABANINDRO NĀTH TAGORE

Page 264

death to returning home. He dismounted from Kantaka for the last time and ordered Channa to lead him home. By him also he sent a message to his father that he should not grieve, but rather rejoice that his son had set forth to find out a means of saving the world from the recurrence of birth and death, from sorrow and pain. "And I am now freed," he said, "from the love due only to relatives; take the horse Kantaka and depart." After many arguments Channa was forced to yield, and he kissed the prince's feet, and Kantaka licked them with his tongue, and those two departed.

Presently the prince, proceeding on his way, met with a hunter, and to him he gave his royal robes in exchange for tattered rags, more suited for a hermit. This hunter was another deva who had assumed a form for that very purpose. Yet another became a barber, and shaved the prince's head. The prince proceeded to the hermitage of a community of Brāhmans, who welcomed him reverently, and he became the pupil of one of the most learned. But he perceived that though their systems might lead to Heaven, yet they provided no means of final deliverance from rebirth on earth or even in Hell.

"Unhappy world," he said, "hating the demon Death, and yet seeking hereafter to be born in Heaven! What ignorance! What delusion!"

The Wanderings of Siddhārtha

So he left the hermitage, to the great grief and disappointment of the yogīs who lived there, and set out for the home of a famous sage named Alara. His system also proved incomplete, and the prince departed, saying: "I seek a system where there shall be no questioning of existence or non-existence, eternity or non-eternity, and the idea of the boundless and illimitable shall be realized, but not talked of." From Alara's hermitage he proceeded to Rājagriha, and was welcomed there by King Bimbisara. This king endeavoured to persuade the prince to abandon his wandering life; but he would not hear of it, and proceeded farther to a village near Gayā and took up his abode in a neighbouring wood, eating daily a modicum of millet seed, just sufficient to maintain life. Then his skin became wrinkled, his flesh fell away, and his eyes grew hollow, and all those who beheld him felt a strange feeling of fear and reverence because of these austerities.

During all these years his father, Suddhodana, sent messengers from time to time praying his son to return, and setting before him every argument and inducement; they came also to Gayā, when the prince was at the point of death; but he would have none of their sayings, and gave them this order, if he should die before attaining Perfect Enlightenment, to take back his bones to Kapilavastu and say: "These are the relics of a man who died in the fixed prosecution of his resolve."

But the prince found that these austerities benefited nothing; rather he experienced less of the illumination of wisdom than heretofore. He resolved, therefore, to nourish his body, and accepted food and attention. The story is told, in particular, of one Sujāta, a daughter of a village lord, who was forewarned by an angel, and prepared food as follows: she collected a thousand cows, and with their milk fed five hundred others, and with theirs two hundred and fifty others, and so on down to fifteen cows, and then, mixing their milk with rice, she prepared a dish of the greatest purity and delicacy. When the Bodhisattva went into the village to beg for food she offered him this rice-milk on a golden dish, and it seemed to him a good omen. He took the food and went out of the village and bathed in a river, and would have crossed to the other side, but the current carried him away, and had it not been that a deva dwelling in a certain great tree on the farther bank stretched out his jewelled arm to draw him to land, he would have been drowned. He reached the shore, however, and sat down to take his meal; after which he cast the golden dish into the river, where it was caught by a nāga, who took it to his palace. Sakra, however, in the form of a garuda,[1] snatched it from the nāga's hand and carried it to the *Tusita* heavens.

Meanwhile the Bodhisattva proceeded toward the Wisdom-tree, beneath which the previous Buddhas had attained enlightenment. As he walked along the forest path hundreds of kingfishers approached him and, circling thrice about him, followed; after them came five hundred peacocks and other birds and beasts; so that he walked on surrounded by devas, nāgas, asuras, and creatures of every kind towards the Tree of Wisdom.

A nāga king who dwelt near the path and was very old, having seen more than one of the former Buddhas come by that way, chanted his praise; and his wife, with countless snake-girls, welcomed him with flags and flowers and jewelled ornaments, and kept up a perpetual song of praise. The devas of the Worlds of Form hung flags and banners on the Wisdom-tree and on the trees that led to it, so that the Bodhisattva might find the way easily. As he went he reflected that not only this host of friendly beings, but also Māra, the evil one, should witness his victory; and this thought, like a ray of glory from his brow-spot, penetrated to Māra's abode, and brought him dreams and portents. A messenger came also in haste to Māra

[1] A mythical bird, hereditary enemy of serpents (*nāgas*).

warning him of Bodhisattva's approach to the Wisdom-tree. Then Māra assembled his army. A horrible sight was that. There were some with a hundred thousand mouths, some with heads or hands or eyes or feet misshapen, some with fiery tongues, some devouring serpents, some drinking blood, others pot-bellied and bandy-legged, and all with spears and bows and clubs and weapons and armour of every sort. All these marched toward the Wisdom-tree.

The Wisdom-Tree

The Bodhisattva, however, approached the tree, shining like a mountain of pure gold, and took his seat on its eastern side, vowing never to rise again till he had attained enlightenment. Then the earth quaked six times. Then Māra took the form of a messenger arriving post-haste from Kapilavastu with the news that Devadatta, Buddha's cousin, had usurped the government and was practising every sort of cruelty and tyranny, and praying the Bodhisattva to return and restore good government and order. But he reflected that Devadatta acted so from lust and malice, and the Shākya princes permitted it only from cowardice, and thus reflecting upon human weakness, the Bodhisattva was all the more determined to attain to something higher and better.

Meanwhile the deva of the Wisdom-tree rejoiced, and cast her jewels before his feet, and prayed him to persevere. The devas of other trees came to inquire of her who was the glorious being seated there; and when she informed them that it was the Bodhisattva they cast down flowers and perfumes about him, and exhorted him by words and songs to go forward. Then Māra ordered his three beautiful daughters to tempt the Bodhisattva in every way, and they went to sing and dance before him.

They wooed him with song and dance and every artifice of love; but he remained unchanged in face or mind, like a lily resting on quiet waters, and firm as Mount Meru, like the iron walls that gird the universe. Then they argued with him, depicting the pleasures and duties of worldly life, and the difficulty and danger of the search for wisdom; but he answered:

Pleasure is brief as the lightning flash—
Why should I, then, covet the pleasures you describe?

And Māra's daughters, recognizing their failure, left him with a prayer for his success:

That which your heart desires may you attain!
And finding for yourself deliverance, deliver all.

The Defeat of Māra

Then Māra himself engaged in argument; and when he also was unsuccessful, he led on his demon army to the attack. All the devas were terrified and fled away, leaving the Bodhisattva alone. Of every shape, kind, and colour, uttering every unearthly sound, filling the air with darkness and shaking the ground, the horrid army advanced with threatening gestures toward the Bodhisattva; but the spears stuck to their hands, their limbs were paralysed, and though they would have ground him to dust or burnt him with fiery tongues, they could not hurt so much as a hair; he sat unmoved, while the weapons showered upon him fell at his feet as flowers. Māra exhausted every resource, and when all had failed he took up his terrible discus, and mounting the elephant Cloud-mountain, himself approached the prince. Now this weapon, if it were thrown against Mount Meru, would cut it in twain like a bamboo; if it were thrown into the sky, it would prevent the falling of rain for twelve years; yet it refused to touch the Bodhisattva, but floated through the air like a dry leaf and remained above his head like a garland of flowers in the air. Then Māra was enraged like a fire into which oil is poured again and again, and he came close to the prince and bade him "Begone!" But he answered: "This throne is mine by virtue of the merit I have acquired in many long ages. How canst thou possess it who have no merit?" Then Māra boasted: "My merit is greater than thine," and called his army to witness, and all his warriors called out: "We witness," so that a sound like the roar of the sea rose to the very sky. But Bodhisattva replied: "Your witnesses are many and partial; I have one and an impartial witness"; and he stretched out his hand from his robe like lightning from an orange cloud and touched the earth and called on her to witness to his merit. Then the Earth Goddess rose at his feet and cried with a hundred thousand voices like the sound of a cosmic drum: "I witness"; and Māra's army fled and returned to Hell like leaves that are scattered by the wind. Cloud-mountain curled up his trunk and put his tail between his legs and fled away. Māra himself fell prostrate and made acknowledgment of the Bodhisattva's power, and rose only to rush away and hide his shame; for his mind was filled with sorrow to know all his efforts had failed, and the prince would soon obtain enlightenment and would preach the truth by which thousands of creatures should reach Nirvāna.

Perfectly Enlightened

The sun had not yet set when Māra was defeated. Buddha remained seated beneath the Wisdom-tree. Gradually through the night the enlightenment for which he sought dawned in his heart: at the tenth hour he perceived the exact conditions of all beings who have ever been in the infinite and endless worlds; at the twentieth hour he gained the divine insight by which all things far or near appeared as if close at hand. Then he obtained the knowledge that unfolds the causes of the repetition of existence; then the privileges of the four paths and their fruition; and at dawn of day he became a Supreme Buddha, the Perfectly Enlightened. Then rays of six colours spread far and wide from his shining body, penetrating to the uttermost bounds of space and announcing the attainment of Buddhahood. Not even a hundred thousand tongues could proclaim the wonders that therewith were manifested.

Then the Buddha himself proclaimed his victory in a song of triumph:

Through many diverse births I have passed
Seeking in vain the builder of the house.

Ah, house-framer, now I have seen thee!
Never again shalt thou build me a house.
I have broken thy rafters,
I have destroyed the king-post.
My mind is detached;
Desire is extinguished.

Then Buddha remained seven days in meditation; for seven days more he fixed his gaze on the Wisdom-tree; again he walked seven days rapt in thought upon a golden ambulatory prepared by the devas; then he sat for seven days in a golden palace, where every event of the remainder of his life became known to him and the whole of the *dharma* became clear to his mind, from the first to the last word of his teaching; in the fifth week he sat under the tree Ajapāla and experienced detachment (Nirvāna); during the sixth week he sat by the Lake Muchalinda, where a nāga of the same name sheltered him from storms of rain; in the seventh week he sat in a grove of Nyagrodha trees.

The Merchants

It was now forty-nine days since he had received the milk-rice from Sujāta. It so happened that two merchants were passing through the forest with their caravan. For many ages and in many lives they had desired the opportunity to make some offering to a Buddha. In the same forest was a *devī*—in fact, a dryad—who had once been their relative: now, to fulfil their desire she caused the wheels of their carts to stick fast in deep mud. The merchants made an offering of lights and perfumes, and prayed to the god whom they supposed responsible for the misfortune. The devī appeared to them, commanded them to make an offering of food to the Buddha, and released the wagons. The merchants, overjoyed, made their way to him with a gift of honey. Now Buddha had no alms-bowl, for Brahmā's bowl, given when Sujāta brought the rice-milk, had vanished, and the golden dish she herself had given had been transported to Snake-land. Now, therefore, the guardian gods of the four quarters appeared with emerald bowls, and when Buddha would not accept these they offered in turn bowls of stone. Then as each desired that his own bowl might be accepted, the Buddha received the four and made them appear like one. In that bowl he received the honey, and in return he taught the *triple formula* to the merchants, and they became lay-disciples. They also received from him a lock of hair as a relic.

In the eighth week the Buddha seated himself under the Ajapāla tree, and there reflected that the doctrine is deep, while men are neither good nor wise. It appeared to him useless to proclaim the law to those who could not understand it. But Brahmā, perceiving this doubt, cried out: "The world will perish!" and the cry was echoed by the devas of the wind and rain and by all other brahmās and devas innumerable. Then Brahmā appeared before the Buddha and said: "My lord, the Buddhahood is hard to obtain; but you have obtained it that you might release the beings of the world from existence; therefore proclaim the law that this may come to pass. O wise one, let the *dharma* be taught!" Then Buddha agreed that it should be so, and looked about for one to whom he should first preach. He thought first of two of his old disciples, but he perceived that they were now dead. He therefore set out for Benāres, intending to instruct the five hermits with whom he had formerly practised austerities.

The Hermits of Benāres

When the five hermits saw him from afar they said: "Siddhārtha has recovered his strength and beauty; he comes to us, having failed to accomplish the penance. As he is of royal birth, let us offer him a seat, but we will not rise or go to meet him." Buddha perceived their thoughts and directed his loving-kindness towards them. Immediately, just as a withered leaf is helplessly swept away in a torrent, so they helplessly, overcome by the force of his love, rose and went to do him honour. They washed his feet and inquired of his welfare, and he informed them that he was now become a Supreme Buddha. Then the whole universe rejoiced, knowing that the Law would be preached for the first time. The evening, like a beautiful lady, came to worship him; Meru danced for joy; the seven mountain ranges bowed before him; and the beings of every world assembled to receive the nectar of the good doctrine. They stood in circles, ever more and more crowded by fresh arrivals, till at last they were so close that a hundred thousand devas occupied a space no more than the point of a needle; all the heavens of the devas and brahmās were emptied. The sound was like that of a storm, but when the lords of the various heavens blew their conchs there was utter silence. Then Buddha opened his mouth.

"There are two things," he said, "that must be avoided by one who becomes a hermit, viz. wrong desires and mortification of the body." This was the subject-matter of the first discourse, and it seemed to each hearer that it was spoken in his own tongue, and every kind of animal heard him with the same impression. Myriads of devas entered the first and the second and third and fourth paths.

The Preaching of Buddha

From that time onward Buddha turned the Wheel of the Law—that is to say, he preached the Good Doctrine to all who heard him. He converted the worshippers of fire by many miracles; Bhīmasaha, king of Rājagriha, became his disciple. Buddha also visited his native city. This was the manner of the visit. King Suddhodhana, hearing of the Buddhaship of his son, sent an embassy of noblemen asking him to visit Kapilavastu; but all the nobles, hearing the Buddha's doctrine, became disciples and remained with him. The same thing happened with many others. At last the king sent a most trusted messenger, the noble Kaludā, who had been Buddha's playfellow from infancy. He also became a disciple, but when the spring season came, and the roads grew green, and the trees blossomed, he went to the Buddha and began to speak of Kapilavastu. "Your father looks out for your coming," he said, "as the water-lily looks for the rising sun; and the queens expect you, as the night-lily expects the moon." Buddha perceived that the time had come when it would be proper for him to visit his native city. The king prepared a beautiful garden for his comfort. At last he arrived, surrounded by no less than twenty thousand priests, his disciples. At first the Shākya princes would not do him homage; but he rose into the air, and displayed first the issuing of streams of water from his body, extending over the whole of the ten thousand worlds, and sprinkling all who desired it; then the issuing of fire, which extended throughout the whole universe, but burnt not so much as a cobweb. Other wonders he showed; then Suddhodhana worshipped his son, saying:

"My lord, my Buddha, my Prince Siddhārtha, though I am indeed thy father, never again shall I call thee my child; I am not worthy to be thy slave. Again and again I worship thee. And were I to offer thee my kingdom, thou wouldst but account it as ashes." When the king bowed low the princes also made their obeisance, like the bending of a forest of bamboos before the wind.

The next day the Buddha proceeded on foot to the city to ask for alms. At every step there arose a lotus-flower beneath his feet, and vanished as he passed on; rays of light arose from his head and mouth; and because of these wonders all citizens came forth to meet him. All were astonished, for as yet this manner of asking alms was unknown. When Yashodarā heard of it she came to the palace door and worshipped him, and said: "O Siddhārtha, that night Rāhula was born thou didst go away in silence and rejectedst thy kingdom; now hast thou a more glorious kingdom instead." The king remonstrated with Buddha for seeking his food in such a manner; but he replied: "It is the custom of my race," meaning of all the former Buddhas. Then he addressed the king and taught him the Law, so that he entered the first and second paths, becoming the Buddha's disciple.

The Princess is comforted

The king then sent to inform Yashodarā that she might also come to worship Siddhārtha. Buddha, however, proceeded to her palace; as he went he informed his disciples Seriyut and Mugalāna that the princess would obtain Release. "She grieves for me," he said, "and her heart will break if her sorrow be suppressed. She will indeed cling to my feet, but do not hinder her, for the end will be that she and her companions will embrace the Law." When Yashodarā heard that the Buddha was coming she cut off her hair and went in humble garments to meet him, followed by five hundred of her ladies. Because of her abounding love, she was like an overflowing vessel and might not contain herself, but, forgetting that she was only a woman, she fell at the Buddha's feet and clung to him, weeping. But recollecting that her father-in-law was present, she presently rose and stood a little apart. Indeed, not even Brahmā may touch the body of a Buddha; but he suffered Yashodarā to do so. The king spoke of her faithfulness. "This is no sudden expression of her love," he said; "for all these seven years she has done what thou hast done. When she heard that thou didst shave thy head, or put on mean garments, or didst eat only at appointed times and from an earthen bowl, she did the same, and has refused every offer of remarriage; therefore

XXI

BUDDHA AS MENDICANT

Abanindro Nāth Tagore

Page 276

pardon her." Then Buddha related how, in a former life, Yashodarā had formed the wish to become the wife of a Buddha, and thereafter in many long ages had been his companion and helper. By this means the princess was comforted. Not long afterward Rāhula was admitted to the order of monks. Buddha, however, refused to admit Yashodarā to the order of priesthood. Many years afterward he instituted the order of Buddhist nuns, to which Yashodarā was admitted; and she, who had been born on the same day as Buddha, attained to Nirvāna two years before his own decease.

Buddha visits the Tavatimsa Heaven

Upon another occasion Buddha visited the devaloka or heaven known as the *Tavatimsa* and remained there three months. Indra hastened to prepare his throne for the Buddha to sit upon, but feared it would be too large; and, indeed, it measured some fifteen leagues in height, while the height of Buddha was twelve cubits. No sooner did Buddha approach, however, than it shrank to a convenient height. It remained, however, of the original length, and Buddha therefore performed the miracle of extending his robe on all sides for a distance of more than a thousand miles, so that the throne appeared like a seat expressly prepared for a preacher. The devas, led by Matru, who had lately been the mother of Buddha, requested the Buddha to expound the *abhidharma*. Many myriads of devas and brahmās entered the paths.

When the time came for Buddha to return to earth, Indra caused three ladders to extend from Heaven to earth, two of gold and one of silver. On one of the golden ladders, which had steps alternately of gold, silver, coral, ruby, emerald, and other gems, Buddha descended, preceded by

Indra blowing his conch. On the other golden ladder proceeded the devas with instruments of music; and on the silver ladder the brahmās, carrying umbrellas. Thus Buddha returned to his own hermitage.

Buddha prevents a War

Upon a certain occasion Buddha prevented a war which was on the point of breaking out between the Shākyas and the Kolis. Between the cities of Kapilavastu and Koli ran the river Rohini; across this river a dam had been built which enabled the people of both countries to irrigate their fields. It so happened that there was a great drought, and the husbandmen on each side claimed the sole right to the little water that remained. The rival claimants called each other by the worst possible names; and the matter, coming to the ears of the princes of each country, much exaggerated by rumour, led to the outbreak of war, and matters had gone so far that the armies of the Shākyas and the Kolis were encamped over against each other on opposite banks of the diminished river. At this crisis Buddha perceived what was going on, and proceeding through the air, at the same time making himself visible, he arrived at the place of battle. The Shākyas threw down their weapons out of respect for him whom they regarded as the jewel of their race, and the Kolis followed their example. Buddha inquired if they were assembled for a water-festival, and being informed that it was for battle, asked the cause. The princes said that they were not quite sure, but would inquire of the generals; they in turn asked their under-officers, and so on downward until it came to the original husbandmen. When Buddha was informed of the cause he asked the value of water, and being told that it was very little, he asked what was the value of men, and was told that it was very great. "Why then," he asked, "do you propose to throw away that which is of great value for the sake of that of little value?" This convincing argument sufficed to end the matter.

At the same time it was resolved that two hundred and fifty princes of each party should become disciples of Buddha. They did so unwillingly and not of their own choice. Their wives also no sooner heard of it than they complained bitterly. Buddha, however, was able to prevail upon the princes to think better of it, and it was not long before they entered the paths to Release and became *Arhats*. They remained quite indifferent when their wives again sent messages imploring them to return home.

The Admission of Women

This matter led to the first admission of women to the order of priesthood—the wives of the five hundred princes, together with the queen-mother Prajāpatī, co-wife with Māyādevī and now widow of Suddhodhana, who had lately died. She requested that they might be admitted to the order of priesthood. Buddha refused her request three times, after which she did not like to ask again. After returning home, however, the ladies determined to act more vigorously; they cut off their hair, assumed mean garments, and set out on foot for the place where Buddha was residing. They, who had been accustomed to walk on smooth marble and to be protected from the heat of the sun and the violence of the wind, were soon exhausted, and only reached the hermitage in a quite helpless and fainting condition. Again Prajāpatī asked to be admitted. Ānanda now pleaded for them on account of the hardships they had endured. Buddha still refused.

Then Ānanda inquired whether a woman, if admitted, could enter the paths and attain Release. Buddha could only reply by asking if Buddhas were born in the world solely for the benefit of men. "The way is open for women as for men," he said. Again Ānanda reminded him that on a former occasion he had announced that at a later time women would be admitted. Buddha then saw that the time had come to establish the order of nuns. His reluctance had been caused from his knowledge that the doing so would lead to doubts and scandal spoken of his order by those who were not yet his followers.

Devadatta plots Evil

The ministry of Buddha was not entirely unopposed. Not only were Brāhman philosophers often his keen opponents in controversy, but his cousin Devadatta, who through countless past births had been his bitter enemy, even attempted to murder him. Though Devadatta by meditation and asceticism had attained great powers, yet owing to his evil nature, these powers, so far from helping him toward Release, involved him in utter ruin. He established himself at the court of the king of Sewet, with five hundred monks of his own, and, supported by Prince Ajasat, obtained much influence. By Devadatta's advice Ajasat first attempted to murder his father by violence, and afterward starved him to death, in order to obtain the kingdom for himself. Not long after the accession of Ajasat Devadatta asked for a band of five hundred archers to kill Buddha. He chose thirty-one of these, and ordered the first to slay Buddha, the next two to slay the first, the next four to slay the two, and the last sixteen he intended to slay himself, in order that the matter might be kept secret. Buddha, however, though well aware of their intentions, received the first and all the other archers in turn very kindly, and preached to them, so that they entered on the path to Release and became priests. On another occasion Devadatta himself projected a great rock at Buddha as he was walking below a high cliff, but it broke into two pieces and merely inflicted an insignificant wound on Buddha's foot.

Devadatta next laid a deeper plot. There was a fierce elephant named Malagiri, accustomed to drink every day eight measures of beer. Devadatta commanded that on a certain day he should receive sixteen measures; a royal proclamation was also issued to the intent that no persons should remain in the streets; it was hoped thus that the elephant would destroy the Buddha as he went out in search of alms. News of this reached him in good time, but he would not change his custom; and next day all the balconies were lined with friends and enemies of Buddha, the former eager to behold his victory, the latter expecting his death. When Buddha approached, the elephant was loosed, and soon began to destroy the houses and show its evil temper in other ways. The friars entreated Buddha to escape, as the elephant was evidently unacquainted with his merit. Then many of the friars asked to be allowed to stand before Buddha to protect him; but he replied that his own power was one thing, that of the disciples another. When at last Ānanda took it upon himself to go in front, Buddha by will-power compelled him to remain behind. Presently a little child ran out of a house, and the elephant was about to kill her; but Buddha called out: "You were not intended to attack anyone but me; do not waste your strength on anyone else." But when the elephant beheld Buddha all its fury abated, and it approached him in the gentlest way and kneeled to him.

Buddha charged the creature never to hurt anyone again, but to be kind to all; and the elephant repeated the five commandments aloud in the presence of all the people; indeed, had he not been a four-legged creature he might have entered the path to Release. When the people saw this wonder the noise of clapping and shouting was like the sea or the thunder. They covered the elephant with jewels, and eighty-four thousand people entered the path. Not long after this Ajasat was converted and became a supporter of Buddha's party. When Ajasat departed from the monastery after this event Buddha remarked: "Had not the king murdered his father he might to-day have entered the first path. As it is, he will be saved from the lowest hell, where otherwise he must have remained a whole age. He will spend sixty thousand years in the other hells; then after long ages spent with the gods he will be born on earth and become a private Buddha."

Devadatta was now in disgrace, but hated Buddha all the more. However, he collected another band of disciples, five hundred in number. But Buddha sent two of his wisest followers to preach to those of Devadatta; and while he slept they all departed to follow Buddha. Devadatta then fell ill, and remained so for nine months; after which he determined to go and seek Buddha's forgiveness. Buddha felt no ill-will toward Devadatta; but he informed the friars: "Devadatta will not see the Buddha; so great are his crimes that not even a thousand Buddhas could save him." Devadatta, borne in his palanquin, came nearer and nearer to Buddha's monastery; but when he set foot to the ground at the entrance flames rose up from the lowest hell and wrapped his body in their folds, first his feet, then his middle, then his shoulders. He cried out to Buddha for help and repeated a verse of a hymn, by which he accepted the three gems, the Buddha, the Law, and the Church; and this will help him eventually, though he none the less went to Hell and received a body of fire sixteen hundred miles in height.

Buddha's Final Release

This was the manner of Buddha's death, called *Parinirvāna*, or Final Release. In the forty-fifth year of his ministry the Buddha suffered from a severe illness, and declared that he would not live long. While residing in the city of Pāwa he was entertained by a good smith named Chunda. He prepared an offering of pork, which was the cause of a sickness resulting in death. Buddha became very faint, and though he set out for Kushinagara, had to rest many times on the way. All this was endured that others might be reminded that none are exempt from old age, decay, and death. At last the Buddha reached the city, and there he addressed Ānanda as follows: "Inform the smith Chunda that his offering will bring a great reward, for it will be the immediate cause of my attaining *Nirvāna*. There are, indeed, two offerings which will bring great reward: one was given by the lady Sujāta before I reached the supreme wisdom, the other has just now been made by Chunda. These are the two foremost gifts." The Buddha spoke thus lest Chunda should feel remorse, or should be blamed by others; but he had given strict orders that the remainder of the offering was to be buried. Buddha lay down on a couch in a grove of sāl-trees near Kushinagara. He sent a message informing the Mālwā princes of his arrival, knowing that their regret, if he died without their once more beholding him, would be very great. Thus it was that a great company of kings and princes, nobles and ladies of the court, beside innumerable priests, and the devas and brahmās of the ten thousand worlds, assembled about the Buddha's death-bed. All these wept and wrung their hands, and bowed themselves to the ground in their grief. This occasion has been made the subject of countless pictures, similar in sentiment to the Christian *Pietas*. Buddha inquired if the priests had any last questions to put to him; but as they had no doubts on any point they remained silent. A Brāhman of Kushinagara, however, arrived, and desired to argue certain matters; Buddha would not have him denied, and in the end he became a disciple. None of his disciples was more stricken with grief than Ānanda. Buddha had given him instructions about his burial and about the rules to be observed by the monks and nuns. Then he said: "Now I depart to Nirvāna; I leave with you my ordinances; the elements of the all-knowing one will indeed pass away, but the three gems will remain." But Ānanda broke down and wept bitterly. Then Buddha continued: "O Ānanda, do not let yourself be troubled; do not weep. Have I not taught you that we must part from all that we hold most dear and pleasant? No being soever born or created can overcome the tendency to dissolution inherent in itself; a condition of permanence is impossible. For a long time, Ānanda, your kindness in act and thought and speech has brought you very near to me. You have always done well; persevere, and you, too, shall win to perfect freedom from this thirst of life, this chain of ignorance." Then he turned to the other mourners and commended Ānanda to them. He said also that the least of those present who had entered the path to Release should never entirely fail, but should at last prevail and reach Nirvāna. After a pause he said again: "Mendicants, I now impress it upon you that the parts and powers of man must be dissolved; work out your salvation

XXII

THE FINAL RELEASE

ABANINDRO NĀTH TAGORE

Page 284

with diligence." Shortly afterward the Buddha became unconscious and passed away.

The Mālwā princes, after they had a little recovered from their sorrow, wrapped the body in fold upon fold of finest cloth, and for six days the body lay in state. Then it was burnt on a magnificent pyre in the coronation hall of the princes. They were unable to set fire to the pyre, but in the end it ignited spontaneously. The body was entirely consumed, leaving only the relics like a heap of pearls. The chief of these, afterward enshrined in glorious monuments, were the four teeth, two cheek-bones, and the skull.

CHAPTER VI : SHIVA

The Supremacy of Shiva

THIS story is related by Brahmā in answer to an inquiry of the gods and rishis:

"In the night of Brahmā, when all beings and all worlds are resolved together in one equal and inseparable stillness, I beheld the great Nārāyana, soul of the universe, thousand-eyed, omniscient, Being and non-Being alike, reclining on the formless waters, supported by the thousand-headed serpent Infinite; and I, deluded by his glamour, touched the eternal being with my hand and asked: 'Who art thou? Speak.' Then he of the lotus-eyes looked upon me with drowsy glance, then rose and smiled, and said: 'Welcome, my child, thou shining grandsire.' But I took offence thereat and said: 'Dost thou, O sinless god, like a teacher to a pupil, call me child, who am the cause of creation and destruction, framer of the myriad worlds, the source and soul of all? Tell me why dost thou thus speak foolish words to me?' Then Vishnu answered: 'Knowest thou not that I am Nārāyana, creator, preserver, and destroyer of the worlds, the eternal male, the undying source and centre of the universe? For thou wert born from my own imperishable body.'

"Now ensued an angry argument between us twain upon that formless sea. Then for the ending of our contention there appeared before us a glorious shining *lingam*, a fiery pillar, like a hundred universe-consuming fires, without beginning, middle, or end, incomparable, indescribable. The divine Vishnu, bewildered by its thousand flames, said unto me, who was as much astonished as himself: 'Let us forthwith seek to know this fire's source. I will descend;

do thou ascend with all thy power.' Then he became a boar, like a mountain of blue collyrium, a thousand leagues in width, with white sharp-pointed tusks, long-snouted, loud-grunting, short of foot, victorious, strong, incomparable—and plunged below. For a thousand years he sped thus downward, but found no base at all of the lingam. Meanwhile I became a swan, white and fiery-eyed, with wings on every side, swift as thought and as the wind; and I went upward for a thousand years, seeking to find the pillar's end, but found it not. Then I returned and met the great Vishnu, weary and astonished, on his upward way.

"Then Shiva stood before us, and we whom his magic had guiled bowed unto him, while there arose about on every hand the articulate sound of '*Om*,' clear and lasting. To him Nārāyana said: 'Happy has been our strife, thou God of gods, forasmuch as thou hast appeared to end it.' Then Shiva answered to Vishnu: 'Thou art indeed the creator, preserver, and destroyer of the worlds; do thou, my child, maintain this world both moving and inert. For I, the undivided Overlord, am three, am Brahmā, Vishnu, and Rudra, who create, maintain, destroy. Cherish this Brahmā, for he shall be born of thee in an ensuing age. Then shall ye twain behold myself again.' Therewith the Great God vanished. Thereafter has the worship of the lingam been established in the three worlds."

Satī

Very long ago there was a chief of the gods named Daksha. He married Prasuti, daughter of Manu; she bore him sixteen daughters, of whom the youngest, Satī, became the wife of Shiva. This was a match unpleasing to her father, for he had a grudge against Shiva, not only for his disreputable habits, but because Shiva, upon the occasion of a festival to which he had been invited, did not offer homage to Daksha. For this reason Daksha had pronounced a curse upon Shiva, that he should receive no portion of the offerings made to the gods. A Brāhman of Shiva's party, however, pronounced the contrary curse, that Daksha should waste his life in material pleasures and ceremonial observances and should have a face like a goat.

Meanwhile Satī grew up and set her heart on Shiva, worshipping him in secret. She became of marriageable age, and her father held a *swayamvara*, or own-choice, for her, to which he invited gods and princes from far and near, except only Shiva. Then Satī was borne into the great assembly, wreath in hand. But Shiva was nowhere to be seen, amongst gods or men. Then in despair she cast her wreath into the air, calling upon Shiva to receive the garland; and behold he stood in the midst of the court with the wreath about his neck. Daksha had then no choice but to complete the marriage; and Shiva went away with Satī to his home in Kailās.

This Kailās was far away beyond the white Himālayas, and there Shiva dwelt in royal state, worshipped by gods and rishis; but more often he spent his time wandering about the hill like a beggar, his body smeared with ashes, and with Satī wearing ragged robes; sometimes also he was seen in the cremation grounds, surrounded by dancing imps and taking part in horrid rites.

One day Daksha made arrangements for a great horse sacrifice, and invited all the gods to come and share in the offerings, omitting only Shiva. The chief offerings were to be made to Vishnu. Presently Satī observed the departure of the gods, as they set out to visit Daksha, and turning to her lord, she asked: "Whither, O lord, are bound the gods, with Indra at their head? for I wonder what is toward." Then Mahādeva answered: "Shining lady, the good patriarch Daksha has prepared a horse sacrifice, and thither the gods repair." She asked him: "Why dost thou not also go to this great ceremony?" He answered: "It has been contrived amongst the gods that I should have no part in any such offerings as are made at sacrifices." Then Devī was angry and she exclaimed: "How can it be that he who dwells in every being, he who is unapproachable in power and glory, should be excluded from oblations? What penance, what gift shall I make that my lord, who transcends all thought, should receive a share, a third or a half, of the oblation?" Then Shiva smiled at Devī, pleased with her affection; but he said: "These offerings are of little moment to me, for *they* sacrifice to me who chant the hymns of the *Sāmaveda*; my priests are those who offer the oblation of true wisdom, where no officiating Brāhman is needed; that is *my* portion." Devī answered: "It is not difficult to make excuses before women. Howbeit, thou shouldst permit me at least to go to my father's house on this occasion." "Without invitation?" he asked. "A daughter needs no invitation to her father's house," she replied. "So be it," answered Mahādeva, "but know that ill will come of it; for Daksha will insult me in your presence."

So Devī went to her father's house, and there she was indeed received, but without honour, for she rode on Shiva's bull and wore a beggar's dress. She protested against her father's neglect of Shiva; but Daksha broke into angry curses and derided the "king of goblins," the "beggar," the "ash-man," the long-haired yogī. Satī answered her father: "Shiva is the friend of all; no one but you speaks ill of him. All that thou sayest the devas know, and yet adore him. But a wife, when her lord is reviled, if she cannot slay the evil speakers, must leave the place, closing her ears with her hands, or, if she have power, should surrender her life. This I shall do, for I am ashamed to own this body to such as thee." Then Satī released the inward consuming fire and fell dead at Daksha's feet.

The Anger of Shiva

Nārada bore the news to Shiva. He burned with anger, and tore from his head a lock of hair, glowing with energy, and cast it upon the earth. The terrible demon Vīrabhadra sprang from it; his tall body reached the high heavens, he was dark as the clouds, he had a thousand arms, three burning eyes, and fiery hair; he wore a garland of skulls and carried terrible weapons. This demon bowed at Shiva's feet and asked his will. He answered: "Lead my army against Daksha and destroy his sacrifice; fear not the Brāhmans, for thou art a portion of my very self." Then this dread sending appeared with Shiva's *ganas* in the midst of Daksha's assembly like a storm of wind. They broke the sacrificial vessels, polluted the offerings, and insulted the priests; finally Vīrabhadra cut off Daksha's head, trampled on Indra, broke the staff of Yama, and scattered the gods on every side; then he returned to Kailās. There Shiva sat unmoved, plunged in the deepest thought, forgetful of what had passed.

The defeated gods sought Brahmā and asked his counsel. He, with Vishnu, had abstained from attending the festival, for they had foreseen what would befall. Now Brahmā advised the gods to make their peace with Shiva, who could destroy the universe at his will. Brahmā himself went with them to Kailās. They found Shiva plunged in deep meditation in the garden of the kinnaras called Fragrant, under a great pipal-tree a hundred leagues in height, its branches spreading forty leagues on either side. Brahmā prayed him to pardon Daksha and to mend the broken limbs of gods and rishis, "for," he said, "the offerings are thine; receive them and permit the sacrifice to be completed." Then Shiva answered: "Daksha is but a child; I do not think of him as one who has committed sin. His head, however, has been burnt; I shall bestow on him a goat's head, and the broken limbs shall be made whole." Then the devas thanked Shiva for his gentleness, and invited him to the sacrifice. There Daksha looked on him with reverence, the rite was duly performed, and there also Vishnu appeared riding upon Garuda. He spoke to Daksha, saying: "Only the unlearned deem myself and Shiva to be distinct; he, I, and Brahmā are one, assuming different names for the creation, preservation, and destruction of the universe. We, as the triune Self, pervade all creatures; the wise therefore regard all others as themselves."

Then all the gods and rishis saluted Shiva and Vishnu and Brahmā, and departed to their places; but Shiva returned to Kailās and fell once more into his dream.

Note on Daksha and Shiva

It happens constantly in the history of Indian literature that a new wave of theology becomes the occasion for a recapitulation of an older theory of the origin of the universe. This fact is the good fortune of later students, for without it we should have had no clue whatever in a majority of cases to the ancient conceptions. Of such an order, we may take it, is the story of Daksha. It was held by the promulgators of Aryan and Sanskritic views that Brahmā had, vaguely speaking, been the creator of the worlds. But amongst those to whom he was sacred there grew up, we must remember, the philosophy of the inherent evil and duality of material existence. And with the perfecting of this theory the name of a new god, Shiva or Mahādeva, embodying spiritual enlightenment, became popular. Now what part could have been played, in the evolution of the cosmos, by these different divinities? This was a world in which good brought forth evil, and evil brought forth good, and good without evil was a mere contradiction in terms. How, then, could the Great God be made responsible for anything so disastrous? Plainly, he could not. So the myth was elaborated that Brahmā had at first created four beautiful youths to be the progenitors of mankind, and they had sat down to worship on the banks of Lake Mānasarovara. Suddenly there came to them Shiva in the form of a great swan—the prototype of the Paramahamsa, or supreme swan, the title of the emancipated soul—who swam hither and thither, warning them that the world about them was an illusion and a bondage, and that their one way of escape lay in refusing to become fathers. The young men heard and understood, and, plunging into meditation, they remained on the shores of the divine lake, useless for any of the purposes of the world. Then Brahmā created the eight lords of creation, the Prajāpatis, and they it was who made up the muddle that is called this world.

The history of ideas is perhaps the only history that can be clearly followed out in India, but this is traceable with a wonderful distinctness. At this point in the history of Brahmā, where he creates the Prajāpatis, in a story whose evident object it is to show the part played by Shiva in the process of creation, it is obvious that we are suddenly taking on board the whole of a more ancient cosmogony. The converse fact, that the gods of that mythology are meeting for the first time with a new series of more ethical and spiritual conceptions than have hitherto been familiar to them, is equally indisputable as the story proceeds. One of the new Prajāpatis has an established conviction—incongruous enough in a new creation, but not unnatural in a case of great seniority—that he himself is Overlord of men and gods, and it is greatly to his chagrin and disgust that he finds his rank and pretensions ignored by that god who is known as Shiva or Mahādeva. In this very fact of the suddenness of the offence given, and the unexpectedness of the slight, we have an added indication that we are here dealing with the introduction of a new god into the Hindu pantheon. He is to be made a member of its family circle by a device that is at once old and eternally new. The chief Prajāpati—Daksha by name—out of wounded pride, conceives a violent feud against Shiva, the Great God. But Daksha had a daughter called Satī, who is the very incarnation of womanly piety and devotion. This maiden's whole soul is given up in secret to the worship and love of the Great God. Now she is the last unmarried daughter of her father, and the time for her wooing and betrothal cannot be much longer delayed. It is announced, therefore, that her *Swayamvara*—the ceremony of choosing her own husband performed by a king's daughter—is about to be held, and invitations are issued to all the eligible gods and princes. Shiva alone is not invited, and to Shiva the whole heart of Satī is irrevocably given. On stepping into the pavilion of the bridal choice, therefore, with the marriage garland in her hand, Satī makes a supreme appeal. "If I be indeed Satī," she exclaims, throwing the garland into the air, "then do thou, Shiva, receive my garland!" And immediately he was there in the midst of them with her garland round his neck. The story of the further development of the feud is related above. Ancient as is now the story of the wedding of the daughter of the older Lord of Creation with the new-comer amongst the gods, it is clear at this point that Daksha was already so old that the origin of his goat's head had been forgotten, and was felt to require explanation by the world of the day that accepted Shiva. To an age before the birth of Buddhism he may have been familiar enough, but the preaching of that faith throughout the length and breadth of India must by this time have educated the people to demanding moral and spiritual attributes in their deities instead of a mere congeries of cosmic powers, and so trained they came back, it would appear, to the conception of Daksha as to something whose significance they had forgotten.

Suggestions of Earlier Myths

Traces of something still more ancient are to be seen in the next act of this sacred drama, when Shiva, drunk with sorrow, strides about the earth, all destroying, bearing the form of the dead Satī on his back. The soil is dried up, plants wither, harvests fail. All nature shudders under the grief of the Great God. Then Vishnu, to save mankind, comes up behind Shiva and, hurling his discus time after time, cuts the body of Satī to pieces till the Great God, conscious that the weight is gone, retires alone to Kailās to lose himself once more in his eternal meditation. But the body of Satī has been hewn into fifty-two dieces, and wherever a fragment touches earth a shrine of mother-worship is established, and Shiva himself shines forth before the suppliant as the guardian of that spot.

This whole story brings vividly back to us the quest of Persephone by Demeter, the Great Goddess, that beautiful Greek myth of the northern winter; but in the fifty-two pieces of the body of Satī we are irresistibly reminded of the seventy-two fragments of another dead body, that of Osiris, which was sought by Isis and found in the cypress-tree at Byblos. The oldest year is said to have been one of two seasons, or seventy-two weeks. Thus the body of Osiris would perhaps signify the whole year, divided into its most calculable units. In the more modern story we find ourselves dealing again with a number characteristic of the weeks of the year. The fragments of the body of Satī are fifty-two. Does she, then, represent some ancient personification which may have been the historic root of our present reckoning?

In a general way goddesses are, as we know, long anterior to gods, and it is interesting to see that in the older myth of Egypt it is the woman who is active, the woman who seeks and carries off the dead body of man. The comparative modernness of the story of Shiva and Satī is seen, amongst other things, in the fact that the husband seeks and finds and bears away the wife.

Umā

Satī was reborn as the daughter of the great mountain Himālaya, when her name was Umā, surnamed Haimāvatī from her birth; another name she had was Pārvatī, daughter of the mountain. Her elder sister was the river Gangā. From her childhood Umā was devoted to Shiva, and she would steal away at night to offer flowers and fruits and to burn lights before the lingam. A deva, too, one day predicted that she would become the wife of the Great God. This awakened her father's pride, and he was anxious that she should be betrothed; but nothing could be done, for Shiva remained immersed in profound contemplation, oblivious of all that went on, all his activity inward-turned. Umā became his servant and attended to all his requirements, but could not divert him from the practice of austerities or awaken his love.

About this time a terrible demon named Tāraka greatly harassed the gods and the world, perverting all seasons and destroying sacrifices; nor could the gods defeat him, for in a past age he had won his power from Brahmā himself by the practice of austerities. The gods therefore proceed to Brahmā and pray his help. He explains that it would not be fitting for him to proceed against the demon, to whom he himself had given power; but he promises that a son should be born to Shiva and Pārvatī, who should lead the gods to victory.

The chief of the gods, Indra, next betook himself to Kāmadeva, or Desire, the god of Love, and explained the need of his assistance. Desire agreed to give his aid, and set out with his wife Passion and his companion the Spring to the mountain where Shiva dwelt. At that season the trees were putting forth new flowers, the snow had gone, and birds and beasts were mating; only Shiva stayed in his dream unmoved.

Even Desire was daunted till he took new courage at the sight of Umā's loveliness. He chose a moment when Shiva began to relax his concentration and when Pārvatī approached to worship him; he drew his bow and was about to shoot when the Great God saw him and darted a flash of fire from his third eye, consuming Desire utterly. Shiva departed, leaving Passion unconscious, and Pārvatī was carried away by her father. From that time Ananga, Bodiless, has been one of Kāmadeva's

XXIII

THE ASCETICISM OF UMĀ

NANDA LĀL BOSE

Page 296

names, for he was not dead, and while Passion lamented her lost lord a voice proclaimed to her: "Thy lover is not lost for evermore; when Shiva shall wed Umā he will restore Love's body to his soul, a marriage gift to his bride."

Pārvatī now reproached her useless beauty, for what avails it to be lovely if no lover loves that loveliness? She became a *sannyāsinī*, an anchorite, and laying aside all jewels, with uncombed hair and a hermit's dress of bark, she retired to a lonely mountain and spent her life in meditation upon Shiva and the practice of austerities such as are dear to him. One day a Brāhman youth visited her, offering congratulations upon the constancy of her devotion; but he asked her for what reason she thus spent her life in self-denial since she had youth and beauty and all that heart could desire. She related her story, and said that since Desire is dead she saw no other way to win Shiva's approval than this devotion. The youth attempted to dissuade Pārvatī from desiring Shiva, recounting the terrible stories of his inauspicious acts: how he wore a poisonous snake and a bloody elephant-hide, how he dwelt in cremation grounds, how he rode on a bull and was poor and of unknown birth. Pārvatī was angered and defended her lord, finally declaring that her love could not be changed whatever was said of him, true or false. Then the young Brāhman threw off his disguise and revealed himself as no other than Shiva, and he gave her his love. Pārvatī then returned home to tell her father of her happy fortune, and the preliminaries of marriage were arranged in due form. At last the day came, both Shiva and his bride were ready, and the former, accompanied by Brahmā and Vishnu, entered Himālaya's city in triumphal procession, riding through the streets ankle-deep in scattered flowers, and Shiva bore away the bride to Kailās; not, however, before he had restored the body of Desire to his lonely wife.

For many years Shiva and Pārvatī dwelt in bliss in their Himālayan paradise; but at last the god of fire appeared as a messenger from the gods and reproached Shiva that he had not begotten a son to save the gods from their distress. Shiva bestowed the fruitful germ on Fire, who bore it away and finally gave it to Ganges, who preserved it till the six Pleiades came to bathe in her waters at dawn. They laid it in a nest of reeds, where it became the god-child Kumāra, the future god of war. There Shiva and Parvātī found him again and took him to Kailās, where he spent his happy childhood. When he had become a strong youth the gods requested his aid, and Shiva sent him as their general to lead an army against Tāraka. He conquered and slew the demon, and restored peace to Heaven and earth.

The second son of Shiva and Pārvatī was Ganesha;[1] he is the god of wisdom and the remover of obstacles. One day the proud mother, in a forgetful moment, asked the planet Saturn to look upon her son: his baleful glance reduced the child's head to ashes. Pārvatī asked advice of Brahmā, and he told her to replace the head with the first she could find: that was an elephant's.

Umā's Sport

Mahādeva sat one day on a sacred mountain of Himālaya plunged in deep and arduous contemplation. About him were the delightful flowering forests, numerous with birds and beasts and nymphs and sprites. The Great God sat in a bower where heavenly flowers opened and blazed

[1] See above, p. 18.

with radiant light; the scent of sandal and the sound of heavenly music were sensed on every side. Beyond all telling was the mountain's loveliness, shining with the glory of the Great God's penance, echoing with the hum of bees. All the Seasons were present there, and all creatures and powers resided there with minds firm-set in *yoga*, in concentred thought.

Mahādeva had about his loins a tiger-skin and a lion's pelt across his shoulders. His sacred thread was a terrible snake. His beard was green; his long hair hung in matted locks. The rishis bowed to the ground in worship; by that marvellous vision they were cleansed of every sin. There came Umā, daughter of Himālaya, wife of Shiva, followed by his ghostly servants. Garbed was she like her lord, and observed the same vows. The jar she bore was filled with the water of every *tīrtha*, and the ladies of the Sacred Rivers followed her. Flowers sprang up and perfumes were wafted on every side as she approached. Then Umā, with a smiling mouth, in playful mood covered the eyes of Mahādeva, laying her lovely hands across them from behind.

Instantly life in the universe waned, the sun grew pale, all living things cowered in fear. Then the darkness vanished again, for one blazing eye shone forth on Shiva's brow, a third eye like a second sun. So scorching a flame proceeded from that eye that Himālaya was burnt with all his forests, and the herds of deer and other beasts rushed headlong to Mahādeva's seat to pray for his protection, making the Great God's power to shine with strange brightness. The fire meanwhile blazed up to the very sky, covering every quarter like the all-destroying conflagration of an æon's end. In a moment the mountains were consumed, with all their gems and peaks and shining herbs. Then Himālaya's daughter, beholding her father thus destroyed, came forth and stood before the Great God with her hands joined in prayer. Then Mahādeva, seeing Umā's grief, cast benignant looks upon the mountain, and at once Himālaya was restored to his first estate, and became as fair as he had been before the fire. All his trees put forth their flowers, and birds and beasts were gladdened.

Then Umā with folded hands addressed her lord: "O holy one, lord of creatures," she said, "I pray thee to resolve my doubt. Why did this third eye of thine appear? Why was the mountain burned and all its forests? Why hast thou now restored the mountain to his former state after destroying him?"

Mahādeva answered: "Sinless lady, because thou didst cover up my eyes in thoughtless sport the universe grew dark. Then, O daughter of the mountain, I created a third eye for the protection of all creatures, but the blazing energy thereof destroyed the mountain. It was for thy sake that I made Himālaya whole again."

Shiva's Fishing

It befell one day that Shiva sat with Pārvatī in Kailās expounding to her the sacred text of the Vedas. He was explaining a very difficult point when he happened to look up, and behold, Pārvatī was manifestly thinking of something else; and when he asked her to repeat the text she could not, for, in fact, she had not been listening. Shiva was very angry, and he said: "Very well, it is clear you are not a suitable wife for a yogī; you shall be born on earth as a fisherman's wife, where you will not hear any sacred texts at all." Immediately Pārvatī disappeared, and Shiva sat down to practise one of his deep contemplations. But he could not fix his attention; he kept on thinking of Pārvatī and feeling very uncomfortable. At last he said to himself: "I am afraid I was rather hasty, and certainly Pārvatī ought not to be down there on earth, as a fisherman's wife too; she is my wife." He sent for his servant Nandi and ordered him to assume the form of a terrible shark and annoy the poor fishermen, breaking their nets and wrecking their boats.

Pārvatī had been found on the seashore by the headman of the fishermen and adopted by him as his daughter. She grew up to be a very beautiful and gentle girl. All the young fishermen desired to marry her. By this time the doings of the shark had become quite intolerable; so the headman announced that he would bestow his adopted daughter in marriage upon whoever should catch the great shark. This was the moment foreseen by Shiva; he assumed the form of a handsome fisher-lad and, representing himself as a visitor from Madura, offered to catch the shark, and so he did at the first throw of the net. The fishermen were very glad indeed to be rid of their enemy, and the headman's daughter was given in marriage to the young man of Madura, much to the disgust of her former suitors. But Shiva now assumed his proper form, and bestowing his blessing on Pārvatī's foster-father, he departed with her once more to Kailās. Pārvatī reflected that she really ought to be more attentive, but Shiva was so pleased to have Pārvatī back again that he felt quite peaceful and quite ready to sit down and take up his interrupted dreams.

THE SAINTS OF SHIVA

Tiger-foot (Vyaghrapāda)

A certain pure and learned Brahman dwelt beside the Ganges. He had a son endowed with strange powers and gifts of mind and body. He became the disciple of his father; when he had learnt all that his father could teach him, the sage bestowed his blessing, and inquired of his son: "What remains that I can do for thee?" Then the son bowed down to his father's feet, saying: "Teach me the highest form of virtue amongst those of the hermit rule." The father answered: "The highest virtue is to worship Shiva." "Where best may I do that?" asked the youth. The father answered: "He pervades the whole universe; yet there are places on earth of special manifestation, even as the all-pervading Self is manifest in individual bodies. The greatest of such shrines is Tillai, where Shiva will accept thy adoration; there is the lingam of pure light."

The young ascetic left his parents and set out on his long journey to the south. Presently he came to a beautiful lake covered with lotus-flowers, and beside it he saw a lingam under a banyan-tree. He fell on his face in adoration of the lord and made himself its priest, doing the service of offering flowers and water with unfailing devotion day by day. Not far away he built himself a little hermitage and established a second lingam in the forest. But now he found it difficult to accomplish perfectly the service of both shrines. For he was not content with the flowers of pools and fields and shrubs, but desired to make daily offering of the most exquisite buds from the summits of the lofty forest trees. However early he would start, still the sun's fierce rays withered half of these before he could gather enough, nor could he see in the dark hours how to choose the most perfect flowers.

In despair of perfect service he cast himself upon the ground and implored the god to help him. Shiva appeared and, with a gentle smile, bestowed a boon on the devoted youth. He prayed that he might receive the hands and feet of a tiger, armed with strong claws and having keen eyes set in them, that he might quickly climb the highest trees and find the most perfect flowers for the service of the shrine. This Shiva granted, and thus the youth became the "Tiger-footed" and the "Six-eyed."

Eye-Saint (Kan-Appan)

There dwelt long ago a forest chieftain who spent all his days in hunting, so that the woods resounded with the barking of his dogs and the cries of his servants. He was a worshipper of Subrahmanian, the southern mountain deity, and his offerings were strong drink, cocks and peafowl, accompanied with wild dances and great feasts. He had a son, surnamed the Sturdy, whom he took always with him on his hunting expeditions, giving him the education, so they say, of a young tiger-cub. The time came when the old chief grew feeble, and he handed over his authority to the Sturdy one.

He also spent his days in hunting. One day a great boar made his escape from the nets in which he had been taken and rushed away. The Sturdy one followed with two servants, a long and weary chase, till at last the boar fell down from very weariness, and Sturdy cut it atwain. When the retinue came up they proposed to roast the boar and take their rest; but there was no water, so Sturdy shouldered the boar and they went farther afield. Presently they came in sight of the sacred hill of Kalaharti; one of the servants pointed to its summit, where there was an image of the god with matted locks. "Let us go there to worship," he said. Sturdy lifted the boar again and strode on. But as he walked the boar grew lighter and lighter, rousing great wonder in his heart.

He laid the boar down and rushed on to seek the meaning of the miracle. It was not long before he came to a stone lingam, the upper part of which was shaped into the likeness of the god's head; immediately it spoke to his soul, prepared by some goodness or austerity of a previous birth, so that his whole nature was changed, and he thought of nothing but the love of the god whom now he first beheld; he kissed the image, like a mother embracing a long-lost son. He saw that water had recently been poured upon it, and the head was crowned with leaves; one of his followers, just coming up, said that this must have been done by an old Brāhman devotee who had dwelt near by in the days of Sturdy's father.

It came into Sturdy's heart then that perhaps he himself might render some service to the god. He could scarcely bring himself to leave the image all alone; but he had no other choice, and hurrying back to the camp, he chose some tender parts of the roasted flesh, tasted them to see if they were good, and taking these in a cup of leaves and some water from the river in his mouth, he ran back to the image, leaving his astonished followers without a word, for they naturally thought he had gone mad. When he reached the image he sprinkled it with water from his mouth, made offering of the boar's flesh and laid upon it the wild flowers from his own hair, praying the god to receive his gifts. Then the sun went down, and Sturdy remained beside the image on guard with bow strung and arrow notched. At dawn he went forth to hunt that he might have new offerings to lay before the god.

Meanwhile the Brāhman devotee who had served the god so many years came to perform his customary morning service; he brought pure water in a sacred vessel, fresh flowers and leaves, and recited holy prayers. What was his horror to see that the image had been defiled with flesh and dirty water! He rolled in grief before the lingam, asking the Great God why he had allowed this pollution of his shrine, for the offerings acceptable to Shiva are pure water and fresh flowers; it is said that there is greater merit in laying a single flower before the god than in offering much gold. For this Brāhman priest the slaying of creatures was a hideous crime, the eating of flesh an utter abomination, the touch of a man's mouth horrible pollution, and he looked on the savage woodland hunters as a lower order of creation. He reflected, however, that he must not delay to carry out his own customary service, so he cleansed the image carefully and did his worship according to the Vedic rite as usual, sang the appointed hymn, circumambulated the shrine, and returned to his abode.

For some days this alternation of service of the image took place, the Brāhman offering pure water and flowers in the morning, the hunter bringing flesh at night. Meanwhile Sturdy's father arrived, thinking his son possessed, and strove to reason with the young convert; but it was in vain, and they could but return to their village and leave him alone.

The Brāhman could not bear this state of things for long; passionately he called on Shiva to protect his image from this daily desecration. One night the god appeared to him, saying: "That of which thou dost make complaint is acceptable and welcome to me. He who offers flesh and water from his mouth is an ignorant hunter of the woods who knows no sacred lore. But regard not him, regard his motive alone; his rough frame is filled with love of me, that very ignorance is his knowledge of myself. His offerings, abominable in thy eyes, are pure love. But thou shalt behold to-morrow the proof of his devotion."

Next day Shiva himself concealed the Brāhman behind the shrine; then, in order to reveal all the devotion of Sturdy, he caused the likeness of blood to flow from one eye of the image of himself. When Sturdy brought his customary offering, at once he saw this blood, and he cried out: "O my master, who hath wounded thee? Who has done this sacrilege when I was not here to guard thee?" Then he searched the whole forest to seek for the enemy; finding no one, he set himself to stanch the wound with medicinal herbs; but in vain. Then he remembered the adage of the doctors, that like cures like, and at once he took a keen-edged arrow and cut out his own right eye and applied it to the eye of the image of the god; and lo! the bleeding ceased at once. But, alas! the second eye began to bleed. For a moment Sturdy was cast down and helpless; then it flashed upon him that he still had the means of cure, of proved efficacy. He seized the arrow and began to cut away his other eye, putting his foot against the eye of the image, so that he might not fail to find it when he could no longer see.

But now Shiva's purpose was accomplished; he put forth a hand from the lingam and stayed the hunter's hand, saying to him: "It is enough; henceforth thy place shall be for ever by my side in Kailās." Then the Brāhman priest also saw that love is greater than ceremonial purity; and Sturdy has been evermore adored as Eye-Saint.

Mānikka Vāçagar and the Jackals

This saint was born near Madura; by his sixteenth year he had exhausted the whole circle of contemporary Brāhman learning, especially the Shaiva scriptures; the report of his learning and intelligence reached the king, who sent for him and made him prime minister. At the Pāndian court he enjoyed the luxury of Indra's heaven, and moved amongst the courtiers like the silver moon amongst the stars, arrayed in royal robes, surrounded by horses and elephants, attended by the umbrella of state; for the wise king left the government entirely in his hands. Still the young minister did not lose his head; he reminded himself that these external pleasures are but bonds of the soul, and must be forsaken by those who would obtain Release. He felt great compassion for the toiling multitudes who pass from birth to birth suffering remediless griefs. His soul melted in passionate longing for Shiva. He continued to administer justice and to rule well, but ever hoped to meet with a Master who would reveal to him the "Way of Release." Like the bee that flits from flower to flower, he went from one to another of the Shaiva teachers, but found no satisfying truth. One day a messenger came to court announcing that a ship had arrived in the harbour of a neighbouring king bringing a cargo of splendid horses from abroad. The king at once dispatched his minister with great treasure to buy the beautiful horses, and he set out in state, attended by regiments of soldiers. This was the last great pageant of his secular life.

Meanwhile Shiva himself, as he sat in his court in Heaven with Umā by his side, announced his intention to descend to earth in the shape of a human *guru* or Master, that he might initiate a disciple for the conversion of the South and the glory of the Tamil speech. He took his seat accordingly under a great spreading tree, surrounded by many servants in the form of Shaiva saints, his disciples. At his advent the trees put forth their blossoms, the birds sang on every branch of the grove near by the seaport where the lord had taken his seat. Then the young envoy passed by, attended by his retinue, and heard the sound of Shaiva hymns proceeding from the grove. He sent a messenger to learn the source of the divine music, and was told that there was seated a saintly Master, like to Shiva himself, beneath a great tree, attended by a thousand devotees. He dismounted and proceeded reverently toward the sage, who appeared to his vision like Shiva himself, with his blazing third eye. He made inquiries as to the divine truths taught by the sage and his disciples; he was converted and threw himself at the Master's feet in tears, renouncing all worldly honour; he received a solemn initiation, and became a *Jīvan-mukta*, one who attains Release even while still incarnate in human form. He adopted the white ashes and braided locks of a Shaiva yogī. Moreover, he made over to the Master and his attendants all the treasure entrusted to him for the purchase of the horses.

The noble retinue now approached the converted minister, and remonstrated with this disposal of his master's property; but he bade them depart, "for why," he asked, "would you bring me back to mundane matters such as this?" They therefore returned to Madura and announced to the king what had taken place. He was not unnaturally enraged, and sent a curt order for the minister's immediate return. He only answered: "I know no king but Shiva, from whom not even the messengers of Death could lead me." Shiva, however, bade him return to Madura and fear nothing, but to say that the horses would arrive in due course. The god also provided him with a suitable equipage and a priceless ruby. The king at first accepted his assurances that the horses would arrive; but the story of the other courtier prevailed, and two days before the promised arrival of the horses the young minister was thrown into prison.

The lord, however, cared for his disciple. He gathered together a multitude of jackals, converted them into splendid horses, and sent them to court, with hosts of minor deities disguised as grooms; he himself rode at the head of the troops, disguised as the merchant from whom the horses were supposed to have been purchased. The king was of course delighted, and released the minister with many apologies. The horses were delivered and sent to the royal stables; the disguised gods departed, and all seemed well.

Before dawn the town was aroused by awful howlings; the horses had turned into jackals and, worse still, were devouring the real horses in the king's stables. The king perceived that he had been deceived, and seized the wretched minister and had him exposed to the noonday sun, with a heavy stone upon his back. He prayed to his lord; Shiva in answer released the waters of Gangā from his matted locks and flooded the town. Again the king perceived his error; he restored the sage to a place of honour, and set about erecting a dam to save the town. When this was accomplished, the king offered to resign his kingdom to the saint; but Mānikka Vāçagar preferred to retire to the seaport where he first beheld the lord. There he took up his place at the feet of the *guru*. Shiva's work, however, was now accomplished; he departed to Heaven, leaving it a charge upon Mānikka Vāçagar to establish the faith throughout Tamilakam. Thereafter the saint spent his life in wandering from town to town, singing the impassioned devotional hymns from which is derived his name of "Him whose Utterance is Rubies." At last he reached Chitambaram, the sacred city where Shiva's dance is daily beheld, the abode also of the saint named Tiger-foot; here the sage dwelt until his passing away into the lord. This was the manner of that beatification. After a great controversy with Buddhist heretics from Ceylon there appeared a venerable but unknown devotee who prayed to be allowed to write down all the saint's songs from his own lips. This he did, and then disappeared; for it was no other than Shiva himself, who took the songs to heaven for the gladdening of the gods. Next morning a perfect copy was found, a thousand verses in all, signed by the god himself, beside his image in Chitambaram. All the devotees of the temple hastened to the saint for an explanation; he told them to follow him, and led them to the image of Shiva in the Golden Court. "That is the meaning," he said, and therewith he disappeared, melting into the image itself, and he was seen no more.

A Legend of Shiva's Dance

It came to the knowledge of Shiva that there resided in Tāragam forest ten thousand heretical rishis, who taught that the universe is eternal, that souls have no lord, and that the performance of works alone suffices for the attainment of salvation. Shiva determined to teach them the truth. He bade Vishnu accompany him in the form of a beautiful woman, and the two entered the wild forest, Shiva disguised as a wandering yogī, Vishnu as his wife. Immediately all the rishis' wives were seized with violent longing for the yogī; the rishis themselves were equally infatuated with the seeming yogī's wife. Soon the whole hermitage was in an uproar; but presently the

XXIV

THE DANCE OF SHIVA

KHITINDRA NĀTH MAZUMDAR

Page 310

hermits began to suspect that things were not quite what they seemed; they gathered together, and pronounced quite ineffectual curses on the visitors. Then they prepared a sacrificial fire, and evoked from it a terrible tiger which rushed upon Shiva to devour him. He only smiled, and gently picking it up, he peeled off its skin with his little finger, and wrapped it about himself like a silk shawl. Then the rishis produced a horrible serpent; but Shiva hung it round his neck for a garland. Then there appeared a malignant black dwarf with a great club; but Shiva pressed his foot upon its back and began to dance, with his foot still pressing down the goblin. The weary hermits, overcome by their own efforts, and now by the splendour and swiftness of the dance and the vision of the opening heavens, the gods having assembled to behold the dancer, threw themselves down before the glorious god and became his devotees.

Now Pārvatī descended on the white bull, and Shiva departed with her to Kailās. Vishnu was thus left alone with his attendant, the serpent Āti-Sheshan, Ananta, the Infinite, upon whom he rests on the ocean of milk during the night of Brahmā. Each was dazed with the beauty of Shiva's dance, and Āti-Sheshan especially longed to see the vision again. Vishnu therefore released the serpent from his service, appointing his son to take his place; he advised his late servant to repair to Kailās and to obtain the favour of Shiva by a life of asceticism. So the serpent devotee, with his thousand jewelled heads, departed to the northern regions to lay aside his secular glory and become the least of Shiva's devotees. After a time, Shiva, assuming the form of Brahmā riding upon his swan, appeared to test the devotee's sincerity; he pointed out that already enough had been endured to merit the delights of paradise and a high place in Heaven, and he offered a boon. But the serpent answered: "I desire no separate heaven, nor miraculous gifts; I desire only to see for ever the mystic dance of the Lord of all." Brahmā argued with him in vain; the serpent will remain as he is, if need be until death and throughout other lives, until he obtains the blessed vision. Shiva then assumed his own form, and riding beside Pārvatī on their snow-white bull, he approached the great snake and touched his head.

Then he proceeded like an earthly guru—and for the Shaivites every true Master is an incarnation of God—to impart ancient wisdom to his new disciple. The universe, he said, is born of Māyā, illusion, to be the scene of countless incarnations and of actions both good and evil. As an earthen pot has for its first cause the potter, for material cause the clay, and instrumental cause the potter's staff and wheel, so the universe has illusion for its material cause, the *Shakti* of Shiva—that is, Pārvatī—for its instrumental cause, and Shiva himself for its first cause. Shiva has two bodies, the one with parts and visible, the other without parts, invisible and transcendental. Beyond these again is his own essential form of light and splendour. He is the soul of all, and his dance is the creation, preservation, and destruction of the universe, and the giving of bodies to souls and their release. The dance is ceaseless and eternal; Āti-Sheshan shall behold it again at Tillai, Chitambaram, the centre of the universe. "Meanwhile," said Shiva, "thou shalt put off thy serpent form and, born of mortal parents, shalt proceed to Tillai, where thou shalt find a grove, where is a lingam, the first of all lingams, tended by my servant Tiger-foot. Dwell with him in the hermitage that he has made, and there shall come a time when the dance shall be revealed to thee and him together."

Such is the story of the revelation of Shiva's dance in the forest of Tāragam.

Note on Shiva's Dance

The above is but one of many legends of Shiva's dance. The dance itself represents the activity of Shiva as the source of all movement within the universe, and especially his five acts, creation, preservation, destruction, embodiment, and release; its purpose is to release the souls of men from illusion. It is frequently emphasized that the place of the dance, the sacred shrine of Tillai or Chitambaram, is in reality within the heart; the human soul attains release when the vision is beheld within itself. It will be seen that Shiva has many forms, "evil" as well as "good." This must ever be so if we are not to postulate a separate "devil." As dancer in the burning-ground, the most terrible and unclean of places, he is essentially a pre-Aryan demon; he is also "The Terrible" and "The Destroyer." Later Shaivate thought makes effective use of this dramatic imagery, not merely arguing that the demons also must be a portion of God, nor simply transferring the place of the dance to the sacred shrine at Chitambaram, but accepting the dance as it is, and finding a new meaning in the cremation-ground, the heart of the devotee, waste and desolate, the place where the self and its deeds are burnt away, and all is destroyed but the dancer himself.

CHAPTER VII: OTHER STORIES FROM THE PURĀNAS, EPICS, AND VEDAS

The Churning of the Ocean

IT happened long ago that Indra, king of the gods, was cursed by the great rishi Durvasas, a portion of Shiva, for a slight he put on him. Thenceforward Indra and all the three worlds lost their energy and strength, and all things went to ruin. Then the *daityas* or asuras put forth their strength against the enfeebled gods, so that they fled to Brahmā for protection; he then advised them to seek aid from Vishnu, the tamer of demons, the undying God, creator, preserver, and destroyer. So Brahmā spoke, and himself led the gods along the northern shore of the sea of milk to Vishnu's seat, and prayed his aid. Then the Supreme Deity, bearing his emblems of conch and disc and mace, and radiant with light, appeared before the grandsire and other deities, and to him again they all made prayer. Then Hari smiled and said: "I shall restore your strength. Do now as I command: Cast into the Milky Sea potent herbs, then take Mount Mandara for churning-stick, the serpent Vāsukī for rope, and churn the ocean for the dew of life. For this you need the *daityas*' aid; make alliance with them, therefore, and engage to share with them the fruit of your combined labour; promise them that by drinking the ambrosia they shall become immortal. But I shall see to it that they have no share of the water of life, but theirs shall be the labour only."

Thus the gods entered into alliance with the demons, and jointly undertook the churning of the sea of milk. They cast into it potent herbs, they took Mount Mandara for

XXV

SHIVA DRINKING THE WORLD-POISON

NANDA LĀL BOSE

Page 314

the churning-stick and Vāsukī for the rope.[1] The gods took up their station by the serpent's tail, the *daityas* at its head. Hari himself in tortoise shape became a pivot of the mountain as it was whirled around; he was present also unseen amongst the gods and demons, pulling the serpent to and fro; in another vast body he sat upon the summit of the mountain. With other portions of his energy he sustained the serpent king, and infused power into the bodies of the gods. As they laboured thus the flames of Vāsukī's breath scorched the faces of the demons; but the clouds that drifted toward his tail refreshed the gods with vivifying showers.

First from the sea rose up the wish-bestowing cow Surabhi, gladdening the eyes of the divinities; then came the goddess Varunī, with rolling eyes, the divinity of wine; then upsprang the Parijata tree of paradise, the delight of Heaven's nymphs, perfuming all the world with the fragrance of its flowers; then rose the troops of apsarās, of entrancing loveliness and grace. Then rose the moon, whom Mahādeva seized and set upon his brow; and then came a draught of deadly poison, and that also Mahādeva took and drank, lest it should destroy the world: it is that bitter poison that turned his throat blue, wherefore he is known as Nīlakantha, blue-throat, ever after. Next came Dhanwantarī, holding in his hand a cup of the dew of life, delighting the eyes of the *daityas* and the rishis. Then appeared the goddess Shrī, the delight of Vishnu, radiant, seated on an open lotus; the great sky-elephants anointed her with pure

[1] The Indian milk-churn is a stick round which a long rope is twisted, and pulled alternately from opposite ends. The rope itself holds up the stick in a vertical position, and the turning of it to and fro accomplishes the churning.

water brought by Gangā and poured from golden vessels, while the enraptured sages sang her praises. The Milky Sea adorned her with a wreath of unfading flowers; Vishvakarmā decked her with celestial jewels. Then she, who was in sooth the bride of Vishnu, cast herself upon his breast, and there reclining turned her eyes upon the delighted gods. But little pleased were the *daityas*, for now were they abandoned by the goddess of prosperity. The angry *daityas* snatched the cup of nectar from Dhanwantarī and bore it off. But Vishnu, assuming an exquisite and ravishing woman-form, deluded and fascinated them, and while they disagreed amongst themselves he stole away the draught and brought it to the gods, who drank deep from the cup of life. Invigorated thereby, they put the demons to flight and drove them down to Hell, and worshipped Vishnu with rejoicing. The sun shone clear again, the Three Worlds became once more prosperous, and devotion blossomed in the hearts of every creature. Indra, seated upon his throne, composed a hymn of praise for Lakshmī; she, thus praised, granted him wishes twain. This was the choice, that never again should she abandon the Three Worlds, nor should she ever forsake any that should sing her praise in the words of Indra's hymn.

Whoso hears this story of the birth of Lakshmī from the Milky Sea, whosoever reads it, that goddess of good fortune shall never leave his house for generations three; strife or misfortune may never enter where the hymn to Lakshmī is sung.

The Birth of Gangā

There was once a king of Ayodhyā, by name Sagara. He eagerly desired children, but had no issue. His elder wife was Keshinī, the second Sumatī, sister of Garuda. With these twain he came to Himālaya to practise an austere penance. When a hundred years had passed, the rishi Brigu, whom he had honoured, granted him his wish. "Thou shalt attain unparalleled renown amongst men," he said. "One wife of thine, Keshinī, shall bring forth a son who will perpetuate thy race; the other shall give birth to sixty thousand sons." Those daughters of kings were glad, and worshipping the rishi, they asked: "Who of us shall have one son and who many we would know." He asked their will. "Who wishes for which boon?" he said, "a single perpetuator of the line, or sixty thousand famous sons, who yet shall not carry on their race?" Then Keshinī chose the single son, and Garuda's sister chose the many. Thereafter the king revered the saint with circumambulation and obeisance and returned again to his city.

In due course Keshinī bore a son, to whom was given the name of Asamanja. Sumatī bore a gourd, and when it burst open the sixty thousand sons came forth; the nurses fostered them in jars of ghee until they grew up to youth and beauty. But the eldest son, the child of Keshinī, loved them not, but would cast them in the Sarayu river and watch them sink. For this evil disposition and for the wrongs he did to citizens and honest folk Asamanja was banished by his father. But he had himself a son named Sumān, fair-spoken to all and well-beloved.

When many years had passed Sagara determined to celebrate a mighty sacrifice. The place thereof was in the region between Himālaya and Vindhya. There the horse was loosed, and Anshumat, a mighty chariot-fighter, followed to protect it. But it befell that a certain Vasava, assuming the form of a rākshasī, stole the horse away. Then the Brāhman priests informed the king, and commanded him to slay the thief and bring back the horse, lest the sacrifice should fail and misfortune should follow all concerned.

Then Sagara sent forth his sixty thousand sons to seek the horse. "Search ye the whole sea-girt earth," he said, "league by league, above the ground or under it." Then those great princes ranged the earth. Finding not the horse upon its surface, they began to delve with hands like thunderbolts and mighty ploughshares, so that the earth cried out in pain. Great was the uproar of the serpents and the demons that were slain then. For sixty thousand leagues they dug as if they would reach the very lowest deep. They undermined all Jambudwīpa, so that the very gods feared and went into counsel unto Brahmā. "O great grandsire," they said, "the sons of Sagara are digging out the whole earth and many are slain therefor. Crying that one hath stolen Sagara's horse, they are bringing havoc on every creature." Then Brahmā answered: "This entire earth is Vāsudeva's consort; he is indeed her lord, and in the form of Kapila sustains her. By his wrath the sons of Sagara will be slain. The far-sighted have foreseen the fated digging out of earth and the death of Sagara's sons; therefore ye should not fear." Then having riven the entire earth and ranged it all about, the sons returned to Sagara and asked what they should do, for they could not find the horse. But he commanded them again to burrow in the earth and find the horse. "Then cease," he said, "not before." Again they plunged into the depths. There they came on the elephant Virūpāksha, who bears on his head the whole world with its hills and forests, and when he shakes his head that is an earthquake. Him they duly worshipped and passed on. To the south they came next, to another mighty elephant, Mahāpadmā, like a mountain, bearing the earth upon his head; in like wise they came also to the western elephant named Saumanasā, and thence to the north, where is Bhadra, white as snow, bearing the earth upon his brow. Passing him by with honour, they came to the quarter east of north; there they beheld the eternal Vāsudeva in the shape of Kapila, and hard by him they saw the horse browsing at his will. They rushed on Kapila in fury, attacking him with trees and boulders, spades and ploughs, crying: "Thou art the thief; now thou hast fallen into the hands of the sons of Sagara." But Kapila uttered a dreadful roar and flashed a burning flame upon the sons that burned them all to ashes. No news of this came back to Sagara.

Then Sagara addressed his grandson Sumān, bidding him seek his uncles and learn their fate, "and," said he, "there be strong and mighty creatures dwelling in earth; honour such as do not hinder thee, slay those that stand against thee, and return, accomplishing my desire." He came in turn to the elephants of east and south and west and north, and each assured him of success; at last he came to the heap of ashes that had been his uncles; there he wailed with heavy heart in bitter grief. There, too, he beheld the wandering horse. He desired to perform the funeral lustrations for the uncles, but he might find no water anywhere. Then he beheld Garuda passing through the air; he cried to Anshumat: "Do not lament; for these to have been destroyed is for the good of all. The great Kapila consumed these mighty ones; therefore thou shouldst not make for them the common offerings of water. But there is Gangā, daughter of Himālaya; let that purifier of every world lave this heap of ashes; then shall the sixty thousand sons of Sagara attain to Heaven. Do thou also take back the horse and bring to completion thy grandfather's sacrifice." Then Anshumat led back the horse, and Sagara's ceremony was completed; but he knew not how to bring to earth the daughter of Himālaya. Sagara died and Anshumat was chosen king. He was a great ruler, and at last resigned the kingdom to his son and retired to dwell alone in the Himālayan forests; in due time he also passed away and reached Heaven. His son, King Dilipa, constantly pondered how to bring down Gangā, that the ashes might be purified and Sagara's sons attain to Heaven. But after thirty thousand years he, too, died, and his son Bhāgīratha, a royal saint, followed him. Ere long he consigned the kingdom to the care of a counsellor and went to the Himālayan forests, performing terrible austerities for a thousand years to draw down Gangā from the skies. Then Brahmā was pleased by his devotion, and appeared before him, granting a boon. He prayed that the ashes of the sons of Sagara should be washed by the water of Gangā, and that a son might speedily be born to him. "Great is thy aim," replied the grandsire, "but thou shouldst invoke Mahādeva to receive the falling Gangā, for earth may not sustain her. None but he who sways the trident may sustain her fall."

Then for a year Bhāgīratha worshipped Shiva; and he, well pleased, undertook to bear the mountain-daughter's fall, receiving the river upon his head. Then Gangā, in mighty torrent, cast herself down from Heaven on to Shiva's gracious head, thinking in her pride: "I shall

XXVI

THE BIRTH OF GANGĀ

KHITINDRA NĀTH MAZUMDAR

Page 320

sweep away the Great God in my waters, down to the nether regions." But when Gangā fell on Shiva's tangled locks she might not even reach the earth, but wandered there unable to escape for many a long year. Then Bhāgīratha again engaged in many hard austerities, till Shiva would set the river free; she fell in seven streams, three to the east, three to the west, while one followed after Bhāgīratha's car. The falling waters made a sound like thunder; very wonderful the earth appeared, covered with fallen and falling fishes, tortoises, and porpoises. Devas, rishis, gandharvas, and yakshas witnessed the great sight from their elephants and horses and self-moving chariots; every creature marvelled at the coming down of Gangā. The presence of the shining devas and the brightness of their jewels lit up the sky as if with a hundred suns. The heavens were filled with speeding porpoises and fishes like flashes of bright lightning; the flakes of pale foam seemed like snow-white cranes crossing heavy autumn clouds. So Gangā fell, now directly onward, now aside, sometimes in many narrow streams, and again in one broad torrent; now ascending hills, then falling again into a valley. Very fair was that vision of the water falling from Heaven to Shankara's head, and from Shankara's head to earth. All the shining ones of Heaven and all the creatures of the earth made haste to touch the sacred waters that wash away all sin. Then Bhāgīratha went forward on his car and Gangā followed; and after her came the devas and rishis, asuras, rākshasas, gandharvas and yakshas, kinnaras and nāgas and apsarās, and all creatures that inhabit water went along with them. But as Gangā followed Bhāgīratha she flooded the sacrificial ground of the puissant Jahna, and he was greatly angered, and in his wrath he drank up all her wondrous waters. Then the deities besought and prayed him to set her free, till he relented and released her through his ears, and again she followed Bhāgīratha's car. At last she came to the mighty river Ocean and plunged into the nether regions; there she laved the heap of ashes, and the sixty thousand sons of Sagara were cleansed of every sin and attained to Heaven.

Then Brahmā spoke to Bhāgīratha. "O most puissant of men," he said, "the sons of Sagara have now gone up to Heaven, and shall endure there so long as Ocean's waters endure on earth. Gangā shall be called thy daughter and receive thy name. Now do thou make offerings of this sacred water for thy ancestors, Sagara and Anshumat and Dilipa, and do thou thyself bathe in these waters and, free from every sin, ascend to Heaven, whither I now repair."

"And, O Rāma," said Vishvāmitra, "I have now related to thee the tale of Gangā. May it be well with thee. He that recites this history wins fame, long life, and Heaven; he that heareth attains to length of days, and the fulfilment of desires, and the wiping out of every sin."

Manasā Devī

Manasā Devī was the daughter of Shiva by a beautiful mortal woman. She was no favourite of her step-mother, Bhagavatī, or Pārvatī, Shiva's wife; so she took up her abode on earth with another daughter of Shiva, named Netā. Manasā desired to receive the worship due to goddesses; she knew that it would be easy to obtain this if she could once secure the devotion of a very wealthy and powerful merchant-prince of Champaka Nagar, by name Chānd Sadāgar. For a long time she tried to persuade him; but he was a stout devotee of Shiva himself, whom he was not going to desert for a goddess of snakes. For Manasā was a goddess and queen of serpents.

Chānd had made a beautiful garden on the outskirts of the city, a veritable earthly paradise, where he was used to eat the air and enjoy the flowers every evening. The first thing Manasā did was to send her snakes to reduce the garden to ashes. But as Chānd had received from Shiva himself the magic power of restoring the dead to life, it was an easy matter for him to restore the garden to all its beauty by merely uttering the appropriate charms. Manasā next appeared to Chānd in the shape of a beautiful girl, so silvery and radiant that even the moon hid herself behind the clouds when she saw her. Chānd fell madly in love with her, but she would not hear a word till he promised to bestow his magic power upon her; and when he did so, she vanished away and appeared in the sky in her own form, and said to Chānd: "This is not by chance, nor in the course of nature. But even now worship me, and I will restore your power." But he would not hear of it. Then she destroyed the garden again. But Chānd now sent for his friend Shankara, a great magician, who very soon revived the flowers and trees and made the garden as good as before. Then Manasā managed to kill Shankara by guile, and destroyed the garden a third time; and now there was no remedy. Every time one of these misfortunes befell Chānd she whispered in his ear: "It is not by chance," &c.

Then she sent her serpents to kill every one of his six sons; at the death of each she whispered the same message in Chānd's ear, saying: "Even now worship me, and all shall be well." Chānd was an obstinate man, and sad as he was, he would not give in. On the contrary, he fitted out his ships for a trading voyage and set forth. He was very successful, and was nearing home, with a load of treasure and goods, when a storm fell on the ships.

Chānd at once prayed to Bhagavatī, the wife of Shiva, and she protected his ship. Manasā, however, represented to her father that this was not fair. "Is she not content with banishing me from Heaven, but must also interfere with all my doings?" So Shiva persuaded his wife to return to Heaven with him. He began by swearing: "By the heads of your favourite sons, Ganesh and Kārtikkeya, you must come away at once, Bhagavatī, or——"

"Or what?" she said.

"Well, never mind," he replied; "but, my dear, you should be reasonable. Is it not fair that Manasā should have her own way for once? After all, she has been very badly neglected, and you can afford to be generous."

So Bhagavatī went away with Shiva, the boat sank, and Chānd was left in the sea. Manasā had no intention of letting him drown, so she cast her lotus throne into the water. But Manasā had another name, Padmā, and this also is the name of the lotus; so when Chānd saw that the floating object by which he was going to save himself was actually a *padmā* he left it alone, preferring drowning to receiving any help from a thing bearing the hated name of his enemy. But she whispered: "Even now worship me, and all will be well."

Chānd would have been quite willing to die; but this would not suit Manasā at all; she brought him ashore. Behold, he had arrived at the city where an old friend, Chandraketu, had his home. Here he was very kindly treated, and began to recover a little; but very soon he discovered that Chandraketu was a devotee of Manasā, and that her temple adjoined the house. At once he departed, throwing away even the garments his friend had bestowed upon him.

He begged some food, and going down to the river, took his bath. But while he was bathing Manasā sent a large mouse, who ate up his rice, so that he had nothing to eat but some raw plantain-skins left by some children on the river-bank. Then he got service in a Brāhman family as a reaper and thresher ; but Manasā turned his head so that he worked quite stupidly, and his master sent him off. It was a very long time before he found his way back to Champaka Nagar, and he hated Manasā Devī more than ever.

Now Manasā had two great friends, apsarās of Indra's heaven. They made up their minds to win over the obstinate merchant. One was to be reborn as Chānd's son, the other as the daughter of Sāha, a merchant of Nichhani Nagar and an acquaintance of Chānd's. When Chānd reached home he found his wife had presented him with a beautiful son ; and when the time came for his marriage there was no one so beautiful or so wealthy as Behulā, the daughter of Sāha. Her face was like an open lotus, her hair fell to her ankles, and the tips of it ended in the fairest curls ; she had the eyes of a deer and the voice of a nightingale, and she could dance better than any dancing girl in the whole city of Champaka Nagar.

Unfortunately, the astrologers predicted that Chānd's son, whose name was Lakshmindara, would die of the bite of a snake on the night of his marriage. All this time, of course, the two apsarās had forgotten their divine nature, and only thought themselves ordinary mortals very much in love; also they were both devoted to the service of Manasā Devī. Chānd's wife would not allow the marriage to be postponed, so Chānd had to go on with the preparations, though he was quite sure that

Manasā was going to have her own way in the matter. However, he had a steel house built, taking care that there were no cracks in it large enough for even a pin to enter. The house was guarded by sentinels with drawn swords; mungooses and peacocks were let loose in the park around it, and every one knows that these creatures are deadly enemies of snakes. Besides this, charms and antidotes and snake-poisons were strewn in every corner.

But Manasā appeared to the craftsman who built the house and threatened to kill himself and all his family if he would not make a tiny hole in the steel wall. He was very unwilling to do it, for he said he could not betray his employer; at last he gave in from sheer fright, and made a hole the size of a hair, hiding the opening with a little powdered charcoal.

Then the marriage day came, and many were the evil omens; the bridegroom's crown fell off his head, the pole of the marriage pavilion broke, Behulā accidentally wiped off the marriage mark from her own forehead after the ceremony as if she had already become a widow.

At last the ceremonies were all over, and Lakshmindara and Behulā were left alone in the steel house. Behulā hid her face in her hands, and was much too shy to look at her husband, or let him embrace her; and he was so tired by the long fasting and ceremonies of the marriage that he fell asleep. Behulā was just as tired, but she sat near the bed and watched, for it seemed to her too good to be true that such a lovely thing as Lakshmindara could be really her husband; he seemed to her like an enshrined god. Suddenly she saw an opening appear in the steel wall, and a great snake glided in; for some of Manasā's snakes had the power of squeezing themselves into the tiniest space and expanding again at will. But Behulā

XXVII

MANASĀ DEVĪ

KHITINDRA NĀTH MAZUMDAR

Page 326

offered the snake some milk, and while it was drinking she slipped a noose over its head and made it fast. The same thing happened with two more snakes. Then Behulā grew so heavy she could not keep awake; she sat on the bed and her eyes closed, opening every now and then with a start to watch the hole in the wall. At last she fell asleep altogether, stretched across Lakshmindara's feet. Then there crept in the serpent Kāl-nāginī, the same who had destroyed Chānd's pleasure-garden, and bit the sleeping bridegroom; he cried out to Behulā, and she woke just in time to see the snake going out by the hole in the wall.

In the morning Lakshmindara's mother came to the bridal-chamber and found him dead, while Behulā lay sobbing by his side. Every one blamed Behulā, for they did not believe a snake could have entered the steel house, and accused her of witchcraft; but presently they saw the three snakes tied up, and then they knew that the bridegroom had died of snake-bite. But Behulā did not attend to what they said, for she was wishing that at least she had not refused her husband's first and last request when she had been too shy to let him embrace her.

It was the custom when anyone died of snake-bite that the body should not be burnt, but set afloat on a raft, in the hope, perhaps, that some skilful physician or snake-charmer might find the body and restore it to life. But when the raft was ready Behulā sat down beside the body and said she would not leave it till the body was restored to life. But no one really believed that such a thing could happen, and they thought Behulā was quite mad. Every one tried to dissuade her, but she only said to her mother-in-law: "Adored mother, the lamp is still burning in our bridal-chamber. Do not weep any more, but go and close the door of the room, and know that as long as the lamp burns I shall still hope that my lord may be restored to life." So there was no help for it; but Behulā floated away, and very soon Champaka Nagar was out of sight. But when she passed by her father's house her five brothers were waiting, and they tried to persuade her to leave the dead body, saying that though she was a widow they wanted to have her back, and they would take every care of her and make her very happy. But she said she could not bear the idea of living without her husband, and she would rather stay even with his dead body than go anywhere else. So she floated away far down the river. It was not very long before the body began to swell and decay; still Behulā protected it, and the sight of this inevitable change made her quite unconscious of her own sufferings. She floated past village after village, and every one thought she was mad. She prayed all day to Manasā Devī, and though she did not restore the body to life, still the goddess protected it from storms and crocodiles, and sustained Behulā with strength and courage.

Behulā was quite resigned; she felt a more than human power in herself. She seemed to know that so much faith and love could not be in vain. Sometimes she saw visions of devils who tried to frighten her, sometimes she saw visions of angels who tempted her to a life of comfort and safety; but she sat quite still and indifferent; she went on praying for the life of her husband.

At last six months went by, and the raft touched ground just where Manasā's friend Netā lived by the river-side. She was washing clothes, but Behulā could see by the glory about her head that she was no mortal woman. A beautiful little boy was playing near her and spoiling all her work; suddenly she caught hold of the child and strangled him, and laid the body down beside her and went on with her work. But when the sun set and her work was done, she sprinkled a few drops of water over him, and he woke up and smiled as if he had just been to sleep. Then Behulā landed and fell at the washerwoman's feet. Netā carried her up to Heaven to see if the gods might be moved to grant her prayer. They asked her to dance, and she pleased them so much that they promised her to bring her husband back to life and to restore all Chānd's losses. But Manasā Devī did not agree to this until Behulā undertook to convert her father-in-law and persuade him to honour and worship the goddess. Behulā promised.

Then Behulā and Lakshmindara set out on their way home. After a long time they came to her father's house, and they stopped to visit her father and mother. But they would not stay, and set out the same day for Champaka Nagar. She would not go home, however, until she had fulfilled her promise to Manasā Devī. The first people she saw were her own sisters-in-law, who had come to the river-bank to fetch water. She had disguised herself as a poor sweeper, and she had in her hand a beautiful fan on which she had the likeness of every one in the Chand family depicted. She showed the fan to the sisters, and told them her name was Behulā, a sweeper-girl, daughter of Sāha, a sweeper, and wife of Lakshmindara, son of the sweeper Chānd. The sisters ran home to show the fan to their mother, and told her its price was a lac of rupees. Sanakā was very much surprised, but she thought of the lamp in the steel house, and when she ran to the bridal-chamber that had been shut tight for a year, behold the lamp was still burning. Then she ran on to the river-side, and there was her son with Behulā. But Behulā said: "Dear mother, here is your son; but we cannot come home till my father-in-law agrees to worship Manasā Devī; that is why I brought you here by a trick."

Chānd was not able to resist any longer; Manasā Devī had conquered. He worshipped her on the eleventh day of the waning moon in the very same month. It is true that he offered flowers with his left hand, and turned away his face from the image of Manasā; but, for all that, she was satisfied, and bestowed on him wealth and prosperity and happiness, and she restored his friend Shankara to life. Ever since then Manasā Devī's claim to the worship of mortals has been freely admitted.

Note on Manasā Devī

This legend of Manasā Devī, the goddess of snakes, who must be as old as the Mykenean stratum in Asiatic culture, reflects the conflict between the religion of Shiva and that of feminine local deities in Bengal. Afterwards Manasā or Padmā was recognized as a form of *Shakti* (does it not say in the Mahābhārata that all that is feminine is a part of Umā?), and her worship accepted by the Shaivas. She is a phase of the mother-divinity who for so many worshippers is nearer and dearer than the far-off and impersonal Shiva, though even he, in these popular legends, is treated as one of the Olympians with quite a human character.

"In the month of Shrāvana [July–August]," writes Bābu Dinesh Chandra Sen, "the villages of Lower Bengal present a unique scene. This is the time when Manasā Devī is worshipped. Hundreds of men in Sylhet, Backergunge, and other districts throng to the river-side to recite the songs of Behulā. The vigorous boat-races attending the festivity and the enthusiasm that characterizes the recitation of these songs cannot but strike an observer with an idea of their vast influence over the masses. There are sometimes a hundred oars in each of the long narrow boats, the rowers singing in loud chorus as they pull them with all their might. The boats move with the speed of an arrow, even flying past the river steamers. These festivities of Manasā Pūjā sometimes occupy a whole month . . . how widespread is the popularity of these songs in Bengal may be imagined from the fact that the birthplace of Chānd Sadāgar is claimed by no less than nine districts"—and by the fact that the *Manasā Mangal*, or Story of Manasā, has been told in as many as sixty versions by poets whose names are known, dating from the twelfth century onward to the present day.

"It must be remembered," adds Dinesh Bābu, "that in a country where women commonly courted death on their husband's funeral pyre this story of Behulā may be regarded as the poet's natural tribute at the feet of their ideal."

The Elephant and Crocodile

There dwelt a royal elephant on the slopes of Triple Peak. He wandered through the forests with his herd of wives. Fevered with the juice exuding from his temples, he plunged one day into a lake to quench his thirst; after drinking deep, he took water in his trunk and gave it to his wives and children. But just then an angry crocodile attacked him, and the two struggled for an endless time, each striving to draw the other toward himself. Piteously the elephants trumpeted from the bank, but they could not help. At last the royal elephant grew weak, but the crocodile was not yet weary, for he was at home in his own element.

Then the royal elephant prayed ardently and with devotion

to the Adorable, the Supreme Being; at once came Vishnu, seated upon Garuda, attended by the devas. He drew forth the crocodile and severed its neck with a cast of his discus, and so saved the royal elephant.

This was the working out of an old curse; the elephant was a gandharva who in another life had cursed a rishi who disturbed him at play. That rishi was the crocodile. By another rishi's curse the gandharva had become an elephant.

The elephant of the story stands for the typical human soul of our age, excited by desires; given over too much to sensual pleasure, the demon would have carried him away, he knew not where. There was no salvation for him until he called on Vishnu, who speedily saves all those who call upon him with devotion.

Nachiketas and Yama

There was a cowherd of the name of Vājashrava; desiring a gift from the gods, he made offerings of all he owned. But the kine he had were old, yielding no milk and worthless; not such as might buy the worshipper a place in Heaven. Vājashrava had a son; he would have his father make a worthier offering. To his sire he spoke: "To which god wilt thou offer me?" "To Death I give thee."

Nachiketas thought: "I shall be neither the first nor last that fares to Yama. Yet what will he do with me? It shall be with me as with others; like grass a man decays, like grass he springeth up again." So Nachiketas went his way to Death's wide home, and waited there three days; for Death was on a journey. When Death returned his servants said: "A Brāhman guest burns like a fire; Nachiketas waits three days unwelcomed; do thou

XXVIII

YAMA AND NACHIKETAS

NANDA LĀL BOSE

Page 332

soothe him with an offering of water, for all is lost to him in whose abode a Brāhman waits unfed."

Then Death spake to Nachiketas: "Since thou, an honoured guest, hast waited in my house three days unfed, ask of me three boons in return, and I shall grant them." Then first he prayed: "Grant to my father peace and to know and welcome me when I return." Death answered: "Be it so."

Nachiketas asked again: "In Heaven-world the folk are quit of thee; there is neither hunger, nor eld, nor fear of death. Reveal to me the sacred fire that leads to Heaven." Then Death described the sacred fire—what stones for its altar, and how disposed; and Nachiketas said it over, learning the lesson taught by Death. Death spoke again: "I grant thee, furthermore, that this sacred fire be known for ever by thy name; thine is the fire that leads to Heaven, thy second boon."

Nachiketas asked again: "The great mystery of what cometh after death; he is, some say; others say, he is no more. This great doubt I ask thee to resolve." Death replied: "Even the gods of old knew not this; this is a matter hard to be learnt; ask me, O Nachiketas, any other boon, though it be a hundred sons, or untold wealth, or broad lands, or length of days. All that a man can desire shall be thine, kingship, wealth, the fairest songstresses of Indra's heaven; only ask not of death." Nachiketas answered: "These be matters of a day and destroy the fiery energy of men; thine be the wealth, thine the dance and song. What avails wealth whenas thou dost appear? How shall a man delight in life, however long, when he has beheld the bliss of those who perish not? This doubt of the Great Hereafter I ask thee to resolve; no other boon I ask."

Death replied: "Duty is one, delight another; these twain draw a man in diverse paths. Well is it for him that chooses duty; he goes astray who seeks delight. These twain, wisdom and folly, point to diverse ends. Well has Nachiketas spoken, seeking wisdom, not goaded by desires. Even the learned abide in delusion, blind led by the blind; while to the fool is naught revealed. This world, and no other, he thinketh; and so cometh again and again into my power.

"But he is great who tells of the One, of whom the many may never hear, whom the many, though they hear, may not know; a marvel is he who knoweth the Brāhman. Untold is he, no path leads to him.

"Having heard and well grasped him with insight, attaining to that subtle One, a mortal is gladdened and rejoices for good cause. Wide is the gate for Nachiketas, methinks."

Nachiketas answered:

"Other than good, other than evil, other than formless or than forms, other than past or future—declare thou That."

Death resumed:

"That goal of sacred wisdom, of goodly works and faith, is *Om!* This word is Brāhman, the supreme. He who doth comprehend this word, whatsoever he desires is his.

"For that Singer is not born, nor does he ever die. He came not anywhence, nor anything was he. Unborn, eternal, everlasting, ancient; unslain is he, though the body be slain.

"If the slayer thinks he slays, or the slain deems he is slain, they err; That neither slayeth nor is slain.

"Smaller than small, greater than great, that Self indwells in every creature's heart.

"Sitting, he travels far; lying, he speedeth everywhere; who knoweth him hath no more grief.

"This Self is not obtainable by explanation, nor by intellection, nor by much hearkening to scripture; whom he chooses, to him That is revealed. But he that knoweth that all things are Self, for him what grief, what delusion lingers, knowing all things are That One?

"When all desires that linger in the heart are driven forth, then mortal is made immortal, he becometh Brāhman.

"When every knot of the heart is loose then doth he win immortal Being. Thus far the teaching."

Thus having learnt the wisdom taught by Death, and finding Brāhman, Nachiketas was freed from death. So verily shall he be free who knoweth that Supreme Self.

The Story of Kacha and Devayānī

Many were the battles of old between the gods and demons, for each desired the sovereignty and full possession of the three worlds. The devas appointed Brihaspati as their priest, master of sacrificial rites; the asuras, Ushanas. Between these two great Brāhmans there was fierce rivalry, for all those demons that were slain in battle with the gods were brought to life by Ushanas, and fought again another day. Many also were the gods slain by the demons; but Brihaspati knew not the science of bringing to life as Ushanas knew it, therefore the gods were greatly grieved. They went, therefore, to Brihaspati's son Kacha and asked him to render them a great service, to become the disciple of Ushanas and learn the secret of bringing to life. "Then shalt thou share with us in the sacrificial offerings. Thou mayst easily do this, since thou art younger than Ushanas, and it is therefore meet that thou shouldst serve him. Thou mayst also serve his daughter Devayānī, and win the favour of both. From Devayānī thou shalt surely win that knowledge," said they. "So be it," answered Kacha, and went his way.

To Ushanas he said: "Receive me as thy disciple. I am the son of Brihaspati, and my name is Kacha. Be thou my master, and I shall practise restraint for a thousand years." Ushanas welcomed him, and the vow was made. Then Kacha began to win the favour of Ushanas and Devayānī. He was young, and sang and played on divers instruments; and she, who was also young, was not hard to please. He gave her flowers and fruits and did her service. She, too, with songs and pleasant manners served him. Thus passed five hundred years, half of the time appointed in the vow.

Then Kacha's purpose became known to the demons, and they slew him in wrath in a lonely part of the forest, where he was tending his master's cows. They cut his body in many pieces and gave it to the wolves and jackals. When twilight came the cows returned to the fold alone. Then Devayānī said to her father: "The sun has set, the evening fire is lit, the cattle have returned alone. Kacha has not come; he is either lost or dead. And, O father, I will not live without him." Then Ushanas said: "I will bring him to life by saying: 'Let him come,'" and summoned him. At once Kacha appeared before his master, tearing the bodies of the wolves that had devoured him. When Devayānī asked him what had hindered his return, he answered that the asuras had fallen upon him in the forest and given his body to the wolves and jackals; "but brought to life by the summons of Ushanas, I stand before you none the less."

Again it befell that Kacha was in the forest, seeking flowers desired by Devayānī, and the demons found him and slew him, and grinding his body into paste, they mixed it with the waters of the ocean. As before, Devayānī told her father that Kacha had not returned, and Ushanas summoned him, so that he appeared whole and related all that had befallen.

A third time he was slain, and the asuras burnt his flesh and bones to ashes and mixed the ashes with the wine that Ushanas drank, for in those days the Brāhmans yet drank wine. Then Devayānī said to her father again: "O father, Kacha has gone to gather flowers, but he comes not back. Surely he is lost or dead. I will not live without him!" Ushanas answered: "O my daughter, surely Brihaspati's son has gone to the realm of the dead. But what may I do, for though I bring him back to life, he is slain again and again? O Devayānī, do not grieve, do not cry. Thou shouldst not sorrow for a mortal, for thou art daily worshipped by the gods." But Devayānī answered: "Why should I not grieve for the son of Brihaspati, who is an ocean of ascetic virtue? Kacha was the son and grandson of a rishi. He, too, kept the rule of self-restraint, and was ever alert and skilful. I will starve and follow him. Fair was Kacha and dear to me."

Then Ushanas was grieved and cried out against the asuras, who slew a disciple under his protection; and at Devayānī's prayer he began to summon Kacha back from the jaws of death. But he answered feebly from within his master's stomach: "Be gentle unto me, O master; I am Kacha that serveth thee. Consider me as thine own son." Ushanas said: "How, O Brāhman, camest thou into my stomach? Forsooth, I shall desert the asuras and join the gods!" Kacha answered: "Memory is mine and all the virtue of my discipline, but I suffer intolerable pain.

Slain by the asuras and burnt to ashes, I was mixed with thy wine."

Then Ushanas said to Devayānī: "What can I do for thee, for it is by my death that Kacha can have back his life? He is within me, and may not come forth without the tearing of my stomach." She answered: "Either evil is alike to me. If Kacha dies, I will not live; and if thou die, I also die." Then Ushanas said to Kacha: "Success is thine, since Devayānī looks on thee so kindly. Receive, therefore, from me the lore of Bringing-to-life, and when thou comest forth from me thou shalt restore my life in turn." Then Kacha came forth from the master's stomach like the full moon in the evening; and seeing his teacher lying lifeless, he revived him by the science he had received and worshipped him, calling him father and mother as the giver of knowledge. Thereafter Ushanas decreed that no Brāhman ever should drink wine. Also he summoned the asuras, and announced to them: "Ye foolish demons, know that Kacha has attained his will. Henceforth he shall dwell with me. He who has learnt the science of Bringing-to-life is even as Brāhman himself." The demons were astonished, and departed to their homes; but Kacha stayed with the master for a thousand years until the time came for him to return to the gods. He received permission from Ushanas to depart; but Devayānī, seeing him about to go, said to him: "Hear me; remember my affection to thee during thy vow of self-restraint; now the time thereof is ended, do thou set thy love on me and take my hand according to the sacred rites." But Kacha answered: "Behold, I honour thee as much as, nay more than, even thy father; dearer than life thou art, my master's daughter. Yet thou shouldst not say these words to me." She answered again:

"Thou art likewise my father's teacher's son, and I must honour thee. Recollect my affection when the asuras had slain thee. I am altogether thine; do not abandon me without a fault." Kacha replied: "Tempt me not to sin; be gentle unto me, thou of fair brows. Where thou hast been in the body of the sage, there have I also been: thou art my sister. Therefore speak not thus. Happy days we have spent together, thou slender-waisted; grant me leave to go to my home now, and thy blessing that my journey may be safe. Think of me as one who would not sin." Then Devayānī cursed him: "Since thou refusest me, thy knowledge shall be fruitless."

Kacha answered: "I have refused thee only because thou art my master's daughter and my sister, not for any fault. Curse me if thou must, though I deserve it not. But thou speakest from passion, not for duty's sake, and thy wish shall fail. Behold also, no rishi's son shall wed with thee. Thou sayest that my knowledge shall bear no fruit; be it so, but in him it shall bear fruit to whom I shall impart it." Then Kacha took his way to the dwellings of the gods and was greeted by Indra, who honoured him, saying: "Great is the boon thou hast achieved for us; be thou hereafter a sharer in the sacrificial offerings: thy fame shall never die."

Thus far the tale of Kacha and Devayānī.

Note on Kacha and Devayānī

Even the planets must sooner or later have shared in the general process of the spiritualizing of stellar myths, and a significant instance seems to be the story of Devayānī and Kacha, from the opening volume of the Mahābhārata. Here it would appear that we have a very ancient fragment, for as a poetic episode the story stands loosely connected with an archaic genealogical relation—not unlike the Semitic account of Sara and Hagar—in which appear mixed marriages between Brāhmans and Kshatriyas, polygamy, and the matriarchal custom and ideal of proposals made by a woman held binding upon the man. All these features of the legend are felt by the final editor to be highly anomalous, and time and words are inartistically spent in arguments for their justification by the characters involved. But this is a very common feature in the dressing-up of old tales to take a place in new productions, and the arguments only confirm the perfect naturalness of the incidents when first related. How Devayānī, the daughter of the planet Shukra,[1] of Brāhman rank, became the ancestress of certain royal or asura princes and tribes, and how the king whom she wedded was also the progenitor of three other purely asura races, or dynasties—these things may have been the treasured pedigrees of families and clans. From a national point of view it may have been binding on the annalist to include them in every version of the epic chronicles. As a poet, however, the point that interested the last editor of the Mahābhārata was a matter that also interests us—a romance that occurred to Devayānī in her youth, and stamped her as a daughter of the planetary order, though wedded to a king.

The mythos comes down from that age when there were constant struggles for supremacy between the gods (devas) and the demons (asuras). Who were these asuras? Were they long-established inhabitants of India, or were they new invaders from the North-West? They are not classed with the aboriginal tribes, it is to be marked, or

[1] *I.e.*, Venus, masculine in Hindu astrology. Also named Ushanas, as above.

referred to as Dāsyus or slaves. There still remain in the country certain ancient metal-working communities who may represent these asuras in blood, as they certainly do in name. And the name of Assyria is an abiding witness to the possibility of their alien origin. In any case it would appear as an accepted fact, from the story of Devayānī, that the asuras were proficients in magic. It is told that they obtained a Brāhman to act as their sacrificial priest, who was in some vague way an embodiment of Shukra, the planet Venus. The gods, on the other hand—meaning perhaps the Aryans, who were Sanskrit-speaking—were served in the same capacity by a Brāhman representing the influence and power of Brihaspati, or Jupiter. The planetary allusions in these names are confirmed by the reproachful statement of the gods that "Shukra always protects the asuras, and never protects us, their opponents." No one could grumble that the archbishop of a rival people did not protect them. But the complaint that a divinity worshipped by both sides shed protecting influences on one alone is not unreasonable.

What were the original fragments from which this story was drawn? Was the whole thing a genealogical record, on the inclusion of which in a national history certain tribes and clans had a right to insist? And is the whole incident of Devayānī and Kacha a sheer invention of the latest editor to explain what had in his time become the anomalous tradition of the marriage of Devayānī, daughter of a Brāhman, to Yayati, of the royal caste? It may be so. And yet as against this we have that statement, so like a genuine echo from the past, that "there were in former times frequent contests between gods and demons for the possession of the whole Three Worlds." In bringing about the highly dovetailed condition of the story as it now stands we may be sure that the latest poet has had a large hand, but in all probability the parts themselves, even to this romance of Kacha and Devayānī, are now as they were in long-inherited lore.

The latest poet feels his own sentiment as much outraged as our own by the unwomanly insistence of Devayānī on the acceptance of her hand by Kacha. But, as a matter of fact, the tale probably came down to him, as to us, from the age of the Matriarchate, when it was the proper thing for a man to become a member of his wife's kindred; and Devayānī, in the first inception of her romance, may not have striven to make Kacha her husband so much as to pledge him to remain amongst the asuras. Even in this she was prompted, we may suppose, more by the desire of preserving the magical knowledge of her people from betrayal than by personal motives. And Kacha, similarly, whatever he may urge, in the hands of his latest narrator, as the reason of his refusal, was really moved, in the earliest version, by the idea that this is the last and supreme temptation that confronts his mission. His one duty is, in his own eyes, to fulfil the task as he undertook it in his youth, namely, to leave the demons and return to the gods to impart to them the knowledge they sent him out to win. And finally, the story in this its completed presentment bears more than a trace of that poetizing of the planetary influences of which the ancient art of astrology may be regarded as the perfected blossom and fruit.

Purūravas and Urvashī

There was a king by name Purūravas. Hunting one day in the Himālayas, he heard a cry for help; two apsarās had been carried off by rākshasas from a pleasure-party in the flowery woods. Purūravas pursued and rescued them; they were Urvashī and her friend Chitralekha. He prayed Urvashī for her love; she granted it, with this condition: "Thou shalt not let me see thee naked."

Long she dwelt with him, and time came when she would be a mother. But the gandharvas, who are the friends and companions of the apsarās, missed their fellow, and they said together: "It is long, indeed, that Urvashī dwells with men; find out a way to bring her back." They were agreed upon a way to bring her back. She had a ewe with two small lambs, dear pets of hers, tied to her bed. While yet Purūravas lay beside his darling the gandharvas carried oft a lamb. "Alas!" she cried, "they have carried off my pet as though no hero and no man was with me." Then they carried off the second, and Urvashī made the same complaint.

Purūravas thought: "How can that be a place without a hero and without a man where I am found?" Naked, he sprang up in chase; too long he thought it needed to put on a garment. Then the gandharvas filled the sky with lightning and Urvashī saw him, clear as day; and, indeed, at once she vanished.

The sorry king wandered all over Hindustān wailing for his darling. At last he reached a lake called Anyataplaksha. There he saw a flock of swans; they were the apsarās, with Urvashī, but Purūravas did not know them. She said: "There is he with whom I dwelt." The apsarās said together: "Let us reveal ourselves," and, "So be it," they said again. Then Purūravas saw Urvashī and prayed her sorely: "O dear wife, stay and hear me. Unspoken secrets that are yours and mine shall yield no joy; stay then, and let us talk together." But Urvashī answered: "What have I to do to speak with thee? I have departed like the first of dawns. Go home again, Purūravas. I am like the very wind and hard to bind. Thou didst break the covenant between us; go to thy home again, for I am hard to win."

Then Purūravas grieved and cried: "Then shall thy friend and fellow rush away this day, upon the farthest journey bent, never returning; death will he seek, and the fierce wolves shall have him."

Urvashī answered: "Do not die, Purūravas; do not rush away! Let not the cruel wolves devour thee! Take it not to heart, for lo! there may not be friendship with any woman; women's hearts are as hyenas'. Go to thy home again." But a memory came into her mind of her life with him, and a little she relented; she said to Purūravas: "Come, then, on the last night of the year from now; then shalt thou stay with me one night, and by then, too, this son of thine shall have been born."

Purūravas sought her on the last night of the year: there was a golden palace, and the gandharvas cried him, "Enter," and they sent Urvashī to him. She said: "When morning dawns the gandharvas will offer thee a boon, and thou must make thy choice." "Choose thou for me," he said, and she replied: "Say, 'Let me be one of your very selves.'"

When morning came, "Let me be one of your very selves," he said. But they answered: "Forsooth the sacred fire burns not upon earth which could make a man as one of us." They gave him fire in a dish and said: "Sacrifice therewith, and thou shalt become a gandharva like ourselves." He took the fire, and took his son, and went his way. He set down the fire in the forest, and went with the boy to his own home. When he returned, "Here am I back," he said; but lo! the fire had vanished. What had been the fire was an Asvattha tree; and what the dish, a Shami

XXIX

PURŪRAVAS

Khitindra Nāth Mazumdar

Page 344

tree. Then he sought the gandharvas again. They counselled him: "Make fire with an upper stick of the Asvattha tree, and a lower stick of the Shami; the fire thereof shall be the very fire thou didst receive from us." Then Purūravas made fire with sticks of the Asvattha and the Shami, and making offerings therewith, he was made one of the gandharvas and dwelt with Urvashī evermore.

Sāvitrī

Yudhishthira questioned Mārkandeya if he had ever seen or heard of any noble lady like to Draupadī's daughter.

Mārkandeya answered:

There was a king named Lord-of-Horses; he was virtuous, generous, brave, and well-beloved. It grieved him much that he had no child. Therefore he observed hard vows and followed the rule of hermits. For eighteen years he made daily offerings to Fire, recited *mantras* in praise of Sāvitrī, and ate a frugal meal at the sixth hour. Then at last Sāvitrī was pleased and revealed herself to him in visible form within the sacrificial fire. "I am well pleased," she said, "with thy asceticism, thy well-kept vows, thy veneration. Ask, great king, whatever boon thou wilt." "Goddess," said the king, "may sons be born to me worthy of my race, for the Brāhmans tell me much merit lies in children. If thou art pleased with me, I ask this boon." Sāvitrī replied: "O king, knowing thy wish, I have spoken already with Brahmā that thou shouldst have sons. Through his favour there shall be born to thee a glorious daughter. Thou shouldst not answer again: this is the grandsire's gift, who is well pleased with thy devotion." The king bowed down and prayed. "So be it," he said, and Sāvitrī vanished. It was not long before his queen bore him a shining girl with lotus eyes. Forasmuch as she was the gift of the goddess Sāvitrī, the wife of Brahmā, she was named Sāvitrī with all due ceremony, and she grew in grace and loveliness like unto Shrī herself. Like a golden image the people thought her, saying: "A goddess has come amongst us." But none dared wed that lady of the lotus eyes, for the radiant splendour and the ardent spirit that were in her daunted every suitor.

One holiday, after her service of the gods, she came before her father with an offering of flowers. She touched his feet, and stood at his side with folded hands. Then the king was sad, seeing his daughter of marriageable age and yet unwooed. He said to her: "My daughter, the time for thy bestowal has come; yet none seek thee. Do thou, therefore, choose for thyself a husband who shall be thy equal. Choose whom thou wilt; I shall reflect and give thee unto him, for a father that giveth not his daughter is disgraced. Act thou therefore so that we may not meet with the censure of the gods."

Then Sāvitrī meekly bowed to her father's feet and went forth with her attendants. Mounting a royal car she visited the forest hermitages of the sages. Worshipping the feet of those revered saints, she roamed through all the forests till she found her lord.

One day when her father sat in open court, conversing with the counsellors, Sāvitrī returned, and, seeing her father seated beside the rishi Nārada, bowed to his feet and greeted him. Then Nārada said: "Why dost thou delay to wed thy girl, who is of marriageable age?" The king replied: "It was for this that she went forth, and even now she returns. Hear whom she has chosen for her husband." So saying, he turned to Sāvitrī, commanding her to relate all that had befallen her.

Standing with folded hands before the king and sage, she answered: "There was a virtuous king of the Shālwas, Dyumatsena by name. He grew blind; then an ancient foe wrested the kingdom from his hands, and he, with his wife and little child, went forth into the woods, where he practised the austerities appropriate to the hermit life. The child, his son, grew up in that forest hermitage. He is worthy to be my husband; him have I accepted in my heart as lord."

Then Nārada exclaimed: "Greatly amiss has Sāvitrī done in taking for her lord this boy, whose name is Satyavān; albeit I know him well, and he excels in all good qualities. Even as a child he took delight in horses and would model them in clay or draw their pictures; wherefore he has been named Horse-painter."

The king asked: "Has this Prince Satyavān intelligence, forgiveness, courage, energy?" Nārada replied: "In energy he is like the sun, in wisdom like Brihaspati, brave like the king of gods, forgiving as the earth herself. Eke he is liberal, truthful, and fair to look upon?" Then the king inquired again: "Tell me now what are his faults." Nārada answered: "He hath one defect that overwhelms all his virtues, and that fault is irremediable. It is fated that he will die within a year."

Then the king addressed his daughter: "Do thou, O Sāvitrī, fair girl, choose for thyself another lord; for thou hast heard the words of Nārada." But Sāvitrī answered: "The die can fall but once; a daughter can only once be given away; once only may it be said: 'I give away!' Forsooth, be life short or long, be he virtuous or vicious, I have chosen my husband once for all. I shall not choose twice. A thing is first thought of in the heart, then it is spoken, then it is done; my mind is witness thereof." Then Nārada said to the king: "Thy daughter's heart is unwavering; she may not be turned from the right way. Moreover, none excelleth Satyavān in virtue; the marriage has my approval." The king, with folded hands, answered again: "Whatsoever thou dost command is to be done." Nārada said again: "May peace attend the gift of Sāvitrī. I shall now go on my ways; be it well with all"; and therewith he ascended again to Heaven.

On an auspicious day King Lord-of-Horses with Sāvitrī fared to the hermitage of Dyumatsena. Entering on foot, he found the royal sage seated in contemplation beneath a noble tree; him the king reverenced duly, with presents meet for holy men, and announced the purpose of his visit. Dyumatsena answered: "But how may thy daughter, delicately nurtured, lead this hard forest life with us, practising austerity and following the rule of hermits?" The king replied: "Thou shouldst not speak such words to us; for my daughter knoweth, like myself, that happiness and sorrow come and go, and neither endures. Thou shouldst not disregard my offer." It was arranged accordingly, and in the presence of the twice-born sages of the forest hermitages Sāvitrī was given to Satyavān. When her father had departed she laid aside her jewels and garbed herself in bark and brown. She delighted all by her gentleness and self-denial, her generosity and sweet speech. But the words of Nārada were ever present in her mind.

At length the hour appointed for the death of Satyavān approached; when he had but four days more to live Sāvitrī fasted day and night, observing the penance of "Three Nights." By the third day Sāvitrī was faint and weak, and she spent the last unhappy night in miserable reflections on her husband's coming death. In the morning she fulfilled the usual rites, and came to stand before the Brāhmans and her husband's father and mother, and they for her helping prayed that she might never be a widow.

Satyavān went out into the woods with axe in hand, suspecting nothing, to bring home wood for the sacrificial fire. Sāvitrī prayed to go with him, and he consented, if his parents also permitted it. She prayed them sweetly to allow it, saying that she could not bear to stay behind and that she desired exceedingly to see the blossoming trees. Dyumatsena gave her leave, saying: "Since Sāvitrī was given by her father to be my daughter-in-law I cannot remember that she has asked for anything at all. Now, therefore, let her prayer be granted. But do not," he added, "hinder Satyavān's sacred labour."

So Sāvitrī departed with her lord, seeming to smile, but heavy-hearted; for, remembering Nārada's words, she pictured him already dead. With half her heart she mourned, expectant of his end; with half she answered him with smiles, as they passed beside the sacred streams and goodly trees. Presently he fell to work, and as he hewed at the branches of a mighty tree he grew sick and faint, and came to his wife complaining that his head was racked with darting pains and that he would sleep awhile. Sāvitrī sat on the ground and laid his head upon her lap; that was the appointed time of Satyavān's death. Immediately Sāvitrī beheld a shining ruddy deity, dark and red of eye and terrible to look upon; he bore a noose in his hand. He stood and gazed at Satyavān. Then Sāvitrī rose and asked him humbly who he might be and what he sought to do. "I am Yama, Lord of Death," he answered, "and I have come for Satyavān, whose appointed span of life is ended." So saying, Yama drew forth the soul from Satyavān's body, bound in the noose, and altogether helpless; therewith he departed toward the south, leaving the body cold and lifeless.

Sāvitrī followed close; but Yama said: "Desist, O Sāvitrī. Return, perform thy husband's funeral rites. Thou mayst come no farther." But she answered: "Whither my lord is brought or goeth of his own will I shall follow; this is the lasting law. The way is open to me because of my obedience and virtue. Lo, the wise have said that friendship is seven-paced. Relying on friendship thus contracted, I shall say thee somewhat more. Thou dost order me to follow another rule than that of wife; thou wouldst make of me a widow, following not the domestic rule. But the four rules are for those who have not attained their purpose, true religious merit. It is otherwise with me; for I have reached the truth by fulfilment of the duty of a wife alone. It needs not to make of me a widow." Yama replied: "Thou sayest well, and well thou pleasest me. Ask now a boon, whatsoever thou wilt, except thy husband's life." She prayed that Dyumatsena should regain his sight and health, and Yama granted it. Still Sāvitrī would not return, saying that she would follow still her lord, and, besides, that friendship with the virtuous must ever bear good fruit. Yama admitted the truth of this, and granted her another boon; she asked that her father should regain his kingdom. Yama gave his promise that it should be accomplished, and commanded Sāvitrī to return. Still she refused, and spoke of the duty of the great and good to protect and aid all those who seek their help. Yama then granted her a third boon, that her father should have a hundred sons. Still Sāvitrī persisted. "Thou art called the Lord of Justice," she said, "and men ever trust the righteous; for it is goodness of heart alone that inspireth the confidence of every creature." When Yama granted another boon, save and except the life of Satyavān, Sāvitrī prayed for a hundred sons born of herself and Satyavān. Yama replied: "Thou shalt, O lady, obtain a hundred sons, renowned and mighty, giving thee great delight. But thou hast come too far; now I pray thee to return." But she again praised the righteous. "It is the righteous," she said, "who support the earth by their austere life; they protect all." Again Yama was propitiated by Sāvitrī's edifying words, and he granted another boon. But now Sāvitrī answered: "O giver of honour, what thou hast already granted cannot come to pass without union with my husband; therefore I ask his life together with the other boons. Without him I am but dead, without him I do not even desire happiness. Thou hast given a hundred sons, and yet dost take away my lord, without whom I may not live. I ask his life, that thy words may be accomplished."

Then Yama yielded and gave back Satyavān, promising him prosperity and a life of four centuries, and descendants who should all be kings. Granting all that Sāvitrī asked, the lord of the ancestors went his way. Then Sāvitrī returned to Satyavān's body, and she lifted his head upon her lap; behold, he came to life, like one returning home from sojourn in a strange land. "I have slept overlong," he said; "why didst thou not awake me? Where is that dark being who would have carried me away?" Sāvitrī answered: "Thou hast slept long. Yama has gone his way. Thou art recovered; rise, if thou canst, for night is falling."

Then those two returned, walking through heavy night along the forest paths.

Meanwhile Dyumatsena and his wife and all the sages remained in grief. Yet the Brāhmans were of good hope, for they deemed that Sāvitrī's virtue must avail even against fate, and they gave words of comfort to the king. Moreover, Dyumatsena suddenly regained his sight, and all took this for an omen of good fortune, betokening the safety of Satyavān. Then Sāvitrī and Satyavān returned through the dark night, and found the Brāhmans and the king seated beside the fire. Warm was their welcome and keen the questioning; then Sāvitrī related all that had befallen, and all saluted her; then, forasmuch as it was late, all went to their own abodes.

Next day at dawn there came ambassadors from Shālwa to say that the usurper had been slain, and the people invited Dyumatsena to return and be again their king. So he returned to Shālwa and lived long; and he had a hundred sons. Sāvitrī and Satyavān had also the hundred sons bestowed by Yama. Thus did Sāvitrī by her goodness alone raise from a poor estate to the highest fortune herself, her parents, and her lord, and all those descended from them.

"And," said Mārkandeya to Yudhishthira "even so shall Draupadī save all the Pāndavas."

Shakuntalā

This old story, best known to English readers in translations of Kalidāsa's play, is an episode of the Mahābhārata, giving an account of Bharata himself, the ancestor of the warring princes of the great epic, from whom, also, the name of India, "Bharatvarsha," is derived. The story of Shakuntalā given here is taken almost literally from the

Javanese version lately published by D. Van Hinloopen Labberton—a version superior in directness and simplicity to that of the Sanskrit Mahābhārata, and as a story (not of course as a play) superior to Kalidāsa's:

There was a rāja, Dushyanta, whose empire extended to the shores of the four seas. Nothing wrong was done in his reign; goodness prevailed, because of his example. One day he was hunting in the Himālayan forests, and went ever deeper and deeper into the woods; there he came upon a hermitage, with a garden of fair flowers and every sort of fruits, and a stream of clear water. There were animals of every kind; even the lions and tigers were well disposed, for the peaceful mind of the hermit constrained them. Birds were singing on every bough, and the cries of monkeys and bears rang like a recitation of Vedic prayers, delighting the king's heart. He ordered his followers to remain behind, for he desired to visit the hermit without disturbing his peaceful retreat. The garden was empty; but when he looked into the house he saw a beautiful girl, like an apsarā upon earth. She bade him welcome and offered him water to wash his feet and rinse his mouth, in accordance with the custom for guests. The king asked her whose was the hermitage and why it was empty. She answered: "By leave of your highness, it is the hermitage of the sage Kanva. He has gone out to gather fuel for the sacrificial fire; please, Mahārāja, wait here till he returns, as he will very soon come."

While the maiden was speaking the king was struck with love of her. But he answered with a question. "Pardon, fair mother," he said; "I have heard of the saintly Kanva. But it is said that he has naught to do with women; in what relation do you stand to him?" The hermit-maiden replied: "By leave of your highness, he is my father;

and as to the way in which that came to pass, here is a Brāhman guest who may inform you; please ask him regarding the story of my birth."

The Brāhman related the story of the girl's birth. The great yogī Vishvāmitra was once a king; but he renounced his royal estate, desiring to attain the same spiritual dignity as Vāshishtha. He practised such severe penance that Indra himself feared that his kingdom would be taken from him. So he called one of the most beautiful of the dancers in heaven, Menakā, the pearl of the apsarās, and dispatched her to tempt the holy man. She accepted the mission, after reminding Indra that Vishvāmitra was a man of immense occult powers, able at his will to destroy the Three Worlds; to which he replied by sending with her the gods Wind and Desire. She went to the hermitage and disported herself in an innocent manner, and just when Vishvāmitra glanced toward her the Wind came by and revealed her loveliness, and at the same time the god of Desire loosed his arrow and struck him to the heart, so that Vishvāmitra loved the apsarā. When she found herself with child she thought her work was done; she might return to Heaven, she thought. Away she went along the river Malinī and up into the Himālayas; there she bore a girl, and left the child alone, guarded by the birds, and came again to Indra. Kanva found the child, attended only by *shakuni* birds; therefore he named her Shakuntalā. "This Shakuntalā," said the young Brāhman guest, "is the same hermit-maiden that gave your highness welcome."

Dushyanta spoke again to the girl: "Well born thou art," he said, "daughter of an apsarā and of a great sage; do thou, fair one, become my bride, by the rite of mutual consent." But she would not, wishing to wait till Kanva came; only when the king urged her overmuch she gave consent, upon the condition that her son should be the heir-apparent and succeed to the throne. The king agreed, and he and she were bound by the gandharva rite of mutual consent. Then the king departed to his city, saying he would send for Shakuntalā without delay. Soon Kanva came, but Shakuntalā could not meet him for her shyness; but he knew all that had befallen and came to her, and said she had done well, and foretold that she would bear an emperor. After long months she bore a perfect child, a fair boy, and Kanva performed the Kshattriya rite for him. While he grew up he was ever with the hermit, and shared a little of his power, so that he was able to subdue every wild beast, even lions and tigers and elephants, and he won the name of All-tamer. He bore the birth-marks of an emperor.

But all this time no message came from King Dushyanta. Then Kanva sent Shakuntalā with the child in charge of hermits to the court; she came before the king as he was giving audience, and asked him to proclaim the child his heir-apparent. He replied: "I never wedded thee, O shameless hermit-girl! Never have I seen thy face before. Dost think there are no fair girls in the city, then? Away, and do not ask to be made an empress." She returned: "Ah, king, how great thy pride! But thy saying is unworthy of thy birth. Thou thinkest: 'None was there when I wedded Shakuntalā'; such was thy device. But know that the divine Self who dwelleth in the heart was there, yea and the Sun and Moon, and Wind and Fire, the Sky, the Earth, the Waters, and the Lord of Death were there besides; these thirteen witnesses, counting the Day and Night, the Twilights and the Law, cannot be deceived, but are aware of all that passes. I know not if it be a punishment for any former sin that I am now denied. But here stands thy son altogether perfect; yet no father makes him happy! Dost thou feel no love for him who is thine own flesh and so like thyself? Indeed thy heart is evil."

"Ah, Shakuntalā," said the king, "were he my son I should be glad. But see, he is too great; in such a little time no child could have grown so tall. Do not make this pretence against me, but depart." But as the king spoke there came a voice from Heaven. "Ho! Mahārāja," it cried, "this is thy child. Shakuntalā has spoken truth." Then Dushyanta came down from his lion-throne and took All-tamer in his arms; to Shakuntalā he spoke with tears: "Mother Shakuntalā, I was indeed glad when I saw thee. It was because of my kingly state that I denied thee; for how should the people have believed that this was my son and heir? Now the voice from Heaven has made the sonship clear to all, and he shall sit upon my lion-throne and shall come after me as the protector of the world, and his name shall be no more All-tamer, but shall be Bharata, because of the divine voice"; and he prayed Shakuntalā to pardon him; but she stood still with folded hands and downcast eyes, too glad to answer, and too shy, now that all was well.

Bharata's prowess is the cause that there is now a Bharat-land; the history thereof is told in the Mahābhārata.

Nala and Damayantī

There was once a young king of Nishadha, in Central India, whose name was Nala. In a neighbouring country called Vidarbha there reigned another king, whose daughter Damayantī was said to be the most beautiful girl in the world. Nala was a very accomplished youth, well

XXX

DAMAYANTI

KHITINDRA NĀTH MAZUMDAR

Page 356

practised in all the sixty-four arts and sciences with which kings should be acquainted, and particularly skilled in driving horses; but, on the other hand, he was much too fond of gambling. One day as he walked in the palace garden, watching the swans amongst the lotuses, he made up his mind to catch one. The clever swan, however, knew how to purchase its freedom. "Spare me, good prince," it said, "and I will fly away to Vidarbha and sing thy praise before the beautiful Damayantī." Then all the swans together flew away to Vidarbha and settled at Damayantī's feet. Presently one of them began to talk to Damayantī. "There is a peerless prince in Nishadha," he said, "fairer than any man of God. Thou art the loveliest of women; would that ye might be wedded." Damayantī flushed, and covered her face with a veil as if a man had addressed her; but she could not help wondering what Nala was like. Presently she said to the swan: "Perhaps you had better make the same suggestion to Nala himself." She felt quite safe in her father's garden, and hoped that Nala would fall in love with her, for she knew that her father was planning a *Swayamvara*, or own-choice, for her very soon, when she would have to accept a suitor at last.

From that day Damayantī began to grow thin; she would sit alone and dream, so that all her maidens were grieved for her. When Bhīma heard of it he hurried on the preparations for the own-choice, feeling quite sure that the only cure was to get her married and settled. He invited all the neighbouring princes and rājas, and made ready to receive them in great state. Meanwhile Nārada, who had been spending a short time on earth, passed up to Heaven and entered Indra's palace. Indra greeted him and inquired what was going forward, inasmuch as the kings of the earth were not paying him their customary visits. Then Nārada related the story of Damayantī, and described the preparations for the own-choice at Bhīma's court. The gods announced their intention of taking part in the festivity, and mounting their chariots, set out for Vidarbha. It was not long before they met Nala, and struck by his beauty and royal bearing, they addressed him with a command to bear a message on their behalf. "I am yours to command," he answered, and stood with folded hands waiting their will. Indra took up the word. "Know, O Nala," he said, "that I, with Agni, Varuna, and Yama, have come hither from Heaven to seek the love of Damayantī; do thou announce this to her, that she may choose one of us four." Nala was appalled at this command; he prayed the gods to find another messenger. But the gods held him to his promise, and, indeed, he found himself immediately transported to Damayantī's palace. There he beheld the lady whom he already worshipped shining like the silver moon. Damayantī and her maidens were astounded at his appearance there amongst them, and still more astonished at his beauty; each maiden secretly adored him. But Nala, checking his own desire, delivered the message of the gods. "Do thou decide even as thou wilt," he ended. Damayantī answered: "Myself and all I have are thine; wilt thou not love me in return? It is only because of thee that the princes are assembled. If thou wilt not accept me, I shall prefer death to any other." But Nala answered: "How mayst thou choose a mortal when even the gods seek thy hand, who, moreover, shall but slay me if their will be thwarted? Behold, how great are the gods, and what shall be hers who weds with them!" Damayantī answered: "It is my vow to wed with none but thee." Nala replied: "As a messenger I may not plead my own cause, yet do thou remember me when I stand before thee suitor on my own behalf." Damayantī smiled and answered: "Yea, thou mayst surely without sin be present at the *Swayamvara*, though the gods be also there; then will I choose thee for my lord, nor can any blame attach to thee for that." Then Nala bowed, and turning away, immediately stood before the gods, and to them he reported all truly as it had befallen. "As for what remains," he said, "it rests with thee, O chief of the gods."

The day of the *Swayamvara* dawned. Bhīma's golden court was filled with the lords of earth, seated in state, shining like the stars in Heaven, strong as mountain lions, fair as the nāgas, multitudinous as the serpents in Bhogavatī. Then Damayantī was borne in; beside her walked her maidens with the fateful garland, and before her went Sarasvatī herself. She passed before the rows of suitors, refusing each in turn as his name and style were announced. Then she beheld five noble princes seated together, each in the form of Nala. Damayantī beheld them in despair; she could not tell which one was Nala, nor who the others might be. She could not distinguish the gods by their attributes, for they had laid aside their proper shapes. Long was the silence as she stood before the five, until she bethought her to approach them with humble prayer, for not even gods may refuse the prayer of the good and virtuous. "O ye great gods," she said, "forasmuch as I have pledged myself to Nala, do ye reveal my lord." Even as she prayed, the gods assumed their own forms and attributes; shadowless, with unwinking eyes, unfading garlands, not touching the earth, they stood before her. But Nala stood revealed by shadow, fading garland, and perspiring brow. Then Damayantī stooped and touched the hem of his garment, and rose and cast the flower garland about his shoulders amid cries of grief from the rejected suitors and of applause from gods and rishis. Thus did Damayantī choose her lord. Great gifts the gods bestowed on Nala, and took their way again to Heaven. The assembled rājas departed. Bhīma bestowed his daughter upon Nala; great and rich was the marriage feast, and Nala and Damayantī went to their home in Nishadha.

There was, however, a demon of the name of Kali, the spirit of the Fourth Age, who, with his friend Dvāpara, failed to reach the *Swayamvara* in time. Meeting the gods returning from Vidarbha, Kali learnt from them that Damayantī had chosen Nala. His wrath knew no bounds that a mortal should have been preferred to a god. Despite the dissuasion of the gods, he determined to avenge himself for the insult. He asked his friend Dvāpara to enter into the dice, and himself watched for an opportunity to take possession of the king. It was twelve long years before a slight neglect in the observance of ceremonial purity placed Nala at the demon's mercy. Kali entered into him, and immediately invited Nala's brother Pushkara to gamble with the king. When he arrived the two sat down to the game. Nala lost, and lost again. Day after day the play went on till months had passed. In vain the citizens desired audience, in vain the queen besought her lord to meet his ministers. Soon the royal treasure was almost spent, but still Nala gambled. Then Damayantī called his faithful charioteer, and warning him that evil days were at hand, she sent her two children away with him, to be cared for by dear friends in Vidarbha. When all else was lost Pushkara asked his brother to cast the dice for Damayantī; but it was enough. He rose and cast off his jewels and his crown, and took his way out of the city where he had been king, followed by Damayantī, clad in a single garment like her lord. Six days they wandered thus, while Pushkara usurped the kingdom. Then Nala saw some birds and would have caught them for food. He cast his single garment like a net upon them, but they rose and flew away, leaving him naked. As they rose into the air they cried: "Foolish Nala, we are the dice, unsatisfied if thou hast even a single garment left." Then the miserable king turned to his wife and advised her to leave him and find her way to Vidarbha alone; but she replied: "How can I leave thee alone in the wild forest? I will rather serve and care for thee, for there is no helper like a wife. Or let us rather go together to Vidarbha, and my father will give us welcome there." But Nala refused; he would not return in poverty to Vidarbha, where he had been known as a great king. Thus they wandered, speaking of their unhappy lot, and coming to a neglected hut, they rested on the ground, and Damayantī slept. Then Kali wrought in Nala's mind to leave his wife; it seemed to him best for her and for himself. A sword lay on the ground; he drew it forth and severed in two the one garment worn by Damayantī, and put the half upon himself. Twice he left the hut and twice returned, unable to leave his wife behind, and again he went on his way, drawn by Kali, till at last he was far away.

When Damayantī woke and missed her lord she wept and sobbed with grief and loneliness. But soon she thought of him more than herself, and bewailed his sufferings; and she prayed that he who brought this suffering upon Nala might suffer tenfold more himself. Vainly she sought her lord, wandering through the forest, till a great serpent seized her. Then a hunter came and slew the snake and set her free, and asked her story. She told him all as it had befallen; but he gazed on her beauty and desired her for himself. Deep was her anger when she saw his purpose, and she cursed him by an act of truth. "As I am true to Nala," she said, "so may this wicked hunter die this instant," and he fell to the ground without a sound.

Still Damayantī wandered through the forest, and the wild beasts did not hurt her; far she went, weeping for her lord, till at last she came to a lonely hermitage, and bowed to the holy men. They welcomed her as the spirit of the forest or the mountain; but she told her tale. They answered her with words of comfort and assurance of reunion with her lord. But no sooner had they spoken than the hermits and the hermitage vanished. After many days she met with a merchants' caravan crossing a ford. They, too, welcomed her as a lady of the forest or the river till she told her tale. The merchants answered that they were bound for the city of Subāhu, king of Shedi, and they took the weary queen into their company and went on their way. That very night, as the merchants slept, a herd of wild elephants broke into the camp, stampeded all the beasts, and killed more than half the travellers. Those who survived put down all their misfortune to the strange woman they had befriended, and they would have killed her if she had not fled away into the forest again. But after many days' wandering she reached the capital of Shedi, and stood by the palace gate like a homeless maniac, dirty, untidy, and half-clad. There the queen of Subāhu saw her and received her kindly. When she told her story, the queen appointed her a place where she might live in seclusion, seeing none but holy Brāhmans, who might bring news of her husband.

It was not long that Nala had left his wife when he beheld in the forest a blazing fire, from the midst of which there came a voice saying: "Hurry, O Nala; haste to help me; hurry." He ran to the place and beheld a royal nāga coiled upon the ground, encircled by the fire. Said the snake: "By Nārada's curse, I am encircled by this fire till Nala rescues me; I am a king of serpents, great of might and wise in manifold hidden lore. Save thou me, and I shall do much for thee." Then Nala lifted him, who could not move of himself because of Nārada's curse, from the fiery circle into the cool forest, bearing him ten paces from the fire. Suddenly the serpent bit him, and his likeness changed; but the nāga assumed his own royal form. Then the nāga counselled Nala: "I have by my poison altered thy appearance that men may know thee not. This is for the discomfiture of the demon by whom thou art possessed. Do thou fare to Ayodhyā, where Rituparna is king; seek service of him as charioteer, and the time shall come when he will exchange with thee his skill in dice for thine in driving. Grieve not, for all that was thine shall be restored. When thou wouldst resume thine own form, think of me and put on thee this tunic." As Nala received the magic garment the nāga king vanished away.

As foretold, so it befell; Nala became the charioteer of Rituparna. Meanwhile Bhīma's messengers, searching the world for Nala and Damayantī, found the queen at Shedi's capital and brought her home. Again she sent other Brāhman messengers to seek for Nala. They were to search the whole world, asking everywhere: "Where art thou gone, O gambler, who didst leave thy wife with half a dress; why dost thou leave me alone?" If any made reply, they were to bring news forthwith. When they came to Ayodhyā, Nala, now become the charioteer Vāhuka, crooked-limbed and little like his former self, made answer to the Brāhmans, praising the faith and the forgiveness of women, since one whose husband had deserted her yet bore no malice, but sought him through all the world. This news the Brāhmans brought to Vidarbha. Immediately Damayantī sought her mother. "Let the Brāhman who comes from Ayodhyā," she said, "return thither at once to bring my lord. Let him announce before Rituparna that Damayantī, knowing not whether Nala lives or not, holds a second *Swayamvara*, and will wed again at dawn on the morrow of the day when he delivers the message. None but Nala may drive a chariot from Ayodhyā to Vidarbha in a single day."

When Rituparna heard this message he called his charioteer Vāhuka and ordered him to yoke the horses, for he would reach Vidarbha ere the sun set. Vāhuka obeyed; but he said to himself: "Can this be true, or is it a device made for my sake? I shall learn the truth by fulfilling Rituparna's will." Like the wind he drove; once when the king let fall a scarf and would have stayed to recover it, Nala answered: "Nay, time presses, and the scarf is by now five miles behind us." The king wondered who Vāhuka might be; for he knew no driver of horse, save Nala, who might drive so fast and sure. But Rituparna had another gift, the gift of numbers; as they passed a mango-tree he said: "Behold, one hundred fallen fruits, and upon two branches a thousand and ninety-five fruits and fifty million leaves." At once Nala stayed the horses, severed the branches, and counted the fruits; the number was exact. Nala, in amazement, asked the king the secret of his wisdom; he answered: "It is born of my skill in gaming." Then Nala offered to exchange his skill in driving for Rituparna's knowledge of numbers;

and it was agreed. But when Nala received the lore of numbers and skill at dice, immediately Kali left him and assumed his own form. The demon prayed for Nala's mercy, since he had suffered so long from the serpent's poison; and he promised that wheresoever Nala's name was heard the dread of Kali should be unknown. Then the demon, spared by Nala's grace, entered a blasted tree and disappeared. Then Nala was glad, being freed from his enemy, and mounting the car he drove yet swifter than before; by nightfall they reached Vidarbha, and the thunder of the chariot-wheels reached the ears of Damayantī, so that she knew that Nala was come. "If this be not Nala," she said, "I shall die to-morrow." Bhīma welcomed his guest and asked the reason of his coming, for he knew nothing of Damayantī's ruse or that Rituparna had come for his daughter's sake. Rituparna, seeing no sign of a *Swayamvara*, no preparations for the royal guest, answered his host: "I have but come, great Bhīma, to give my salutations unto thee." Bhīma smiled, for he thought: "Not thus, so far and so fast, does the king of Ayodhyā drive for so small a matter." But he let the question drop and courteously appointed chambers and refreshment for the weary king. Vāhuka led the horses to the stables, dressed them, caressed them, and sat him down on the chariot-seat.

Damayantī knew not what to think, for, though she managed to catch a glimpse of the car as it arrived, she saw no Nala. Yet, she thought, Nala must be there or Rituparna must have learnt his skill. She sent a messenger to the charioteer, making many inquiries whether he knew aught of Nala. Vāhuka answered: "Only Nala's self of Nala knows, and Nala will of himself no sign betray." Then the messenger again repeated the Brāhman's question: "Where art thou gone, O gambler?" and in answer Vāhuka praised the constancy of women and let fall some witness to his true self; and the messenger, marking his agitation, returned to Damayantī. She sent the messenger again to keep close watch on the charioteer; she commanded that no service should be done for him, no water fetched or fire prepared. The messenger reported that the charioteer exhibited divine powers, commanding the elements, fire and water, as he would. Now more and more Damayantī suspected that this was Nala in disguise. Sending once more, she bade the messenger bring her a morsel cooked by him; when she tasted it she knew for certain that none but Nala had prepared the dish. Then she sent her children, Indrasena and Indrasen; when the charioteer beheld them he fell a-weeping, so like he thought them to his own long-lost son and daughter. Still he would not reveal himself.

Then Damayantī went to her mother, that the charioteer might be called before her, and it was done. Much was he moved to see her whom he had left in the forest long ago. When she questioned him if he knew naught of Nala, he proclaimed himself and said that the gaming fever and the desertion of his wife were the doing of Kali, not himself. "But how mayst thou, noble lady, leaving thy lord, seek another husband? For thy second *Swayamvara* is proclaimed, and it is for that cause that Rituparna has come and I." Then Damayantī explained her ruse and called the gods to witness that she was faithful to the uttermost; and a voice from Heaven proclaimed: "It is the truth," and flowers fell from the sky and celestial music was heard. Then Nala assumed the magic vest and his own form, and Damayantī came to his arms; that large-eyed lady found her lord again.

Great were the joy and surprise throughout the city and the palace when the news of this reunion spread abroad. Rituparna departed with another charioteer, while Nala remained a month at the court of Vidarbha. Then Nala took his way to Nishadha, and came before his brother Pushkara, challenging him to dice, asking him to contend again, this time for their lives. Pushkara answered confidently: "Be it so; now, at last, Damayantī shall be mine." It was little that Nala did not slay him in his wrath; but he took the dice and threw, and won, and Pushkara lost.

Then Nala pardoned his evil-minded brother and bestowed a city upon him, and sent him forth in peace. Nala himself, with Damayantī, ruled in Nishadha, and all men were happy.

The Virtue of Compassion

Spoken by Bhīshma to Yudhishthira:

There lived a hunter in the city of Benāres. He set forth in search of antelopes, taking a quiverful of poisoned arrows. He found a herd deep in the forest and sped an arrow toward them; but he missed his aim, and the poisoned shaft entered a great forest tree. Hurt by the deadly poison, the great tree withered and shed its leaves and fruits. But a certain saintly parrot had dwelt all its life in a hollow of its trunk, sheltered by the forest lord, and though the tree was now withered, he would not leave his nest, such was his love toward it. Silent and sorrowful, motionless and without food, the grateful and virtuous parrot withered with the tree.

Indra's throne grew hot; looking down on earth, he marvelled at the devotion and extraordinary resolution of the noble bird, faithful alike in happiness and sorrow.

"How," he reflected, "can this bird possess such feelings, that are not found in lower creatures? Yet, maybe, it is not so strange, for every creature is kind and generous to others." Then, to test the matter further, Indra assumed the shape of a holy Brāhman and approached the tree. "Good bird," he said, "why dost thou not desert this withered tree?" The parrot bowed and answered: "Welcome to thee, king of the gods; by the merit of my discipline, I know thee." "Well done!" exclaimed the thousand-eyed deity, marvelling at the bird's wisdom. Then he inquired again: "Why dost thou cling to this leafless tree, unfit to shelter any bird? Do thou forsake it and choose another, for there are many fair trees in the forest round about."

Then the parrot sighed: "I am thy servant. Lo, the reason of this matter: Here in this very tree I came to life; here I learnt all of wisdom that I have; here was I protected from every enemy. Why dost thou seek to turn me from my path, for I am compassionate and grateful? Do not advise me to leave the tree; while it lived it was my protector; how can I forsake it now?" Then Indra was well pleased, and bestowed a boon at will upon the virtuous bird. This boon the parrot sought: "Let the tree revive." Then Indra sprinkled it with the water-of-life, and it was filled with sap and put forth leaves and blossoms.

Thus was the tree restored by virtue of the parrot's merit, and he, too, at the close of life, obtained a place in Indra's heaven. Thus do men obtain what they will by friendship with the virtuous and holy, even as the tree by friendship with the parrot.

The King, the Pigeon, and the Hawk

Spoken by Bhīshma to Yudhishthira:

Once on a time a beautiful pigeon, followed by a hawk, dropped from the sky and sought protection from King Vrishadarbha of Benāres. The single-minded king, seeing the pigeon's terror, said to it: "Be comforted, good bird. How comes it that thou art wellnigh dead with fear? Thou art so beautiful, thy colour like a fresh-blown blue lotus, thy eyes like the flower of an ashoka-tree! Fear not; for none need fear who seek protection here. For thy protection I will surrender all my kingdom; yea, if need be, life itself. Be comforted, my pigeon."

But the hawk took up the king's words. "This bird," he said, "is my appointed food. Thou shouldst not protect my lawful prey, won by hard endeavour. O king, hunger is gnawing at my stomach. The pigeon is my lawful prey, and bears the mark of my talons on his body. Thou hast the right to intervene when human beings fight; but what lawful power hast thou over the birds that range the sky? Or, if thou seekest to earn religious merit by granting thy protection to the pigeon, have regard also to me, who am like to die of hunger." Then said the king: "So be it; let a bull or boar or deer be dressed for thee, for thou shalt not have the bird." But the hawk replied: "I do not eat the flesh of bulls or boars or deer. Pigeons are my appointed food. But, O great king, if thou hast such affection for the pigeon, give flesh from thine own body equal to the pigeon's weight."

Vrishadarbha answered: "Great is thy kindness in suggesting this to me. Yea, what thou sayest shall be done." Saying this, the king began to cut away his own flesh and to weigh it in a scale against the pigeon.

Meanwhile the gold-decked queens and the ministers and servants raised a bitter wail of grief, that rose from the palace like the sound of roaring clouds. Also the earth quaked because of that act of truth. But the king cut flesh from his arms and thighs, filling the scale in vain; for the bird weighed heavier and heavier against the flesh. Then, when the king was nothing but a skeleton, he desired to give his whole body, and stepped himself into the scale.

Then there appeared the gods, headed by Indra, and the sound of heavenly music was heard; a shower of nectar fell on the king whereby all his body was restored. Heavenly flowers fell from the sky, and the gandharvas and apsarās danced and sang; there came a splendid car, and when the king was seated it bore him away to Heaven.

"And, O Yudhishthira," said Bhīshma, "whosoever protects another shall certainly attain the same good end. And he who tells this story shall be cleansed of every sin, and he also that hears it."

The Worth of Kine

Spoken by Bhīshma to Yudhishthira:

Once there was a great rishi named Chyavana. He followed the *Udvasa* rule for twelve years in the forest, free from pride and anger, joy and grief. He inspired all creatures with happy trust, not only those who live on land, but even those of the water; the great sage was as mild to all as is the gentle moon. This was the vow that he observed: Entering the water at the confluence of Jamna and Ganges, there he stood like a lifeless wooden post, bending forward and bearing on his head the fierce and roaring current of the united streams, swift as the wind itself. Sometimes he laid himself down in the water and slept at ease. All creatures in the water came to look upon him as their friend, and used to come to smell his lips.

One day there came some fishermen with nets, bent on catching fish. Well-knit, broad-chested, strong, and fearless, they lived on the earnings of their nets. They cast into the rivers a net of new string, large and wide, and then, walking into the water, dragged the net with great force; each of them was bold and cheerful and resolved to act according to the others' bidding. Many were the fish they caught, and with them they dragged up Chyavana himself. His body was overgrown with river-weeds, his beard and matted locks were green; shells had fastened themselves upon him. When the fishermen beheld the great sage they worshipped him with folded hands and bowed down to the ground; but the fishes, caught in the net and dragged to land, were dying, and the rishi was filled with pity and sighed hard.

The fishermen asked what they might do to atone for their sin in dragging up the sage. He answered: "Hear and obey my will. I shall either die here with the fishes, or do ye sell me with them; for I will not abandon them in such a case." The fishermen were terrified, but with pale faces they took the fishes and the rishi and went to King Nahusha. He addressed the sage with folded hands and obedient mien. Chyavana said: "These men are weary with their labour; do thou pay them the value of the fish and the price that may be set on me." Nahusha offered a thousand coins. Chyavana said: "A thousand coins are not my price. Pay what is fair, according to thine own judgment." Nahusha offered a hundred thousand, and a million; then half his kingdom, then the whole; but the rishi declared all too little. Then Nahusha was stricken with grief; but there came a wild hermit from the woods who lived on roots and fruit; he said to the king: "I shall satisfy both thee and the rishi too; do what I bid, for I never speak in vain." Then said Nahusha: "Name the sage's price; save me in this case, save my kingdom and my race; for Chyavana, if he be angered, will destroy the Three Worlds, much more myself and all my land. Be thou our raft across the stormy sea."

Then said the yogī: "The Brāhmans, O king, are foremost of the four estates of men; no value can be set upon them, however great, for their value is beyond telling. But kine also are of infinite value; therefore, O lord of men, thou shouldst offer a cow in payment for the rishi." Then was Nahusha glad, and offered a cow in payment for Chyavana. The rishi was appeased and said: "Yea, O king, now hast thou bought me at a fair price, for I know no wealth exceeding that of kine. Even to speak of kine or hear them spoken of is a thing that cleanses from all sin. Kine are faultless, the source and root of all prosperity, the chief ministrants at sacrifices, worshipped by every world, full of energy and givers of joy; sinless is that land where kine are glad. Kine are the stairs that lead to Heaven; they are adored in Heaven itself."

Then the fishermen bestowed that cow upon the sage himself and worshipped him, who in energy was like a blazing fire; and he gave his blessing to them, accepting their offering. "Go ye to Heaven forthwith," said he, "and the fishes too." Greatly marvelled King Nahusha when he saw the fishermen ascend to Heaven with the fishes. Then the two rishis bestowed on him numerous boons, until he cried: "Enough!" Then he worshipped them, and each returned to his own place. Such are the holiness and worth of kine.

Gautama's Elephant

The following story was related by Bhīshma to Yudhishthira in order to acquaint him with the various states enjoyed by good men after death:

There was a mild and self-restrained sage, named Gautama, dwelling in a forest hermitage. He found a baby elephant that had lost its mother and was very sad. The good sage nursed it till the little beast grew into a large and mighty elephant.

One day Indra beheld the great creature, huge as any mountain, and he took the form of the king Dhritarāshtra, and seized the elephant and was taking him away. Then Gautama addressed him: "Thankless king, do not take my elephant, who brings me fuel and water, who guards my hermitage when I am away, who is gentle and obedient, and very dear to me." Dhritarāshtra offered him a hundred kine and maidservants and gold and gems. But what did the hermit want with wealth? Dhritarāshtra argued that elephants were royal animals, fit for the service of kings, and would have gone his way, taking the elephant. But said Gautama: "Though thou goest unto Yama's land, I shall take back my elephant from thee." The king replied: "They go to Yama's land who are unbelievers and sinful, and devoted to the gratification of their senses." Gautama answered: "In Yama's land is truth, and there the weak may overcome the strong." But the king replied: "None but the sinful go to Yama; I shall reach a higher place." Gautama answered: "Though thou goest to Vaishrāvana's realm, where dwell the gandharvas and the apsarās, I shall take back my elephant."

Dhritarāshtra answered: "Well, I shall seek a place yet higher." Gautama said: "If thou goest to the summit of Mount Meru, where the flowery woods are echoing with the song of kinnaras, I shall yet pursue and take my elephant again."

So was it said by each of every higher place: the flowery groves of Nārada, resort of all who are given over to dancing and to music; the perfumed land of Soma; the heavens of Indra with the apsarās; the heavens of the rishis; the heavens of Brahmā. "There," said Dhritarāshtra, "thou mayst not discover me." "Even there," replied Gautama, "I shall find thee out and take my elephant. But now I know thee. Thou art Indra, wont to wander through the universe in divers shapes. Pardon my missaying thee, and that I knew thee not."

Then was Indra pleased that Gautama knew him, and bestowed on him a boon. Gautama asked that the elephant should be restored, for, he said: "It is so young; it is only ten years old. I have brought it up as my own child. It has been my dear companion in these woods." Indra answered: "Lo, the elephant that has been so dear comes toward thee and bows his head down to thy feet. Be it well with thee." Then Gautama bowed to the king of gods and took the elephant. But Indra blessed him and took him with himself and with the elephant to Heaven, where even the righteous hardly go.

He also who tells or hears this tale shall reach the same place.

The Throne of Vikramāditya

Indian legend has attached great sanctity and fame of wisdom to the name of Vikramāditya, who is historically a somewhat shadowy king, generally identified with

Chandragupta II (A.D. 375–413); but perhaps the Vikramāditya of this story was an older than he. At any rate it so fell out that in the time of a later king the ancient throne of Vikramāditya was discovered near what had been the old city of Ujjayini. The king had the throne brought to his own capital, and proposed to take his seat upon it with great state, and thence to deliver his daily judgments. The marble seat was supported by thirty-two stone angels. Each day that the king was about to ascend the throne one of these addressed him and, requesting him not to take his seat on the sacred throne, related a story of the wisdom of Vikramāditya.

This is the story related by the eighteenth statue, named Rūp-rekha, Streak of Beauty:

Once there came before King Vikramāditya two hermits with a dispute concerning a matter of philosophy, and requested him to resolve their doubt. The king asked what it was, and the first hermit said: "O king, I maintain that Intellect is superior to Wisdom and Soul, since these and the senses are subject to the Intellect, inasmuch as all Deeds are born in the Mind. Thus Mind rules over all." But the second hermit said: "It is Wisdom that rules the Mind. For Wisdom checks the froward thoughts arising in the Intellect. True, the senses are ruled by Mind, but Mind is ruled by Wisdom. Through Wisdom our senses are controlled, and we progress in yoga."

The king replied: "O ascetics, of a surety this mortal body, wrought of fire, air, earth, and water, is ruled by the Intellect. But by following the dictates of the Mind alone, this body perishes untimely. Therefore I think that Wisdom is greater than the Mind, for it is Wisdom that preserves us from destruction. Again, it is said that one perfect in Wisdom dieth nevermore; and no yogī can attain perfection lacking Wisdom."

Both ascetics were delighted with this judgment, and they gave to the king a piece of chalk, saying: "Whatever thou dost draw therewith in the day will come to life at night." Then they departed.

At once the king shut himself in a room alone and spent the whole day drawing gods and goddesses upon the wall. At night the figures all came to life and cried "Hail! Hail!" to the king and talked together. Next day the king drew on another part of the wall armies of men, horses, elephants, and other creatures, and at night he was delighted to find that they, too, came to life. The next day, again, he drew gandharvas and apsarās with drums and lutes and viols in their hands, and at night they came to life and played exquisitely according to the laws of music.

Thus the king spent his days in drawing and his nights in seeing living pictures, and he neglected all his queens and the duties of the state. One night the queens came to him in their splendid palanquins, weeping and lamenting. Vikramāditya asked them why they wept. "O ladies," he said, "why are your moon-faces pale?" One answered in a sweet voice: "O Mahārāja, you promised never to leave us alone; why, then, do you desert us now?" But the king paid no attention, for he was absorbed in looking at the moving pictures on the wall.

Next day, when all the figures on the wall were still once more, the queens spoke to the king again, praying him not to leave them in distress. He smiled and asked: "What am I to do, then?" "O king," they answered, "if thou art agreed to grant a boon, then give to us the chalk that is in thy right hand." So Vikramāditya gave the chalk, and the queens kept it hidden ever after. Never since have pictures come to life.

The Ashvins

The Ashvins are divine twins, distinguished for their great beauty, and masters of medicine. They were at first refused a place amongst the gods on account of their lowly birth; but the rishi Chyavana, who received from them perpetual youth, secured from Indra that they should participate in the offerings.

This tale is told of Chyavana's attainment of eternal youth: The aged rishi Chyavana had a beautiful wife, Sukanyā—that is to say, Fair-maid. One day the Ashvins beheld her at her bath, bare of any garment. They came to her and asked: "O fair-limbed girl, whose daughter art thou, and what hast thou to do here in these woods?" and she answered shyly: "Know that I am Saryati's daughter and the wife of Chyavana." The Ashvins answered: "Why has thy father given thee to one so aged and near to death, for thou art radiant as summer lightning? We have not seen thy like even in Heaven. Bare of adornment as thou art, none the less thou makest all the forest fair; how much fairer mightst thou appear in gorgeous robes and splendid jewels! Do thou leave thy aged husband and take one of us, for youth will not endure."

She replied: "I am devoted to my husband Chyavana." Again they prayed her, saying: "We are the physicians of Heaven. We will make thy husband young and fair; then choose from us three—ourselves and him—whom thou wilt for lord." Then Fair-maid told to Chyavana what had been said, and he consented.

Then the Ashvins commanded Chyavana, who was eager to regain his youth, to enter water, and they, too, sank into the waters of the pool. Then came forth all three in radiant youthful forms, wearing burnished ear-rings. All were of the same appearance, delightful to behold, and they said to Fair-maid: "Choose one of us to be thy husband. Choose whom thou dost most desire." But Fair-maid found that one appearance was upon them all, and she hesitated long; only when at last she recognized her husband did she choose, and chose no other than himself.

Then Chyavana, well pleased to have both youth and beauty and to have his wife again, promised in return to win for the Ashvins the right to share in the offerings of soma-juice given to the gods. The twins, no less glad, went their way to Heaven, and Chyavana and Fair-maid dwelt together in great joy, even as the gods themselves.

The Story of Dhruva

Of myths that represent a spiritualizing interpretation of the stars, the very jewel is probably the story of Dhruva. It is frankly a statement of how the Pole-star came to be so steady, and the Hindu name for the Pole-star is Dhruva-lok, or place of Dhruva.

Dhruva was a child and a prince, the eldest son of a king and his chief queen. There was, however, a younger wife who had gained great ascendancy over the mind of Dhruva's father, and in consequence of her jealousy and dislike the prince and his mother Sunītī were banished from the court and sent to live in retirement in a cottage on the edge of a great forest. We are here dealing, we must remember, with a Hindu tale of the period when every story forms an epos of the soul, and in the epos of the soul the chief event is that by which arises a distaste for the material world. Young Luther sees his

XXXI

DHRUVA

ASIT KUMAR HALDAR

Page 378

friend struck dead by lightning, and at once enters a monastic order.

This crisis in the history of the child Dhruva arises when he is seven years old. At that age he asks his mother to tell him who is his father. When she has answered he has still another question. May he go and see his father? Permission is readily given, and on the appointed day the child sets forth. Seated on his father's knee, amidst all the joy of his love and welcome—for the little son is the king's darling—the great disillusionment arrives. Dhruva's stepmother enters, and at the sight of the anger in her face the father hastily puts his boy down.

Wounded to the core, the child turns, without speaking, and steals quietly away. He has sought for strength and found none. Even the strongest love in the world, a father's, and that father a king, is without power or courage to be faithful and to protect. On reaching the home of their exile the child has only one question to put to the anxious woman who has watched so eagerly for his return: "Mother, is there anyone in the world who is stronger than my father?"

"Oh yes, my child," said the startled queen; "there is the Lotus-eyed. In him is all strength."

"And, mother," said the child gravely, "where dwells the Lotus-eyed? Where may he be found?"

Was there in the simple words some hint of danger, some note of a parting that was to throw its shadow over all the years to come? There must have been, for the mother gave as if in fear an answer that would fain make search impossible.

"Where dwells the Lotus-eyed, my son?" said she. "Oh, in the heart of the forest, where the tiger lives and the bear lives. There dwells he."

That night when the queen lay sleeping the child stealthily rose to find his way to the Lotus-eyed. "O Lotus-eyed, I give my mother to thee!" he said, as he stood for a moment at her side. And then, as he paused on the threshold of the house: "O Lotus-eyed, I give myself to thee!" and stepped boldly forth into the forest. On and on he went. Difficulty was nothing, distance was nothing. He was a child, and knew nothing of the dangers of the way. On and on, without faltering, he went. After a while, still pursuing his way through that impenetrable forest, he came to the Seven Sages deep in their worship, and paused to ask his road of them. At last he came to the heart of the forest and stood there waiting. As he waited the tiger came, but the child Dhruva stepped up to him eagerly and said: "Art thou he?" And the tiger turned away in shame and left him. Then the bear came, and again Dhruva went forward, saying: "Art thou he?" But the bear, too, hung his head and went away.

And then, as the child of the steady heart still waited and watched, a great sage stood before him who was Nārada himself. And Nārada gave him a prayer and told him to sit down, there at the heart of the forest, and fix his whole mind on the prayer, saying it over and over again, and surely he would find the Lotus-eyed. So there, at the heart of the forest, where we see the Polar Star, sits Dhruva saying his prayer. He has long ago found the Lotus-eyed—found him in his own heart. For he fixed his mind on his prayer with such perfect steadfastness that even when the white ants came and built about him the mighty ant-hill of the midnight sky the child Dhruva never knew it, never moved, but there, stirless, all-absorbed, sat on and sits still, worshipping the Lotus-eyed for ever and ever.

Shani

In the mass of literature called the *Purānas* hundreds of myths are embedded which pass unknown to all but the inquisitive amongst the Hindus of to-day. Yet each one of these must have had importance at the time of its origin, and by careful examination might be induced to yield up its historical secret. One such curious legend concerns Saturn (Shani). At the birth of Ganesha, eldest son of the Mother of the Universe, his cradle was visited, it is said, by gods and demi-gods. Only one exception was there. Shani did not come. At last this fact was noticed by the Great Mother, and she inquired the reason of his absence. She was told that he feared to harm her child, since it was matter of common knowledge that the head of one on whom Shani looked was likely to be burned to ashes at his glance. With easy pride the mother smiled, and assuring him that her son could not be subject to his power, sent him a message of warm invitation and welcome. Accordingly Shani came. But what was the horror of all present when he looked at the babe, and instantly its head disappeared in a flame. How much greater was Shani than anyone had suspected!

At this catastrophe the mother was profoundly disturbed, and commanded her guest somewhat sharply at once to restore the head of her child. But Shani smiled pleasantly, and pointed out that the head as such no longer existed. It lay in ashes before them. "Then send forth a servant and let him bring me the head of the first one he meets," commanded the mother in effect, and Shani had no option save to obey. Only one who is in fault can be subject to Shani, and his emissary found no one inadvertently doing wrong, till suddenly he came upon an elephant sleeping with his head to the north. This trifling fault brought him under the jurisdiction, and hastily the servant cut off his head and returned to put it on the infant's body. It is for this reason that Ganesha wears an elephant-head.

Two or three points are noteworthy here. The intention of the story is, of course, to show the power of Shani, and consequently the necessity for his propitiation. But, as usual in obedience to the Indian instinct for synthesis, the new claimant to more or less divine honours is also made to explain some anomaly in the faith that preceded him. And the faith with which Shani is thus connected, the tree on which the new belief is grafted, is the worship of Ganesha, perhaps the oldest of organized and sacerdotalized popular worships in India. This fact alone is eloquent of the antiquity of the propitiation of Shani. It is interesting also to see that the very point in the image of Ganesha that is so anomalous and tantalizing to ourselves was held similarly inexplicable at the time of the incoming Saturn and the other planets. Whatever piece of symbolism this white head on the red body originally expressed, whether it was the setting sun beneath the clouds or what not, was now long ago forgotten; and the children of Ganesha, not doubting his divinity, were ready to accept any explanation of its origin that might offer itself to them. This explanation came, together with the new-fangled worship of the planets, from some people who feared and propitiated their deities. Long, long ago had the worship of the gentle Ganesha gone out to the nations of the farther East, and now the fear of Shani was added to it in the land of its birth from foreign sources. Was Chaldea by any possibility the centre from which came this worship of the planets?

Star-Pictures

For most of us there has been perhaps a golden hour of childhood when we dreamed ourselves back into the love and reverence of primitive man for the starry sky. In early ages, especially in the hot countries of the South, where day was an agony and night a delight, the coming of sunset must have been looked forward to by thoughtful minds as the opening of a great book, the only book that then existed. Astronomical passion has undeniably decreased with the growth of what we know as civilization. We of Europe could not to-day divide a Church on some difference of opinion about the date of Easter.

Primitive science, such as it was, was inextricably interwoven with the study of the stars, for the simple reason that man early became ambitious of fixing a date. We can hardly doubt that this was the fourth of those great steps by which we emerged into humanity. First the defining and accumulation of language, then the tentative handling of stones as tools, again the long subsequent discovery of fire, and last of all this, the measurement of the year. To-day, with our accomplished theories of the cosmos, the obvious instrument of time-measurement would seem to be the sun, writing the steps of his progress from hour to hour and season to season with the pen of changing shadow-lengths. And in this empiric fashion something of the sort may have lain behind the early sacredness of poles, pillars, and obelisks. As the climax of a great scientific theory on the subject, the sun, however, is only the successor in time-reckoning of the moon, for already of a hoary antiquity when solar measurement was born was the calculation of the year by the coincidence of the full moon with some given constellation.

A glance shows us how the process grew. As nations became organized and consolidated the popular science of rude time-measurement was transformed into a great priestly function and mystery. The year itself was worshipped as a whole, as well as in its component parts. The awe with which the women of Greece regarded certain of their own annual festivals of purification was a relic, doubtless, of an older state of things, in which they had been responsible for the anxious computation of the circling year. The Hindu festivals, scattered up and down the lunar months, were once so many steps by which to make sure of the recurrence of specific days. Calendar-making retains even now something of this its ancient religious character. Thus early science was bound up with religion, and the stars were watched before the moon or the sun was even dimly understood.

A Picture-Book

It would be a mistake, however, to think that man's early regard for the midnight sky was always serious. The blue and silver page was more to him in that far-off age than a world of thought and reverence, more even than a sphere of growing inquiry and enlarging knowledge. It was also a gigantic picture-book, an absorbing wonder-tale. How many of the semi-divine beings of whom his fancy was so full could be seen, the moment night arrived, shining up there against the blue! How soon must have been recognized the hero coursing across the sky, followed by his dog! And the Bengali name of Orion to this day—Kal-Purush, the Time-man—tells us something of that early significance. Strange relations of cause and effect were predicated, doubtless, of that lofty hero-world. Something like theological differences of opinion may have obtained as between different races touching the various functions of a given constellation in the divine economy. Men had long dreamed of an immense bird, whose wings were the clouds, whose movements were felt as the winds, carrying sun and the stars on their ring-like course. And now, searching the heavens most eagerly at the moments of dawn and sunset, or at those turns of the seasons when weather and flood were telling what next to expect of the crops, if the vast outlines of a bird could be dimly descried at evening in the imperfect tracing made by remote suns, what was to hinder Aquila or Garuda, the divine Eagle, from being held the jailer of the disappearing light? One race may well have held the stars of the Great Bear to be the bed, and another the reins, of the sun-god. How many of the most beautiful stories of old mythology might thus be proved to be at bottom grave and simple accounts of astronomical occurrences; how many of the Labours of Herakles, for instance, were in reality stories of his constellation! Whether Alcestis restored to the house of Admetus is not, in truth, the sun brought back to its place amongst the stars, or whether Perseus was not always a hero seen in outline between Andromeda and Cassiopeia—these questions, and others like them, will never, probably, be fully answered. A little we may be able to spell out from the very fringe of the great subject, but the whole story of the psychological origin of mythology we cannot possibly decipher. One thing, however, is fairly certain. The divine world of the stars, the great stage of the shining souls, was, to begin with, a confused world. Man had his luminous points of understanding, for he dedicated given stars to chosen characters by arbitrary acts of piety and wonder; but he could not map out the whole.

Agastya

We can see easily enough that different communities may have adopted different starting-points in their study of the midnight sky or their measurement of time. One tribe perhaps would watch the movements of the star Agastya, as Canopus in Argo is said to have been called. The distinctively Indian idea that the heroes of the sky were meditating souls, plunged in thought and radiant with a light of which they were unconscious, must have been elaborated only gradually; but with its final acceptance the star Agastya would come to be known as Agastya-Muni, or Agastya the Sage, while the tribes that measured their year by Canopus—as the Cholas, Cheras, and Pāndyas in Southern India may have done—would grow to look upon him as a deified or canonized ancestor. There is a valley in the Himālayas containing an ancient village which is known as Agastya-Muni. Is this some prehistoric tribal home, or is the secret of its dedication one we cannot hope to penetrate?

The folk-lore of Hinduism is familiar enough with the name of this Agastya Canopus. According to one story he swallowed the ocean. According to another he set forth on the first of the month for the South, and on his way from the Himālayas to the ocean he passed the Vindhyas. Now for a long time there had been a quarrel between the two ranges of mountains, the Himālayas and Vindhyas, as to which should lift its head the higher. The Vindhyas, by their ambition, had threatened to shut out the light from mortals. As the great Agastya passed by, however, the Vindhyas could not refuse to bow themselves in reverence, whereupon the cunning old sage said: "It is well, my children! Remain thus till I return!"

Alas! on reaching the shores of the South he plunged into the ocean and never returned, for which reason the Vindhyas remain to this day with lowered heads. In reference to this story he who sets forth on the first of the month is always said to perform Agastya-Jatra, the Journey of Agastya, and it is more than hinted that he may not return. Meanwhile the picture of the coming forth from the North to South, the final plunge into the ocean, never to return by the way he came—though he will again be seen on starry nights passing over the head of the Vindhyas from the North—sounds remarkably like a popular rendering of the astronomical observation of a bright star passing below the horizon.

The Great Bear

But Agastya Canopus was not the only stellar progenitor of men. Early fancy played about the seven stars of the Great Bear. Weird tales are told of the deadly arrow—the arrow that slew the sun—shot at the year's end by the Wild Huntsman. And men loved, as they have always loved, the tender light of the Pleiades, the Spinning Women, or the Dancing Maidens, amongst whom shone Rohinī, the Queen of Heaven. Arundhatī, the Northern Crown, was another of the stars that bore a favoured race to fortune. Sirius, the Dog-star, did the same. And personification might in any of those cases, we must remember, by an easy series of transitions become ancestor-worship.

The Pole-star

The earliest of male anthropomorphic gods is said to have been the Pole-star, and there is a touch of humour in the way he is portrayed up and down the pages of ancient mythology. The Pole-star, it seems, from his solitary position at the apex of the stellar system, gave rise to the notion of a god who was one-footed. How ancient is this conception will be guessed when we learn that the wild tribes of Australia have a star-god Turunbulun, who is lord and protector of the Pleiades, and one-eyed and one-footed. After this Odin, or the Cyclopes with their one eye, or Hephaistos, the Smith of Heaven, with his lame foot, need occasion us no surprise. This lame-footed god, again, forms an obvious stepping-stone to the one goat-foot of the great god Pan, that deep and tender Asiatic conception which found its way into Hellenic ideas from the older Phrygia. It is difficult to believe, and yet it is said, that the Pole-star deity was at one time identified with the goat. Thus the Rig-Veda contains numerous references to Aja-Ekapada—a name that may be translated as either the One-footed Goat or the Birthless One-footed One. It is generally assumed that the second of these renderings is correct, and that it points to the sun. And if it had not been for the great god Pan and his one goat-foot, comparative mythology might have had to agree. Indeed, it is not easy to ignore this rendering entirely when we read in the Veda that "he who has one foot has outstripped them that have two." This would sound to a modern more like the sun than the Pole-star. But the ancient singer possibly meant that he who had but one foot had reached to the lordship and height of the universe. In this sense, of apex of the cosmos, Aja-Ekapada is constantly opposed to Ocean and the Dragon of the Deep, who is supposed to be the Rain-Cloud, the womb of all life, and to personify the vast and immeasurable abyss of the southern sky. Thus we have a pair of gods—gods of the North and South.

CHAPTER VIII: CONCLUSION

Summary of Indian Theology

THE following scheme sets out very briefly the fundamental conceptions of Indian theology and cosmology, as assumed in most of the foregoing myths and legends:

The Gods

The One Absolute Reality is Brahman (neuter), which, by the assumption of attributes, becomes Īs vara, god or overlord. Īshvara has three aspects, viz. Brahmā, Shiva, and Vishnu, with their *Shaktis* or energies, Sarasvatī, Devī, and Lakshmī. The sectarian worshippers identify one of these with the highest Īshvara, and regard the two other aspects as merely devas. Hence there appears a certain confusion of status in the legends, according to the particular sectarian standpoint from which they are related. The most important sects are the *Shaivas*, who worship Shiva, the *Vaishnavas*, who worship Vishnu (chiefly in his *avatārs*, as Rāma or Krishna), and the *Shāktas*, who worship Devī as the Supreme. Almost all Indian worship is monotheistic; there is not for the individual worshipper any confusion of God with gods.

Avatārs are special incarnations assumed by portions of the Supreme for helping on the processes of evolution and release. Ten such *avatārs* of the supreme Vishnu are usually recognized, of whom Rāma, Krishna, and Buddha are the last, and Kalki is yet to come. "Whensoever," says Shrī Krishna, "the Law fails and lawlessness uprises, O thou of Bharata's race, then do I bring myself to bodied birth. To guard the righteous, to destroy evildoers, to establish the Law, I come into birth age after age."

Different Names

A source of confusion to the student of Indian mythology at first appears in the many names by which one and the same Supreme Divinity may be known.

The most important of the name identities are, for Shiva, Mahādeva, Hara, Natarāja, and for Vishnu, Hari, Nārāyan. A familiarity with these names is gradually acquired, and it is realized that the different names refer to as many aspects of One Being. For the gods possess a manifold consciousness, and by division of their attributes appear and act in many places and many forms at one and the same time. It will have been observed that every god, whether Īshvara or deva, has a feminine counterpart or aspect. These wives are the Shaktis or powers without whom there could be no creation or evolution. For example, the Shakti of Shiva is Devī, whose other names are Satī, Umā, Durgā, Chandī, Pārvatī, Kālī, &c.; it is she who is worshipped by many millions as the Mother, and all these worshippers speak of God as She. The great sex-distinction pervades the whole universe, and the psychology of sex is everywhere the same: all things that are male are from Shiva, all that are female are from Umā.

Cosmic Powers

Distinct from Īshvara are the devas, Indra, Agni, Varuna, Yama, old personified cosmic powers who alone were worshipped in the old Vedic days, before the emergence of Shiva and Vishnu. These devas dwell in *swarga*, an Olympian paradise; they bestow on their worshippers divers boons, but they are never saviours of souls. Their moral status is like that of men, and *swarga* is a place where all wishes and desires are gratified, where

XXXII

KĀLĪ

SURENDRA NĀTH KAR

Page 390

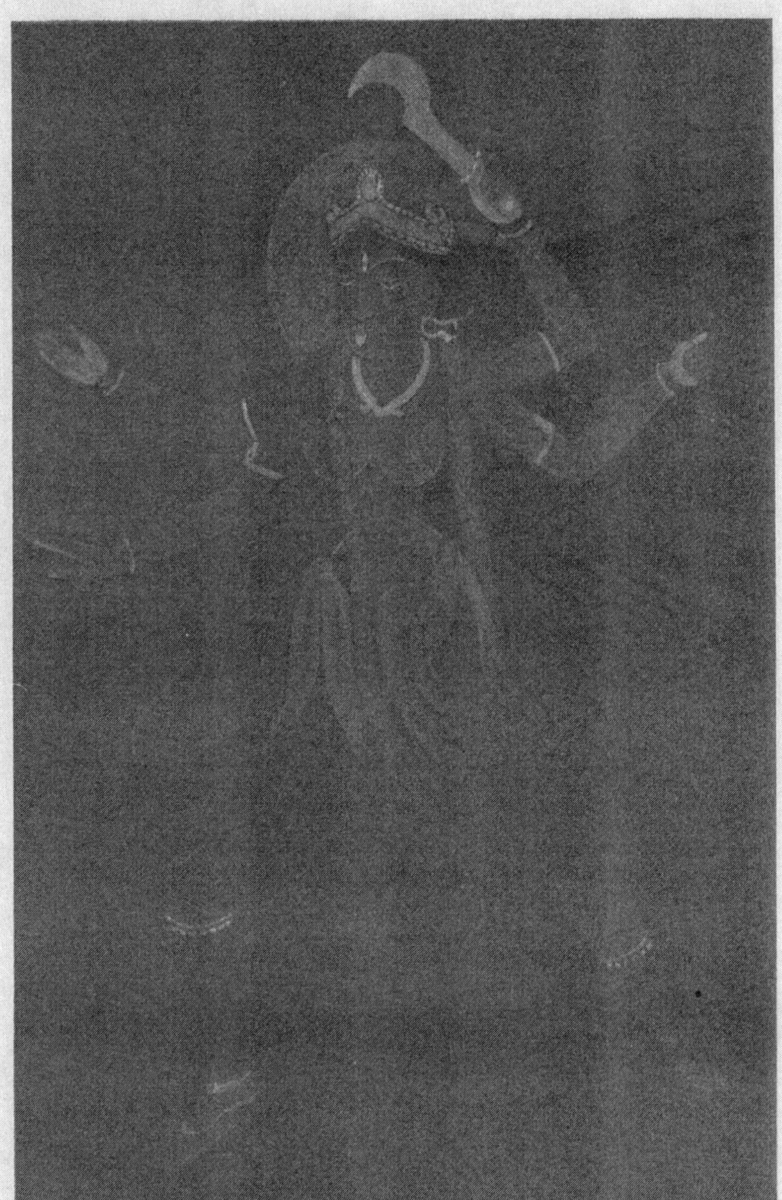

also human beings obtain the reward of good deeds in the intervals between one birth and another. The devas do not perform *tapas* (asceticism) or sacrifice themselves for the world, nor do they incarnate as *avatārs.* Human beings, by *tapas* or ritual sacrifices, and generally by good deeds, may attain a place in *swarga,* and even the status of a deva; but this does not preclude the necessity of rebirth on earth, nor is it to be regarded in any sense as salvation (*mukti, moksha*) or as equivalent to the attainment of *nirvāna. Nirvāna* is a state, *swarga* a place.

Amongst the devas is Kāmadeva and his wife Ratī (desire). Associated with the devas in *swarga* are the rishis (including, *e.g.* Nārada, Vishvāmitra, Vāshishtha, &c.) and the *prajāpatis* (including Daksha); the former are the priests, the latter the worshippers, of the devas. *Swarga* also is the home of a variety of mythical beings, the apsarās, gandharvas, kinnaras, and the special animals who are vehicles of the gods, such as Vishnu's Garuda and Ganesha's rat. The apsarās are the dancing girls of Indra's court; the gandharvas and kinnaras the musicians, and these last have forms which are only partly human, some being partly animal, others partly bird in nature. The apsarās, gandharvas, and kinnaras do not enter into the cycle of human incarnation and evolution, but, like the fairies of Western mythology, may in rare cases make alliances with human beings.

Yama, though one of the devas, is the Lord of Hades, where the bad deeds of human beings are expiated in the intervals between one birth and another. It should be understood that a part of the interval between births is spent in Hades, a part in Heaven, according to the proportion of merit and demerit earned by the individual in question.

The demons (asuras, daityas, rākshasas) are constantly at

war with the devas, who are represented as appealing to Brahmā, Shiva, or Vishnu for assistance.

The Universe

In speaking here of the Hindu cosmology, it is chiefly our solar system that is to be understood; but it will be clear that similar principles are applicable to any other system, or to a whole universe composed of many systems.

No original creation of the universe can be imagined; but there are alternations, partial and complete, of manifestation and withdrawal. At the commencement of a cycle (*kalpa*) the world is created by the Brahmā aspect of Īshvara; during the cycle it is sustained by Vishnu; and at the end, as Shiva, he destroys it. This cosmic process takes place according to the following time scheme:

A cycle, or Day of Brahmā, a *kalpa*, the period of the endurance of the solar system, is 12,000 years of the devas, or 4,320,000,000 earth-years. At the beginning of each Day when Brahmā wakes, the "Three Worlds" so often spoken of in the myths, together with the devas, rishis, asuras, men, and creatures, are manifested afresh according to their individual deserts (*karma*, deeds); only those who in the previous *kalpa* obtained direct release (*nirvāna*, *moksha*), or who passed beyond the Three Worlds to higher planes, no longer reappear. At the close of each Day the Three Worlds, with all their creatures, are again resolved into chaos (*pralaya*), retaining only a latent germ of necessity of remanifestation. The Night of Brahmā is of equal length with the Day.

The life of our Brahmā or Īshvara is one hundred Brahmā-years, at the end of which time not only the Three Worlds, but all planes and all beings—Īshvara himself, devas, rishis, asuras, men, creatures, and matter—are resolved into chaos (*mahā-pralaya*, "great-chaos"), enduring for another hundred Brahmā-years, when there appear a new Brahmā and a new creation. It will be seen that both major and minor alternations of evolution and involution are represented as necessitated by natural law—the latent force of past action (*karma*). Causality governs all conditioned existence. The whole scheme is highly scientific.

The Day of Brahmā is divided into fourteen *manvantaras*, over each of which presides a *Manu*, or teacher. Each *manvantara* is followed by a Deluge, which destroys the existing continents and swallows up all living beings, except the few who are preserved for the repeopling of the earth. The name of our *Manu* is Vaivasvata, who is the source of the Laws of Manu, formulating the basic structure of Hindu society. The Day of Brahmā is also divided into 1000 *yuga*-cycles (*mahā-yuga*), each consisting of four ages, the Satya, Tretā, Dvāpara, and Kali *yugas*, of which the last three are periods of progressive degeneration from the first. The four *yugas* together last 4,320,000 years; the first 1,728,000, the second 1,296,000, the third 864,000, and the last 432,000. The present year (A.D. 1913) is the 5013th of the Kali yuga[1] of the present *mahā-yuga*; this *mahā-yuga* is the twenty-eighth of the seventh *manvantara* of our *kalpa*, called the Varāha kalpa, because in it Vishnu incarnated as a boar (*varāha*); and this *kalpa* is the first day of the fifty-first year of the life of our Brahmā.

The events related in the Mahābhārata took place in the Tretā yuga of our *mahā-yuga*; those of the Rāmāyana in the Dvāpara yuga. The oldest stories of the battles of

[1] The commencement of which Kali yuga was coincident with the Day of the death of Krishna.

the gods and asuras and the legends of the rishis go much further back: the Churning of the Ocean, for example, took place in the sixth *manvantara*; the rescue of the elephant from the crocodile in the fourth; the Boar incarnation in the first; and the emergence of Brahmā, called the lotus-born because of his origin from a lotus sprung from the navel of Nārāyana, at the very beginning of the *kalpa*.

The Three Worlds (*triloki*), to which constant reference has been made, are the physical plane (Bhur), the astral plane (Bhuvar), and Heaven (Swarga); these three only, with the underworlds, are concerned in the daily creation and dissolution. These also constitute the Samsāra or Wandering, the condition of birth and rebirth, where desire (*kāma*) and personality (*ahamkāra*) are the guiding principles of life. Above the Three Worlds are four other planes which endure throughout the life-period of a Brahmā; these are reached by such as pass beyond the Three Worlds without attaining direct release; they go onwards to Īshvara, and attain release with him at the conclusion of the period of a hundred Brahmā-years.

Below the Three Worlds are the seven Pātālas or underworlds (distinct from the realm of Yama); these are inhabited by the nāgas, the semi-human serpents, who possess a rich material civilization of their own. These underworlds are supported on the heads of the nāga Ananta (Infinity), who also supports Nārāyana during his repose in the Night of Brahmā.

The earth is supported by eight elephants, one in each of the eight quarters. There are also guardian gods of the quarters, those for East, South, West, and North being Indra, Yama, Varuna, and Kuvera; according to the Buddhists, however, it is the regents of these gods who are the guardians of the quarters, and it is these regents who are represented in the oldest Indian god-figures, those of the Bharhut Stūpa (second century B.C.). Even earlier the Brāhmans also had representations of the devas, but made in impermanent materials; while the representation of Īshvaras and Supreme Buddhas is a later development, attaining its highest types in the seventh or eighth century A.D.

The prime cause of creation is inexplicable, for in a universe conditioned by causality causes must precede causes backwards for ever. But the process of manifestation or creation is more properly regarded as outside time, and equally past, present, or future. No motive can be assigned for this Will, a fact which is mythically represented by calling the world-process *Līlā*, the Lord's amusement; or, again, by saying that Being desires to behold the reflection of its own perfection mirrored in Non-Being.

Mythical Geography

The mythical geography of our system must also be described. There are seven island-continents surrounded by seven seas. Jambu-dwīpa (the world) is the innermost of these; in the centre of this continent rises the golden mountain Meru, rising 84,000 leagues above the earth. Around the foot of Meru are the boundary mountains of the earth, of which Himālaya lies to the south; the land of Bharat-varsha (India) lies between Himālaya and the salt sea. Meru is buttressed by four other mountains, each 10,000 leagues in height; of these, one is Mandara, used as a pivot for the churning of the ocean. The name of the continent Jambu-dwīpa derives from a Jambu tree that grows on one of these four mountains. Its fruits are as large as elephants; when they are ripe they fall upon the mountain, and their juice forms the Jambu river, whose waters give health and life to those that drink of them. There are also lakes and forests and mountain spurs.

On the summit of Meru is the city of Brahmā, extending 14,000 leagues, renowned in Heaven; around it are the cities of Indra and other regents of the spheres. About the city of Brahmā flows the Ganges, encircling the city; according to one account, the river divides in four, flowing in opposite directions; according to another, Ganges, after escaping from Heaven and from Shiva's tresses, divides into the seven sacred rivers of India. In the foot-hills dwell the gandharvas, kinnaras, and siddhas; the daityas, asuras, and rākshasas in the valleys. All these mountains are included in Swarga (Paradise), where the fruit of good actions is enjoyed. Bharat-varsha (India, or perhaps the whole human world) is one of nine lands situate in areas bounded by the various mountains spoken of. Of these nine, it is in Bharat-varsha only that there are sorrow, weariness, and hunger; the inhabitants of other *varshas* are exempt from all distress and pain, and there is in them no distinction of *yugas*. Bharata is the land of works, where men perform actions, winning either a place in Heaven, or release; or, it may be, rebirth in Hell, according to their merit. Bharata is, therefore, the best of *varshas*; other *varshas* are for enjoyment alone. Happy are those who are reborn, even were they gods, as men in Bharat-varsha, for that is the way to the Supreme.

History of the Theology

With regard to the history of some of the ideas here spoken of:

From the hymns of the Rig-Veda, which go back to a

time when the Aryans were not yet settled in the Ganges valley, but lived amongst the tributaries of the Indus, we learn of a time when there was no caste, no privileged worship, no Brāhmanical system of government, but there were many pastoral tribes governed by hereditary kinglets. The old Vedic religion consisted in the worship of the personified powers of Nature, gods of the sky, the air, and the earth. Gradually the belief in these distinct deities yields to a conviction that they are manifestations of One, who has many names, such as Prajāpati, Vishvakarmā, &c., but is finally called Brahman, a word which in the earlier hymns means nothing but the power of prayer, in a way analogous to the Christian conception of the *Logos*. To this was added the idea that this Brahman was nothing but the all-pervading Self (*ātman*), to know whom is to know all. Thus we get side by side two phases of religion—the old sacrificial cult, whereby men seek to win a place in Paradise by means of moral behaviour and offerings to the gods; and the search for the highest knowledge, the knowledge of the Brahman. This position was reached before the time of Buddha; the fully developed Brāhmanical system above described attained shape in the succeeding centuries.

Philosophy

The prevailing philosophy (there are, of course, other systems also, though all are closely interconnected), the doctrine of esoteric reality to which the above exoteric scheme is related, is a form of uncompromising monism called the Vedānta; it maintains that there is but One Reality, the Brahman, of which naught whatever can be predicated. This is the Unshown, the Unknown God; whatever qualities or attributes one might wish to use to express its nature, in a famous Vedāntic phrase: "It is not that, it is not that" (*neti, neti*). To know this reality is to know all, just as to know clay is to know all that is made of clay—the apparent differences consist only in name and form (*nāmarūpa*). This reality is within ourselves, and we in it. It is, in fact, our only true Self (*ātman*), obscured in us by personality (*ahamkāra*) and attributes (*upādhis*). The knowledge of this Reality is Release (*moksha, nirvāna*), just as when an earthen pot is broken it is realized that the space within is one with the space without. To attain this release is the highest end of life.

The life of each individual soul (*jīvātman*) follows a double path—the primal Will to Experience (*pravritti mārgaya*), and the later Will to Denial (*nivritti mārgaya*), or, briefly, the paths of Pursuit and Return, familiar to the mystics of all ages and countries. The process of Embodiment and Release is always in progress; but inasmuch as the Released return no more, it is clear that the Pursuers must always be in the majority. Yet it is an evil thing for any community if it be composed wholly of those who pursue, without a due leaven of those who return.

Human Society

On this basis the ancient rishis laid down as the four aims of human life, *Dharma*, *Artha*, *Kāma*, *Moksha*, *i.e.* Morality, Wealth-winning, Fulfilment of Desires, and Release. That individual souls are in different stages of development, besides possessing special capacities or tendencies as well as special deserts according to the nature of past action, is reflected in the theory of caste (*varna*, lit. colour), each with its appropriate morality (*sva-dharma*).

"Caste," as Sister Nivedita has said, "is race continuity; it is the historic sense; it is the dignity of tradition and of purpose for the future. It is even more: it is the familiarity of a whole people in all its grades with the one supreme human motive—the notion of *noblesse oblige*."

Marriage

Moksha, or Release, is ultimately attainable by the individual alone, and depends on his or her relation to God. But the secular ends of life, morality, wealth, desire, and, above all, the birth of children, require the co-operation of men and women. Hence in the Hindu social system great stress is laid on marriage; so far from celibacy being recommended to the citizen on religious grounds, it is expressly declared that neither can the citizen attain to Heaven after death, nor can his ancestors remain there, unless he has begotten a son. The Hindu marriage is indissoluble, except in the fourth caste. Polygamy is permitted, but is comparatively rare, as the number of men and women is about equal; the most usual reason for a second marriage is the childlessness of the first. As in so many other systems, the basis of marriage is duty rather than romantic love. The high spiritual status of the Hindu woman is reflected in the mythology; indeed, as we have seen, there are many millions of Hindus who think habitually of God as She.

> *It is She* (says Shankarāchārya) *with whom Shiva seeks shelter . . .*
> *Whose words are sweet,*
> *The Destructress of ills,*
> *Ever and in all places pervading,*
> *Tender creeper of Intelligence and Bliss.*

"The mother," says Manu, "exceedeth a thousand fathers in the right to reverence, and in the function of teacher." And again in the *Kubjikā Tantra*: "Whosoever has seen the feet of woman, let him worship them as those of his teacher."

Renunciation

The life of a citizen is a
feel already in their youth the irresistible call to renunciation (*vairāgya*, turning away), and so become monks or nuns. For such as these asceticism is a vocation. The citizen, on the other hand, as we have seen, is commanded to marry and to bring up children. But life as a citizen is not the whole life, even of an ordinary man; there comes a time when he, too, turns away from the world. His life is planned in four stages (*ashrāmas*), as follows: studentship, life as a householder and wealth-winner, retirement, and finally complete renunciation of all ties. It is the strength of character, the merit accumulated in many lives so ordered, that gradually ripens the individual soul, until at last it feels the irresistible call and bends its whole force toward Release (*nirvāna*).